LOOSE ENDS

LOOSE ENDS

Primary Papers in Archetypal Psychology

James Hillman

Spring Publications
Dallas, Texas

© 1975 by James Hillman. All rights reserved
Sixth Printing 1991
Published by Spring Publications, Inc.
P.O. Box 222069; Dallas, Texas 75222
Printed in the United States of America
on acidfree paper

Library of Congress Cataloging-in-Publication Data
Hillman, James.
Loose ends.
Includes bibliographies.
1. Archetype (Psychology) 2. Jung, C. G. (Carl
Gustav), 1875–1961. I. Title.
BF175.5.A72H55 1986   150.19'54   86–13097
ISBN 0–88214–308–5

CONTENTS

Themes

Theories

Prefatory Note

These papers appeared in different places at different times in different languages. A boxed note at the end of each tells its history. Although some of them — "Betrayal", "Three Ways of Failure and Analysis", "Towards the Archetypal Model for the Masturbation Inhibition" — have already been printed several times, they are included here because they are not easy to get. The paper on Dream Research was given originally in German and this is its first publication in English. The paper on Plotinus, Ficino and Vico has been printed only in Italian; that on the Pothos of the Puer Eternus was given in French and is published here for the first time. Generally, I have kept the papers in their original shape and this accounts for the discrepancies between them in the styles of notes and bibliography, and sometimes even spelling. The papers on Masturbation, the Child, and Dream Research have undergone the most revision, in places *in extenso,* for this edition. I am indebted to Lyn Cowan for her marvelous help with the whole job.

J. H.

Zürich
Groundhog Day, 1975

The first edition of this book included a checklist of my writings in English (1960–1975). This list was deleted because it has been superseded by an exhaustive checklist through 1988, including languages other than English, published as Part Three in my *Archetypal Psychology: A Brief Account*, Dallas: Spring Publications.

J. H.

I

A NOTE ON STORY

From my perspective as depth psychologist, I see that those who have a connection with story are in better shape and have a better prognosis than those to whom story must be introduced. This is a large statement and I would like to take it apart in several ways. But I do not want to diminish its apodictic claim: to have "story-awareness" is *per se* psychologically therapeutic. It is good for soul.

To have had story of any sort in childhood — and here I mean oral story, those told or read (for reading has an oral aspect even if one reads to oneself) rather than watching story on screen — puts a person into a basic recognition of and familiarity with the legitimate reality of story *per se*. It is given with life, with speech and communication, and not something later that comes with learning and literature. Coming early with life, it is already a perspective to life. One integrates life as story because one has stories in the back of the mind (unconscious) as containers for organizing events into meaningful experiences. The stories are means of telling oneself into events that might not otherwise make psychological sense at all. (Economic, scientific, and historical explanations are sorts of "stories" that often fail to give the soul the kind of imaginative meaning it seeks for understanding its psychological life.)

Having had story built in with childhood, a person is usually in better relation with the pathologized material of obscene, grotesque, or cruel images which appear spontaneously in dream and fantasy. Those who hold to the rationalist and associationist theory of mind, who put reason against and superior to imagination, argue that if we did not put in such grim tales in early impressionable years, we would have less pathology and more rationality in later years. My practice shows me rather that the more attuned and experienced is the imaginative side of personality the less threatening the irrational, the less necessity for repression, and therefore the less actual pathology acted out in literal, daily events. In other words, through story the symbolic quality of pathological images and themes finds a place, so that these images and themes are less likely to be viewed naturalistically, with clinical literalism, as signs of sickness. These images find places in story as legitimate. They *belong* to myths, legends, and fairy tales where, just as in dreams, all sorts of peculiar figures and twisted behaviours appear. After all, "The Greatest Story Ever Told", as some are fond of calling Easter, is replete with gruesome imagery in great pathologized detail.

Story-awareness provides a better way than clinical-awareness for coming to terms with one's own case history. Case history too is a fictional form written up by thousands of hands in thousands of clinics and consulting rooms, stored away in archives and rarely published. This fictional form called "case history" follows the genre of social realism; it believes in facts and events, and takes all tales told with excessive literalism. In deep analysis, the analyst and the patient together re-write the case history into a new story, creating the "fiction" in the collaborative work of the analysis. Some of the healing that goes on, maybe even the essence of it, is this collaborative fiction, this putting all the chaotic and traumatic events of a life into a new story. Jung said that patients need "healing fictions", but we have trouble coming to this perspective unless there is already a predilection for story-awareness.

Jungian therapy, at least as I practice it, brings about an awareness that fantasy is the dominant force in a life. One learns in therapy that fantasy is a creative activity which is continually telling a person into now this story, now that one. When we examine these fantasies we discover that they reflect the great impersonal themes of mankind as represented in tragedy, epic, folktale, legend, and myth. Fantasy in our view is the attempt of the psyche itself to re-mythologize consciousness; we try to further this activity by encouraging familiarity with myth and folktale. Soul-making goes hand in hand with deliteralizing consciousness and restoring its connection to mythic and metaphorical thought patterns. Rather than interpret the stories into concepts and rational explanations, we prefer to see conceptual explanations as secondary elaborations upon basic stories which are containers and givers of vitality. As Owen Barfield and Norman Brown have written: "Literalism is the enemy". I would add: "Literalism is sickness". Whenever we are caught in a literal view, a literal belief, a literal statement, we have lost the imaginative metaphorical perspective to ourselves and our world. Story is prophylactic in that it presents itself always as "once upon a time", as an "as if", "make-believe" reality. It is the only mode of accounting or telling about that does not posit itself as real, true, factual, revealed, i.e., literal.

This brings us to the question of content. Which stories need to be told? Here I am a classic, holding for the old, the traditional, the ones of our own culture: Greek, Roman, Celtic, and Nordic myths; the Bible; legends and folktales. And these with the least modern marketing (updating, cleaning up, editing, etc.), i.e., with the least interference by contemporary rationalism which is subject to the very narrowing of consciousness which the stories themselves would expand. Even if we be not Celtic or Nordic or Greek in ancestry, these collections are the fundamentals of our Western culture and they work in our psyches whether we like it or not. We may consider them distorted in their pro-Aryan or pro-male or pro-warrior slant, but unless we understand that these tales depict the basic motifs of the Western psyche, we remain unaware of the basic motives in our psychological dynamics. Our ego psychology still resounds with the motif and motivation of the hero, just as much psychology of what we call "the feminine" today reflects the patterns of the goddesses and nymphs in Greek myth. These basic tales channel fantasy. Platonists long ago and Jung more recently pointed out the therapeutic value of the great myths for bringing order to the chaotic, fragmented aspect of fantasy. The main body of biblical and classical tales direct fantasy into organized, deeply life-giving psychological patterns; these stories present the archetypal modes of experiencing.

I think children need less convincing of the importance of story than do adults. To be adult has come to mean to be adulterated with rationalist explanations, and to shun such childishness as we find in fairy stories. I have tried to show in detail how adult and child have come to be set against each other: childhood tends to mean wonder, imagination, creative spontaneity, while adulthood, the loss of these perspectives (cf. below, "Abandoning the Child"). So the first task, as I see it, is restorying the adult — the teacher and the parent and the grandparent — in order to restore the imagination to a primary place in consciousness in each of us, regardless of age.

I have come at this from a psychological viewpoint, partly because I wish to remove story from its too close association with both education and literature — something taught and something studied. My interest in story is as something lived in and lived through, a way in which the soul finds itself in life.

From *Children's Literature: The Great Excluded,* Vol. III (ed. Francelia Butler and Bennett Brockman), Journal of The Modern Language Association Seminar on Children's Literature, Storrs, Connecticut, 1974, pp. 9-11.

I I

ABANDONING THE CHILD

> Everything that begins in us with the
> distinctness of a beginning is a mad-
> ness of life.
>
> — Gaston Bachelard

Subjectivity

The position of the psychologist at these meetings has its special difficulties, and I would like to start by mentioning them — perhaps as a rhetorical device to gain your sympathy, perhaps as an appropriate subjective prelude to any psychological statement, perhaps to impart something of the nature of psychology, and of my theme, the child. Whereas colleagues who come to this podium must meet the difficulty of making their special knowledge generally understandable, the psychologist begins the other way around. We begin with the general, that which we all share, the all-too-human soul, hoping to make this common event specifically relevant to each individual. So it shall be less a matter of having something new to tell, than of bringing the familiar home, of making the objective subjective.

Owing to this different focus, psychotherapy also has a different purpose than that of the other disciplines. (I use the terms psychotherapy and psychology interchangeably, for a psychology that is not a depth psychology is inevitably superficial and off the mark, and a depth psychology is inevitably a psychotherapy because of its effects upon the unconscious grounds of the psyche.) Because psychotherapy's subject matter is indeed "subject matter", the soul, our field seems to have an obligation to the same soul from which it extracts its ideas. It tries to remain always in relationship with its subject matter, but not merely in the empirical manner of good scientific method, paying respect to facts. Rather, psychology must pay back its ideas to the soul, feed it, be of value to the soul, rather than merely using the psyche to make psychology. Depth psychology may use the soul as its empirical object but this object is at the same time a person, a subject. Since this soul has its locus in each of us, the focus of depth psychology and the purpose of its psychological ideas will be to touch something subjective. The field moves only when its subject matter is moved. "For", as Freud wrote, "a psychoanalysis is not an impartial scientific investigation, but a therapeutic measure. Its essence is not to prove anything, but merely to alter something". ("Analysis of a phobia in a five-year-old boy" [1909], CP III, p. 246.) Depth psychology begins and continues as a therapy whose essence is to affect the human soul.

It has long seemed to me necessary that a psychological lecture participate in the work of psychotherapy. A lecture too aims at altering something, otherwise it is not truly psychological (in the sense I am using that term), but only *about* psychology. If psychotherapy is to move out of the consulting room and into life more generally, then one of the places for general psychotherapy is in the psychological lecture.

This kind of lecture shall have to discover the style suiting its purpose, a style not yet worked out, where subjectivity is paramount, and yet where subject talking to subject is not conceived by older models of altering something, e.g., preaching, personal confessing, or polemical debate, because psychological alteration means affecting subjectivity in depth through the constellation of symbolic and emotional reality. By aiming at the constellation of "subject matter", I shall not be proving something, demonstrating, explaining or even informing. And the way of proceeding, too, will have to be discovered, since we are used to a lecture on a linear model that marshalls evidence and arrives somewhere with a result, ending in a point. But we shall today be entertaining a theme, rather than answering a problem, hoping our method to move us through a series of reflections on the same subject, like a string of water-colors, evoking insights, perspectives, emphasizing metaphorical speech, aiming to suggest and open, and where the aim is not a conclusion, not to close the subject, but to open it further.

Thus in yet another way psychology differs from the other disciplines represented here: it depends so much upon the psychologist. Other fields do have a more or less objective area under observation and the field does more or less show historical advancement in problem-solving. Does psychology move forward in the same way, and is it meant to? Do we or should we have more awareness of psyche today? Has the effect of depth psychology upon the psyche resulted in your soul or mine being more conscious, more loving, more harmonious than was the soul of others a century ago before Freud, or two centuries ago before Rousseau, Pinel and Herbart? And here I am raising less the Kantian question of ethical progress than a psychological question about the relationship between psychology, psychologist, and psyche. In what other discipline are the three so inherently necessary for the movement of any one of them. The psyche requires an adequate psychology to reflect itself, just as psychology depends upon the psyche of the psychologist who in turn exemplifies his psychology. The closer psychology reflects its subject matter, the psyche, the more it merges, as Jung said so often, with the psychologist himself, and becomes like music or painting always a subjective statement.

This is uncomfortable and embarrassing; and well it might be, for embarrassment is a corrective to psychology's pretentiousness. The psyche's subtlety and depth – did not Herakleitos warn of this – will far outreach any psychology which is always bound by its subjective limitations. It is better, despite the embarrassment, to bring up the subjectivity of psychology, than to cover it over with that fantasy of objectivity so infecting our field. So we shall not pretend that the analyst is objective (Freud behind the couch; Jung with his amplificational knowledge), nor shall we entertain this afternoon notions of an objective psyche, an objective level of dreams and objective meaning of psychic events that can be impartially investigated by the psychologist engaged in scientific or scholarly work on objective material: cases, dreams, syndromes, associations. *None of this material exists independent of persons and the psyche of the investigator.* This so-called objective material is the most subjective stuff of life: it concerns what people re-member, how they fantasy, where they love. It is the report of wounds and where life went wrong: it is the scrutiny of secrets and the confession of prayers.

Just here our theme begins: abandoning the child. For the intense subject-ivity of psychology, the discomforting embarrassment we feel with its inadequacy vis-a-vis our older brother disciplines, and its extraordinary bigger-than-big infla-tion, despite the continual re-birth of its problems in which there is no maturing and no advancement so that everything has to be done again anew by each of us entering psychology — this all reflects the archetype of the child. To cast psy-chology in an objective form, to consider it positivistically, a progress, equal to its tasks, to see psychology's strength and not its weakness (and pretention and omni-potence fantasy to understand all and everything) is to cast out the child.

What is the Child?

What is this "child" — that is surely the first question. Whatever we say about children and childhood is not altogether really about children and child-hood. We need but consult the history of painting to see how peculiar are the im-ages of children, particularly when comparing them in their distortions with con-temporary exactitude in depicting landscapes and still lives or the portraits of adults. We need but consult the history of family life, education and economics to realize that children and childhood as we use the terms today are a late inven-tion. (Ariès, Part I.) What is this peculiar realm we call "childhood", and what are we doing by establishing a special world with children's rooms and children's toys, children's clothes, and children's books, music, language, caretakers, doctors, of playing children so segregated from the actual lives of working men and women. Clearly, some realm of the psyche called "childhood" is being personified by the child and carried by the child for the adult. How curiously similar this *daseinsbe-reich* is to the realm of the madhouse some centuries ago and even today, when the madman was considered a child, the ward of the state or under the parental eye of the doctor who cared for his "children", the insane, like for his family. Again, how extraordinary this confusion of the child with the insane, of child-hood with insanity. ("Madness is childhood". — Foucault, 1965, p. 252.)

The confusion between real child and his childhood and the fantasy child that obfuscates perception of child and childhood is classical to the history of depth psychology. You may remember that Freud at first believed that repressed memories causing neuroses were forgotten emotions and distorted scenes from actual childhood. Later he abandoned this child, realizing that a fantasy factor had placed in childhood events that had never actually happened; a fantasy child was at work and not an actual occurrence in the life of the person. He was obliged then to separate child of fact from that of fantasy, outer child events from inner childhood. Nevertheless, he stuck to his belief that the job of therapy was the analysis of childhood. A statement of 1919 is typical:

> Strictly considered...analytic work deserves to be recognized as genuine psycho-analysis only when it has succeeded in removing the amnesia which conceals from the adult his knowledge of his childhood from its beginning (that is, from about the second to the fifth year)...The emphasis which is laid here upon the importance of the earliest experience does not imply any underestimation of the influences of later ones. But the later impressions of life speak loudly enough through the mouth of the patient, while it is the physician who has to raise his voice on behalf of the claims of childhood. ("A child is being beaten", CP II, p. 177.)

What childhood did Freud mean? Actual children, as I pointed out here two years ago, were never analyzed by Freud. He did not analyze children. Was the "childhood" which the analyst had to recapture actual childhood? Here, Freud himself remains ambiguous, for the actual small young human we call "child" merges in Freud with a Rousseauian, even Orphic-Neoplatonic child who is "psychologically a different thing than an adult...". (NIL, p. 190.) ("Childhood has its own ways of seeing, thinking and feeling; nothing is more foolish than to try to substitute our ways". Rousseau, *Emile*, II.) The difference lies in the child's special way of reminiscing: "...a child catches hold on...phylogenetic experience where his own experience fails him. He fills in the gaps in individual truth with prehistorical truth; he replaces occurrences in his own life by occurrences in the life of his ancestors. I fully agree with Jung in recognizing the existence of this phylogenetic inheritance...". "From the history of an infantile neurosis (1918), CP III, pp. 577-78.

The actual child itself was not altogether actual because its experiences consisted in the confabulations of "pre-historic" occurrences, i.e., non-temporal, mythical, archetypal. And childhood thus refers in Freud partly to *a state of reminiscence*, like the Platonic or Augustinian *memoria*, an imaginal realm which provides the actual child with "its own ways of seeing, thinking, and feeling" (Rousseau). This realm, this mode of imaginal existence, is to be found, according to popular and depth psychology, in primitive, savage, madman, artist, genius, and the archeological past; the childhood of persons becomes merged with the childhood of peoples. (Cf. CP III, p. 470: the last paragraph of Freud's discussion of the Schreber case.)

But the child and the childhood are *not* actual. These are terms for a mode of existence and perception and emotion which we still today insist belongs to actual children, so that we construct a world for them following our need to place this fantasy somewhere in actuality. We do not know what children are in themselves, "unadulterated" by our need for carriers of the imaginal realm, of "beginnings", (i.e., "primitivity", "creation"), and of the archetype of the child. We cannot know what children are until we have understood more of the working of the fantasy child, the archetypal child in the subjective psyche.

Freud gave to the child image and to the fantasy of childhood a group of startling attributes which you may remember: child had no super-ego (conscience) like the adult; no free associations like the adult but confabulated reminiscences. The child's parents and problems were external, rather than internal as with the adult, so that the child had no symbolically transferred psychic life (NIL, p. 190). How close to the mental life of "madness", of artist, and how close to what we call "primitive" — this absence of personal conscience, this mixture of behaviour and ritual, of memory and myth.

But more startling than the attributes Freud enunciated are those which we may draw from his ideas. First, Freud gave the child *primacy*: nothing was more important in our lives than those early years and that style of thought and emotion of imaginal existence called "childhood". Second, Freud gave the child *body*: it had passions, sexual desires, lusts to kill; it feared, sacrificed, rejected; it hated and longed and it was composed of erogenous zones, pre-occupied with feces, genitals, and deserved the name polymorphous perverse. Third, Freud gave the child *pathology*: it lived in our repressions and fixations; it was at the bottom of our psychic disorders (CP II, p. 188); it was our suffering.

These are startling attributes indeed if they be compared with the child of Dickens, for Dorrit and Nell, Oliver and David had little passion and little body, and no sexuality at all, especially in view of little Hans and little Anna and other children of psychoanalytic literature. Perversity, when it entered in Dickens at all, came from adults, from industry, education and society; pathology was in deathbed scenes that claimed children back to paradise. Against Dickens we can see Freud's vision most sharply, even if in both the child as fact and the child as image were still not disentangled.

Jung's essay "The Psychology of the Child Archetype" in 1940 moved the matter much further; actual child is abandoned and with it the fantasy of empiricism, the notion that our apperception of the factor in our subjectivity results from empirical observation of actual childhood. Jung writes:

> It may not be superfluous to point out that lay prejudice is always inclined to identify the child motif with the concrete experience "child", as though the real child were the cause and pre-condition of the existence of the child motif. In psychological reality, however, the empirical idea "child" is only the means...by which to express a psychic fact that cannot be formulated more exactly. Hence by the same token the mythological idea of the child is emphatically not a copy of the empirical child...not — and this is the point — a human child (CW 9, 1, p. 161 fn.).

What accuracy can our studies of the human child have so long as we have not recognized enough the archetypal child in our subjectivity affecting our vision? So let us leave the child and childhood to one side and pursue, what Jung calls, the "child motif" and the "childhood aspect of the collective psyche".

Our question now becomes what is the child *motif* which projects so vividly and draws such fantasies onto itself? Jung answers:

> The "child" is all that is abandoned and exposed and at the same time divinely powerful; the insignificant, dubious beginning and the triumphal end. The "eternal child" in man is an indescribable experience, an incongruity, a handicap, and a divine prerogative; an imponderable that determines the ultimate worth or worthlessness of a personality (CW 9, 1, §300).

Jung elaborates these general and special features: futurity, divine heroic invincibility, hermaphroditism, beginning and end, and the motif of abandonment from which my theme is drawn. Jung's elaborations of 1940 should be

11

taken as an addition to those in his previous works where the child motif is related to archaic mythical thinking and the mother archetype (CW 5, *passim*) and to paradisiacal blissfulness (CW 6, §§422f, 442). Some of the aspects which Jung discusses Freud had already described in his language-style. The idea of the creative child occurs in Freud's equation child = penis, and the rejected child in his equation child = feces. " 'Feces', 'child', and 'penis' thus form a unity, an unconscious concept (*sit venia verbo*) — the concept, namely, of a little thing that can become separated from one's body". "From the history of an infantile neurosis", (1918) CP III, p. 562f.

To these features I would add two others from our Western tradition, the first specifically Christian, the second specifically Classical. In the Christian tradition (Légasse) "child" refers also to the simple, the naive, the poor and the common — the orphan — of society and of the psyche, as it did in the language of the Gospels, where child meant outcast, the pre-condition for salvation, and was later placed in association with the feelings of the heart opposed to the learning of the mind. In the Classical tradition the child appears in those configurations of masculine psychology represented specifically by Zeus, Hermes and Dionysos, their imagery, mythemes and cults. The child motif there may be kept distinct from the child-and-mother motifs and also the child-hero motifs which have a distinctly different psychological import.

Our theme follows Jung literally when he says: "The child motif represents something not only that existed in the distant past but something that exists *now* ...not just a vestige but a system functioning in the present whose purpose is to compensate or correct, in a meaningful manner, the inevitable onesidedness and extravagances of the conscious mind" (CW 9, 1, §276). If, according to Freud, the essence of the psychoanalytic method is to alter something, and if the child, according to Jung, is that which acts as psychological corrector, our reflections this afternoon require that we bring the child back from his abandonment even while we speak of him. Then the general theme may become specifically focussed in the private subjectivity of each and may act to alter the onesidedness of consciousness in regard to the child.

12

Abandonment in Dreams

We find the abandoned child first of all in dreams, where we ourselves or a child of ours or one unknown, is neglected, forgotten, crying, in danger or need, and the like. The child makes its presence known through dreams; although abandoned, we can still hear it, feel its call.

In modern dreams we find the child endangered by: drowning, animals, road traffic, being left behind in a car trunk (the "chest" motif), or a pram or supermarket cart (the "basket" motif); kidnappers, robbers, members of the family, incompetents; illness, crippling, secret infections, mental retardation and brain damage (the idiot child); or a wider less specific catastrophe such as war, flood or fire. Sometimes, one wakens in the night with the sensation of having heard a child crying.

Usually the dreamer's response to the motif of abandonment is acute worry, a guilty responsibility: "I should not have let it happen; I must do something to protect the child; I am a bad parent". If it is an infant in the dream, we believe we must keep the sense of this "child" with us all the time, feed it every three hours with thoughtful attention, carry it on our backs like a papoose. We tend to take the child as a moral lesson.

But guilt puts the burden of altering something (Freud) and correcting something (Jung) altogether upon the ego as doer. After all, the dreamer is not only in charge of the child; he also *is* the child. Consequently the emotions of worry, guilt and responsibility, morally virtuous as they may be and even partly corrective of neglect, may also prevent other emotions of fright, loss and helplessness. Sometimes the more we worry over the child the less the child really reaches us. So, as long as we take up any dream mainly from the position of the responsible ego, by reacting to it with guilt and the energetics of seeing matters straight, improving by doing, by changing attitudes, extracting from dreams moral lessons for the ethically responsible ego, we reinforce that ego. We thereby emphasize the parent-child cleavage: the ego becomes the responsible parent, which only further removes us from the emotions of the child.

Crucial in all dream integration — integration, not interpretation, for we are speaking now of integrity with the dream, standing with it and in it, befriending it in all its parts, participating in its whole story — is the emotional experience of

13

all its parts. Gestalt therapy attempts to drive this home by demanding that the dreamer feel himself into all the parts: the distraught parent, but also the wild dogs, the flooding river, the secret infection, and the exposed child. It is as important to collapse with the child's crying, and to hate savagely the childish, as it is to go home from the analytical hour resolved to take better care of the new and tender parts that need help to grow.

As interpretation and ego responsibility may strengthen the parent at the expense of the child, so too may amplification not reach the child who is abandoned. An amplification of the child in the river, wandering lost in the forest or attempting a task beyond his strength, in terms of fairytales and myths and initiation rites may stain the motif accurately so that we see certain aspects clearly — mainly heroic new consciousness emerging — but the staining technique of amplification to bring out the objective meaning may also obliterate the subjective reality of dereliction. Amplification often takes us away from the misery by placing it on a general level. For many psychic events this extension of awareness through amplification is just what is needed, but for precisely this motif it would seem contraindicated because the forsaken child can best be refound by moving closer to subjective misery and noting its precise locus.

Both responsibility and amplification are insufficient methods for this motif. As activities of the reasoned, mature person they distance us yet further from the child.

Abandonment in Marriage

Because every home established, every nest, niche of habit offers the abandoned child a sanctuary, marriage unavoidably evokes the child. Sometimes an early marriage is obviously intended to find a basket for the child that was inacceptable in the parental house. The pattern may continue long afterwards: husband and wife in tacit agreement taking such care of the abandoned child left from their parental homes that they cannot find the child appropriate to themselves.

Being at home, coming home, heading for home — these are emotions which refer to the child's needs. They indicate abandonment. These emotions transform the actual home, its walls and roof. into a picture-book fantasy with psychic walls and psychic roof in which we place our vulnerability and in which we may be safely exposed to the polymorphous perverse fragmentation of our demands. At home, we are not only mother who embraces and father who captains, but also a little child. What is rejected everywhere else must be allowed here at home.

This reality, which some psychotherapists have called "the inner child of the past" and others "neurotic interaction in marriage" is as important in the fantasies which are enacted in a marriage as are the various patterns of the conjunction described by Jung. What prevents the aspirations of the conjunction are the fierce incest demands of the child, whose desires for union are of another order than the marriage quaternio (CW 14 and 16, *passim*) and whose image of "contained" and "container" (CW 17, §331c and following) is wholly in terms of his anxious dereliction. Where else can he go? This is his home too, and more important to him than wife and husband are mother and father, nursing and protection, omnipotence and idealizations.

A purpose of marriage has been defined in terms of procreating and caring for children. But there is also the archetypal child who is constellated by marriage and whose need for care would wreck the actual marriage by insisting that it rehearse archetypal patterns that are 'pre'-marital (uninitiated, infantile, incestuous). Then there occur those struggles between the actual children and the psychic child of the parents as to whom will be abandoned. Then divorce threatens not only the actual children, but the abandoned child of the parents that found containment in marriage.

The concentration of abandonment in marriage because there is no other home for it, makes marriage the principal scene for enacting the child archetype (not the conjunctio). In marriage we find the idealizations of the child: marriage as alpha and omega of life, hermaphroditism lived as "role-sharing", futurity lived as the planning of hopes and fears, and defensive vulnerability. The couple's attempts to contain the child (not each other) produce a familiar pattern alternating between emotionalism and none at all, marriage stiffened into a social norm. Lost in the oscillation is the imagination which the child can bring. Imagination is blown off in affects or concretizes into plans and habits that keep the child cribbed. If we may speak of a "marriage therapy" then it would be based, not on the "neurotic interaction" of the *couple*, but on the child as central factor in marriage, and the child's imagination, i.e., the cultivation of the imaginal psyche, the peculiar fantasy life that plays between your child and mine.

Baptising the Child

Usually we feel something fundamentally wrong in regard to the child, which wrong we then place into or onto the child. Societies have to do something with children in order to make right this wrong. We do not take children as they are given; they must be removed out of childhood. We initiate, educate, circumcise, innoculate, baptise. And if in the Romantic manner we idealize the child — and idealizations are always a sign of distance —, calling the child a *speculum naturae,* we do not altogether trust this nature. Even the child Immanuel (Isaiah 7:14-16) has first to eat butter and honey before he can distinguish between good and evil. The child *per se* makes us uneasy, ambivalent; we are anxious about the human propensities concentrated by the child symbol. It evokes too much of what has been left out or is unknown, becoming easily associated with primitive, mad and mystical.

When one looks at the early controversies over infant baptism one wonders just what psychological content was so exercising these excellent Patristic minds. Their energy spent on the child is comparable to that of ours spent on childhood in modern psychology. At first, though, they (Tertullian, Cyprian) did not urge early baptism, and Gregory of Nazianzus preferred some degree of mind, about the age of three, before baptism. But Augustine was adamant. Because man was born in original sin he brought it with him into the world, as Augustine himself had done from his pagan past. Only baptism could wash this from the child. Augustine was sharp about the child's need of salvation, writing: "Those who plead for the mimesis of children ought not love their ignorance, but their innocence". (*Enar. in Ps.* XLIV, 1.) And what is innocent? "It is the weakness of the *faculties* of the child that is innocent, not the soul". (*Conf.* I, 7, 11.) How Freudian: the child cannot perform with its still-too-young faculties, those latent perversities that are in the soul. The soul carried not mere general sin, but the specific sin of pre-Christian, un-Christian impulses of polytheistic paganism which Freud was later to discover and baptise "polymorphously perverse", and which Jung was later more comprehensively to describe as the archetypes. Baptism could redeem the soul from childhood, from that imaginal world of a multitude of archetypal forms, Gods and Goddesses, their cults and the unchristian practices they substantiated.

16

Inasmuch as the child is not a vestige but a system functioning now and inasmuch as a sacrament is not a vestige of a one-time historical happening, but continues now, then the baptism of the child is *always going on*. We are continually baptising the child, lustrating the psyche's "childhood", its "beginnings", its reminiscing, with the apotropaic rites of our Augustinian culture, cleansing the soul of its polytheistic imaginal possibility which is carried emblematically by the child, thereby taking the child of the psyche a "prisoner for Christ" (Gregory of Nazianzus, "In Praise of Basil"), much as the early church replaced the infants of the hero cults and pagan pantheon with the Jesus child.

This Christening goes on whenever we connect to the child motifs in our dreams and feelings using only Christian models. Then we regard the polymorphic potential of our inherent polytheism as fundamentally in need of updating by transformation into unity. Thus we prevent the child from performing its function of that which alters. We correct it, rather than let it correct us.

Regression, Repression

Baptism served two functions for which we have modern names: it prevented regression; it offered repression. Our most immediate experience of the child today is through these experiences.

What depth psychology has come to call regression is nothing other than a return to the child. Since this is so, we might inquire more fundamentally into psychology's notion of maturity which has regression as its counterpart and into psychology's idea of development which requires that the child be abandoned. Regression is the unavoidable shadow of linear styles of thinking. A developmental model will be plagued by its counter-movement, atavism; and reversion will be seen, not as a return through likeness to imaginal reality along Neoplatonic lines (Proclus, Plotinus), but as a regression to a worse condition. Psychology presents "going back" as "going down", a devolution to prior and inferior patterns. Maturity and regression become incompatible. For regression we lose respect, forgetting the need of living things to "go back" to "beginnings".

Regression is made tolerable in theory today only in terms of a "regression in the service of the ego" (E. Kris, *Psychoanalytic Explorations in Art,* 1952). Even in Jung, regression is mainly compensatory, a *reculer pour mieux sauter.*

In Maslow, Erikson, Piaget, Gesell, as well as in Freudian ego psychology, if we do not advance along certain well-researched paths from stage to stage we become fixated in "childhood" and show regressed behaviour, styles called puerile and infantile. Behind every forward step into "reality" there is the threatening shadow of the child — hedonistic or mystical depending upon how we regard the reversion to primordiality. This child we propitiate with sentimentality, superstition and kitsch, with indulgent holidays and treats, and with psychotherapy which partly owes its existence and earns its living from the regressive pull of the child.

Our model of maturity tends to make regression attractive. At a distance we idealize the angelic state of childhood and its creativity. By abandoning the child we place it in arcadia, borne by the sea, cradled, rocking softly at water level among reeds and rushes, nourished by nymphs who delight in its whims, shepherds, kindly old caretakers who welcome the childish, the regressed. Then of course the counter-movement sets in again; the hero constellates; from the abandoned child the great leap forward, the draining of the Zuyder Zee with which Freud compared the work of psychoanalysis. (NIL, p. 106.)

Because the major content of repression is the child, the contemporary revolution on behalf of the repressed — black or poor, feminine or natural or undeveloped — becomes unavoidably the revolution of the child. The formulations become immature, a touch pathetic, the behaviour regressed, and the ambition invincible and vulnerable at the same time. Hermaphroditism of the archetype also plays its role in the revolution, as does that peculiar mixture of beginning and end: hope exemplified in apocalyptic destruction. Our theme thus touches upon psychology's relation to the times and its struggle with the child, all of which suggests that it might be profitable to reflect the statements of Marcuse, Laing, and Brown concerning the contemporary revolution of the repressed in the light of archetypal psychology, i.e., as expressions of the cult of the child.

Evoking the Child

We are familiar with situations that call the child back from where we have left it. Going backwards into familiar places, sounds, smells; each *abaissement du niveau mental,* new conditions that constellate thrill and the fantasy of complete newness, that one can make of something whatever one wishes; also sudden falls into love, into illness, into depression. The child is also evoked by unfamil-

18

iarity where imagination is asked for and we respond instead with stubborn petulance, inadequacy, tears.

But the regressed condition that no one wants can also be directly prompted in psychotherapy. For here is a haven, to creep out of hiding; here one may show one's unwanted, unlovable, ugly concealments, and one's huge hopes. These feelings have all been given appropriate psychological names: infantile desires, self-destructive fantasies, omnipotence cravings, archaic impulses. But in deriding these names we ought not to forget — and we are each therapists of the psyche since it is a devotion that cannot belong to a profession only — that always these childish *pathological conditions contain futurity.* The very way forward through the condition so unwanted, ugly and preposterously expectant lies just in the conditions themselves. The pathology is also the futurity. In it the insights lie; from it the movement comes.

By recognizing a basic cry we may evoke this child in the pathology; it is as if there were a basic cry in persons that gives direct voice to the abandoned content. For some persons it is: "Help, please help me"; others say, "take me, just as I am, take me, all of me without choice among my traits, no judgement, no questions asked"; or "take me, without my having to do something, to be someone". Another cry may be "hold me", or "don't go away; never leave me alone". We may also hear the content saying simply, "Love me". Or we can hear, "teach me, show me what to do, tell me how". Or, "carry me, keep me". Or the cry from the bottom may say, "Let me alone, all alone; just let me be".

Generally the basic cry speaks in the receptive voice of the infant, where the subject is an object, a "me" in the hands of others, incapable of action yet poignantly enunciating its knowledge of its subjectivity, knowing how it wishes to be handled. Its subjectivity is in the crying by means of which it organizes its existence. So, as well, we hear it in the basic cry a person addresses to his environment, turning his entourage into helpers, or lovers, or constant companions (a *thiasos*) who will nurse, dance attendance, or teach, or accept all blindly, who will never let him alone, or the reverse, from whom he flees in continual rejection. And the cry says how a person is unable to meet his needs himself, unable to help himself, or let himself alone.

It is worth insisting here that the cry is never cured. By giving voice to the abandoned child it is always there, and must be there as an archetypal necessity. We know well enough that some things we never learn, cannot help, fall back to and cry from again and again. These inaccessible places where we are always exposed and afraid, where we cannot learn, cannot love, and cannot help by transforming, repressing or accepting are the wildernesses, the caves where the abandoned child lies hidden. That we go on regressing to these places states something fundamental about human nature: we come back to an incurable psychopathology again and again through the course of life yet which apparently does go through many changes before and after contact with the unchanging child.

Here we strike upon the psychological relationship between what philosophy calls becoming and being, or the changing and the changeless, the different and the same, and what psychology calls growth on the one hand and on the other psychopathy: that which cannot by definition reverse or alter but remains as a more or less constant lacuna of character throughout life. In the language of our theme we have the eternal vulnerability of the abandoned child, and this same child's evolving futurity.

In this conundrum we usually pick up one side or the other, feeling ourselves different, changing, evolving, only to be smashed back by the shattering recurrence of a basic cry which in turn leads to the belief of being hopelessly stuck, nothing moving, just the same as always. The history of psychotherapy has also been driven back and forth by this apparent dilemma. At times degeneration theory (inheritance and constitution, or an idea of predestination) declare character is fate and that we can but move within pre-determined patterns. At other times, such as today in American humanistic developmental psychology, the category of growth through transformation covers all psychic events.

Neither position is adequate. Like the metaphorical child of Plato's *Sophist* (249d) who, when asked to choose, opts for "both", the abandoned child is both that which *never grows,* remaining as permanent as psychopathy, and also that futurity springing from vulnerability itself. The complex remains, and the lacunae; that which becomes different are our connections with these places and our reflections through them. It is as if to change we must keep in touch with the changeless, which also implies taking change for what it is, rather than in terms of development. Evolution tends to become a "means of disowning the past" (T. S. Eliot); what we want to change we wish to be rid of. A subtle psychological perception is required to distinguish in our natures the changeable from the changeless, and to see the two as intimately connected so as not to search in the wrong place for growth and the wrong place for stability, or to presume that change leaves stability behind and that stability is never vulnerable.

The Return of the Child

If the child is repressed in the amnesia of "the second to the fifth year", as Freud wrote, then it is the little child who shall return. Abandonment does not succeed; the murderer's hand fails; fishermen, shepherds, maids appear; the child becomes a foundling to come back and carry the day.

It is not merely that the childish returns in the left-overs of childhood, but *everything that emerges from unconsciousness comes back too young.* Everything begins in youthful folly because the doors to the cellars and gardens of the mind are barred not only by a censor, a flaming sword, or a Cerberus, but by a little boy or girl who magically transforms everything passing over the threshold into its own condition.

Thus, as Freud saw, the world of the unconscious is the world of childhood, not actual childhood or the childhood of the human race, but a condition governed by the archetype of the child; thus, as Jung saw, this archetype is herald, the prefiguration of every change that we go through in depth. Everything comes back too young, implying that the adequate connection with the unconscious will have to show inadequacy. We are not able, still dependent on that child, its whims, its atmosphere of specialness, still needing our hurts, the way it touches our eros, making us each at moments into paedophiles, child-lovers.

Moreover, all the other faces of the repressed, the personally forgotten and the primordially unknown, will return in a child-like style. Besides the revolution, all those other things ostracized from the agora of daily life — art, insanity, passion, despair, vision — will come in with this peculiar childishness which at times we ennoble as the childlikeness of the creative.

The childishness that returns as the personal shadow deserves better treatment than merely the Freudian one. Jung indicated that the treatment of childishness, of psychopathology, at the archetypal level is to *"dream the myth onwards"* (CW 9, 1, §271), to let its prospective nature speak. By allowing the child to be the corrector, it performs one of its archetypal functions: futurity. What comes back points forward; it returns as the repressed and at the same time comes back in order to fulfill a Biblical cure for psychopathology: "and a little child shall lead them" (Isaiah 11:6).

Consequently, the cue to the future is given by the repressed, the child and what he brings with him, and the way forward is indeed the way back. But it is immensely difficult to discriminate among the emotions that come with the child, mainly because he does not return alone.

It is as if the little girl abandoned returns with a protector, a new found father, a strong male figure of muscular will, of arguments and cunning, and his outrage, his blind striking out mingles with her pained tantrums, his sullen melancholy becomes indistinguishable from her withdrawn pouting. Though they coalesce, child and guardian also struggle for separation. In face and gesture there are alternating movements, an alternating look in the eye, appeal for help, resistance to it, bitterness of tears coming grudgingly, fought off, clenched, and then abandoned cataclysmic sobbing. Sometimes the little girl returns as a gamin of the streets, dirty, or a tomboy of the fields, earthy, half-male, hardened from the long neglect and the tutorials of the animus, a girl-child almost wolf-child, all thumbs and elbows, returning yet saying "let me alone".

In the little boy a similar pattern occurs for it is equally difficult to distinguish him from the milkmaids and nymphs and sisters who have succoured him during the repression. The softness and vanity and demands which he brings with him, passivity and vulnerability, the reclusive nursing of himself, hardly differ from what psychology has called anima states.

With the child's return comes childhood, both kinds: actual with its memories and imaginal with its reminiscences. We have come to call this memorial factor with its two kinds of remembrances "the unconscious", personal and collective. But this term, "the unconscious", only adds to the burden of differentiating the complexity of psychic life. It might be more beneficial to separate the child (as the reminiscent factor which returns a person to the primordially repressed of non-actual sub-structures) from a category so indefinite as the unconscious. Then we would be in a better position to free "childhood" as an imaginal mode of perceiving and feeling from its identification with actual childhood which usually had less freedom and joy, less fantasy and magic and amorality than we sentimentally attribute to it. *Our cult of childhood is a sentimental disguise for true homage to the imaginal.* Could childhood be called by its true name — the realm of archetypal reminiscence — then we would not have to become unconscious to find the mythical. We have psychologically confused the "coming up" of events

22

from "the unconscious" with the "coming back" of reminiscence.

Psychology has taken the repressed child to be an axiomatic metaphor of psychic structure. Psychology assumes the repressed is less developed than the repressor, that consciousness is topographically, historically and morally superior to the unconscious, characterized by primitive, amoral and infantile impulses. *Our notion of consciousness inherently necessitates repression of the child.* This constellates our main fear: the return of the inferiority, the child, who also means the return of the realm of archetypal reminiscence. Archetypal fantasy is the most threatening activity of the human soul as we now conceive it, for our Western rational tradition has placed this activity in the ontologically inferior, the primitive amoral realm of actual childhood. (Cf. Bundy, 1927.)

Thus a restoration of the mythical, the imaginal and the archetypal implies a collapse into the infantile realm of the child. Our strong ego-centered consciousness fears nothing more than just such collapse. The worst insult is to be called "childish", "infantile", "immature". So we have devised every sort of measure for defending ourselves against the child — and against archetypal fantasy. These defenses we call the consciousness of the strong, mature and developed ego.

Though ego-consciousness has its defenses, or *is* defenses, the child is defenselessness itself. Exposure, vulnerability, abandonment are its very nature. Its defense is mainly that of innocence. Without structured walls, lost in the woods or afloat on the waters in a frail basket, its predilection is to remain protected by its own helplessness. Its style of defense, of paranoia, is innocence: "I don't know", "I didn't realize", "I didn't mean anything", "It just happened". The world is *systematically* haphazard, afloat; all things held together by spontaneous amazing synchronicities; all things intending the child, pointing to him, keeping him alive in the center of importance, even while he does nothing, wills nothing, knows nothing.

The shadow that we fear most and repress primordially, i.e., the kind of fantasy reminiscence that we name madness, is brought with the child. The fear of yielding control to him governs our profound amnesia. And so we have forgotten an evident psychological truth: anxiety reveals the deepest shadow. Rather than see the child in the shadow, recent psychology has been concentrating upon the shadows of aggression and of moral evil. But aggression can be enjoyable, and moral evil, attractive. They are not fearful, shameful to the same degree as the child. Jungian focus upon the devil and the dark side of the God image has covered over our anxiousness, so that we have neglected the dark side of the Bambino, the other *infans noster* who was the first shadow found in the anxieties of classical analysis. The ruling power contaminating the imaginal with the impulsive is a monster child whom we have been abandoning for centuries.

So, when the cry goes up *"l'imagination au pouvoir"* (Sorbonne rebellion in 1968) we should not feel deceived that a monster has been released, that the revolution becomes puerile nonsense, obscene, scatological, polymorphously perverse. The imagination to power is the child to power, because Western corsciousness with its onesided extravagances of will and reason at the expense of memoria, has abandoned the *mundus imaginalis* to children.

The Fantasy of Independence

"Child", writes Jung in his essay on this archetype, "means something evolving towards independence". In a phrase Jung catches the dilemma, for the child returns not only in the regression, bringing one into the imaginal world of childhood, but also in a striving out of childhood for independence. Abandonment, as Jung pointed out and Neumann elaborated, is the precondition for the independence and invincibility of the child-becoming-hero.

" 'Child' means something evolving towards independence. This it cannot do", continued Jung, "without detaching itself from its origins: abandonment is therefore a necessary condition, not just a concomitant symptom" (CW 9, 1, §287). The child is abandoned in order to reveal its independence. Out of feelings of isolation and rejection arises a fantasy of independence.

There is a similarity of metaphor, as others have observed, between Aristotle's entelechy, Leibniz' monad, and Jung's self of which the child is a primary image. (CW 9, 1, §270, 278.) Entelechy, monad and self coincide in this fantasy of independence: self-substantial entelechy on the course of its actualization and the self-same windowless monad unique to itself different from all others are both recapitulated in Jung's self of individuation unfolding through the tensions of opposites, like a tree. Jung compares child and tree (CW 15, §122), and he writes: "If a mandala may be described as a symbol of the self seen in cross section, then the tree would represent a profile view of it: the self depicted as a process of growth" (CW 13, §304).

The tree is a cherished symbol in depth psychology — the tree test, the analysis of tree-images in clinical paintings and drawings, and the examination of the tree in art in order to grasp the personality of the painter. The tree suits our notion of personality growth, and indeed appears as a spontaneous metaphor for the imperceptible expansion from seed to fullness, in which history can be read, the dry years and wet ones, the blows and diseases, and the same metaphor provides for ancestral roots, vertical movement stretched between heaven and earth, branches, fruits in season, pruning. And we need these metaphors to place our lives and to place the feelings that something besides myself carries my life in a natural process and is uniquely mine, my tree of life.

At the same time, it is the task of psychology to point out what else these metaphors are saying so that consciousness does not become imprisoned in its own favourite images. One job of psychology is to bring archetypal reflection to its own systems, ideas, imagery so that it, unlike the other disciplines, can apply itself to itself, aware of what shadows appear within its statements.

In regard to the tree, its style of independence may so dominate our awareness that we lose sight that we are being carried by it, for we are not trees, but men, not vegetables, but animals, not planted and rooted but roaming, not cyclic only in our rhythms but multiphasic with many processes taking place simultaneously, at different rhythms and in different directions and not necessarily following one overall entelechy. If, on the one hand, the tree fantasy states an independence of the self from the ego the fantasy just as well states the independence of the self from other selves. It emphasizes *separation*, so that we forget that individuation and independent separateness are neither synonymous, nor necessarily involved.

The fantasy of independence comes out again in Jung's "Seven Sermons to the Dead" (1916), where the speaker in Sermon IV tells of two God-devils: the Burning One and the Growing One. The first is Eros, the second, the Tree of Life; the first "bindeth twain together, the second filleth space with bodily forms, growing with 'slow and constant increase' ". "In their divinity", says the speaker, "stand life and love opposed".

Life and love are opposed when life is represented by the tree (CW 13, §459) that grows alone; its habitat, as Jung writes (CW 13, §406), is a mountain or an island, or it grows directly out of the sea water, upon a rock, or extends from a human body part, head or belly (CW 12, figs. 131, 135). Clinical drawings of the tree show the same independence as the alchemical imagery described by Jung.

25

Evidently the slow and constant increase of the tree, representing personality in its individuation process (CW 13, §350), individualized already *in nuce* by its particular "nature", stalwart, memorable, alone, is a process of independence. Tree is the child in which abandonment has become the seed set apart.

Note that this tree does not appear in a community, as a member of a grove, one in an allée or orchard, a part of a forest. We do not see the forest for the tree, and, unless the trees like Philemon and Baucis are joined by their "vegetable love" and united by miraculous intervention, the tree in its independence shows a growth where life and love are opposed. That we may encourage our growth on an island or mountain, producing individuation from heads or bellies, or directly from the psychoid sea of our emotionality through concentration upon the subjective factor may occur, but then at the expense of the other God-devil Eros, who becomes the burning one, feverish to connect that which is isolated and which must be isolated by the very metaphor that does not have the interdependence of connection inherent to its fantasy.

Child and tree associate in mythologems that bring the two together: the child in the tree, born of a tree, hidden there, or carried to its death by the tree; by giving the tree a maternal meaning, matters have been left at that. But we may also regard them as a pair of radical extremes: solitary independence and symbiotic dependency, two fantasies and qualities of emotion that bespeak each other and call each other up. Though child may be abandoned, it is never alone; child does not represent a solitary self, but *a psychic condition in need* and cared for by animals, nurses, foster parents. It may grow, as Jung says, towards independence, and thus be latently heroic, as the tree, a singleton pre-determined in seed, but its essence is dependent. Fundamental to the tree is that it is rooted to its fate and grows from it, and one way only — the tree never regresses; but the child is regression; it can do nothing alone; it must be sheltered, watered, kept.

Thus when we are in the fantasy of independence we are also secretly in the fantasy of dependency, which projects independence as goal, that towards which we are evolving. Furthermore, when we are in the fantasy of independence, dependency seems incommensurable, a contradictory opposite, that which must be left behind; so the child will continually be abandoned which in turn constellates an ever-stronger Burning One and an ever more compulsive dependency upon Eros. To be free of this cycle would mean to abandon the tree of independence as our model of self in order to imagine dependency by means of other metaphors.

For instance, independence could mean widening the areas of dependency, sensitivity toward one's needs for help and following, for a forest of comrades in symbiotic participation, for interchange and cross-fertilization, where life and love are not necessarily opposed.

The Fantasy of Growth

If any single notion now conjoins the disparate schools of therapeutic psychology it is the fantasy of growth. Carl Rogers in a chapter describing "A Therapist's View of the Good Life" uses these phrases: "An increasing openness to experience", "increasing trust in his organism", "a process of functioning more fully", "greater richness of life". Erik Erikson in a chapter called "Growth and Crises of the Healthy Personality" describes psychic health in similar language: "an increased sense of inner unity, with an increase of good judgement, and an increase in the capacity to do well...".

Karen Horney in her main late book *Neurosis and Human Growth* (London, 1951) speaks of the work of psychotherapy as giving "the constructive forces of the real self a chance to grow" (p. 348). The wholeheartedness of psychic health is built upon her "morality of evolution", a belief "that inherent in man are evolutionary constructive forces, which urge him to realize his given potentialities" (p. 15).

These are but three pointed examples. The growth fantasy is easy, appealing to the child: whatever is may become something else, transformed through a "natural" process of increase and in accordance with the "natural" development of inborn basic patterns. The personality is not conceived in original sin but in health, not in *privatio boni* requiring baptism but in *a priori* health and wholeness. We need but conform with the ground plan of our individual being and grow from there. Disease, perversion, insanity, evil — these are secondary accrued phenomena, lacunae or fixations in the growth process which is primary. Jung's cautionary realism about the shadow in all psychic events, including wholeness, and Freud's pessimism reflected by his thanatos hypothesis have been crushed under the juggernaut of therapeutic enthusiasm which is but the recrudescence of messianic hope that no longer finds place in religion. Psychology does not notice that its constructs and interpretations have become dogmatic expressions of a fantasy, so that psychology no longer can reflect the actual psyche in conditions that bespeak neither hoping nor growing and are neither natural nor whole.

Astoundingly, psychology turns to the child in order to understand the adult, blaming adults for not enough of the child or for too many remnants of the child still left in adulthood. *The thinking of psychotherapy and of psychology of personality has been captured by the child archetype and its growth fantasy.* Psychological thought is deliberately childish. It continues the fantasy of creative expansion, widening, enlargening, so essential to the Romantic temperament according to Georges Poulet. This fantasy is hard to reconcile with that feeling of decline in our civilization and our subjective experiences of narrowing specialization, limitation and decay. Psychology's growth fantasy seems a curious left-over of the early twentieth century's colonial, industrial and economic fascination with increase: the bigger the better.

Little wonder that at a certain moment in our lives we feel we have done with psychology, that we feel unable to abide one more psychological explanation, for it is all too simple, too naive, too optimistic. At a certain moment we hear the child speaking through our psychological words, and this one archetypal perspective is inadequate for the complexity of our souls. Moreover, the childishness is not itself provided for by the fantasy of growth which abandons the child in an unsophisticated notion of growing.

Growth, like evolution and development, or like any of the pregnant terms with which psychology operates — unconscious, soul, self, — is a symbolic, emotionally charged word, evocative rather than descriptive, generally hortatory rather than particularly precise. We have confused the general category of motion with one of its varieties, growth, so that all movements and changes become witness to growth. We call adaptation "growth", and even suffering and loss part of "growing". We are urged, nay expected, to "keep growing" in one way or another right into the coffin.

In this one idea of psychology various notions converge: 1) increase in size (or expansion); 2) evolution in form and function (or differentiation); 3) moral progress (or improvement); 4) conjunctions of parts (or synthesis); 5) stages in temporal succession (or maturation); and 6) negentropic self-generation (or spontaneity). These last two need further clarification, in that the process of maturation from stage to stage occurs, according to the growth fantasy, both rationally and spontaneously — not randomly — following the essential goodness of the child. Growth represents this goodness, manifests its activity being realized, and this goodness is part of the child's "instinct", "creative nature", "heart", not part of its intellect or "head" which is later and learned and not so deep.

These interlocking notions form part of what George Boas in his masterly, critical essay has explored as *The Cult of Childhood,* a title which means nothing less than obeisance to the child archetype in our modern Western culture. There is still more to it: added to the six components which I have tried to separate within the growth fantasy, there is also an underlying idea that growth equals health. To stop growing is to be fixated, stuck, neurotic. Moreover, decay, which certainly belongs to less naive models of growth, is apparently forgotten by psychology. What appears here as my simplification merely mirrors the simplifications in psychological theories.

But the idea of growth could be separated from the child's version of it and then it might be less simplified. Psychology could adopt a more sophisticated analysis of growth in terms of change of form as discussed by L. L. Whyte and as presented by Adolf Portmann in many subtle discussions of it here at Eranos. Then we might imagine growth less as increase and linear development, and more as changes in *patterns of significance and imagery.* The precision of this imagery arises in response to the empty non-formed aspects of the psyche. Its lacuna and voids (*increatum*) provide the "negative" background — much as empty areas in leaf patterns provide the characteristics in emerging leaf shapes in Goethean morphology. Psychological significance "grows" out of the negative, meaningless areas of our suffering. Significance occurs in relation with psychopathy; we find significance when the absurd and insignificant nonsense of our complexes takes on changed shape. The changes are formal. Wholeness then would imply less the integration of parts into a unity as in the naive growth fantasy, but more the discrimination of patterns and the freedom of their changes.

We must be clear not to blame biology for the naive growth metaphor. Its origins precede its appearance in biology. Notions such as the "childhood of the race", evolution, and recapitulation by ontogeny of phylogeny indicate that this archetypal fantasy probably played its part in the formation of basic ideas of nineteenth-century biology, anthropology and linguistics. (Much work needs to be done in order to uncover the archetypal patterns in the formation of these ideas.) In psychology many images of growth are of course taken from the naturalist's language: Froebel, speaking of children's education, conjures up flowers blooming, ducks taking to water, chickens scratching at an appointed stage. Erikson understands psychological growth through models of the "growth of organism" from a "ground plan". Gesell compares growth of the mind to that of plants; Koffka entitled his major work in Gestalt psychology (that so stresses wholeness) *The Growth of the Mind.* Piaget finds intelligence can best be accounted for by means of a developmental metaphor: intelligence follows inherent maturational laws producing progressively more stable states of adaptation; we move through smaller stages and larger periods, each stage and period providing foundation for the next. "Genesis is simply transition from one structure to another, nothing more; but this transition always leads from a 'weaker' to a 'stronger' structure..." (Piaget, *Structuralism,* p. 141).

Within and below lies "nature", the governing determinant of growth. To put the fantasy in the language of archetypal psychology: the archetypes of child as growth and its mother, nature, rule psychology's main view of the human being. The idea of nature further mystifies the imprecision, for it is an idea so rich, so varied, so symbolic that over sixty different conceptual connotations have been distinguished. It would be worth a *Tagung,* perhaps several, on this complex subject of health, nature and growth; fortunately our part is only a few reflections on the fantasy in relation to the child.

The Static Child

As Jung and Freud point out in different ways, discussion of the child always involves us with ideas of growth, and the actual child most vividly presents a pattern where all the notions — expansion, differentiation, improvement, maturation and spontaneity — coincide. The child gets bigger and better and more able "naturally". But neglected in these observations which have been elaborated into precise norms for the ages of childhood by Erikson, Koffka, Maslow, Piaget, and Gesell is the *static* child. For the child *archetype* does not grow but remains an inhabitant of childhood, a state of being, and the archetypal child personifies a component that is not meant to grow but to remain as it is as child, at the threshold, intact, an image of certain fundamental realities that necessarily require the child metaphor and which cannot be presented in another manner. Child Zeus and Child Dionysos and Child Hermes do not grow, as do Theseus and Moses for instance.

30

The child is one of the faces — not stages — of the God, one of his ways of being, of revealing his nature. There is no question of moral improvement, of increase, or of differentiation through developmental process in these child images of these Gods unless we use man and his childhood as the measure for archetypal events. Although these Gods fulfill some of the patterns of abandonment, *they do not leave the child behind in order to become "mature"*. The face of the child is eternally theirs, and if we are created in the image of the divine, so a face of the child in us is static, eternal, not able to grow. Perhaps I speak now of men, and the image in which they are made since curiously we do not have comparable images of a Child Athene, a Child Aphrodite, a Child Hera or Demeter.

By giving more favour to this idea of the child that is not meant to grow, we might imagine the child's abandonment and need for rescue as a continuous state, a static necessity that does not evolve towards independence, does not evolve at all, but remains as a requirement of the fulfilled and matured person.

Picasso speaks to our point: "Change does not mean development". "When I hear how people talk of the development of the artist, it seems to me as if they were seeing the artist between two opposed mirrors which were endlessly reflecting his mirror image, and as if they saw the series of images in one mirror as his past and the images in the other mirror as his future, while he himself supposedly stood for his present. They do not realize that all are the same images but on different levels". "I am astounded over the way people let the word development be misused, I don't develop; I am".

And finally, concerning abandonment, Picasso says: "Nothing can come about without loneliness. I have created a loneliness for myself that no one can imagine" (translations mine).

The Fantasy of Origins

The repressed child returns too in the fantasy of origins, a fantasy which seems to affect particularly those whose disciplines require a purgation of subjectivity for the sake of an objective rationality. Scientific scholarship shows much concern with beginnings, with *Ursprungsgeschichte, Urtext* and *Urwort,* with *Quellenforschung.* The search is for origins in roots, elements, sources. In psychology the fantasy of origins occurs elaborately in Freud's "primal horde" and primal scene and Rank's "birth trauma" to mention but two of the most obviously imaginary. But contemporary psychiatry's insistence that neurotic disturbances originate fundamentally in the deprivation during early years of maternal care (Bowlby) is, despite the objective nature of the supporting research and the unimaginative language in which it is presented, also an origin fantasy about babies, breasts and what a mother should be.

There will always be an unease when one deals —as do the scholarly, investigative disciplines (*Geisteswissenschaften*) — with the depths of human nature, because these depths remain always open questions. The *a priori* of law, language, religion and society are difficult to discover not merely because they are "buried in the past". Because these fields display the human spirit, they remain enigmatic in principle, and their riddles give rise to philosophical wonder — and to psychological anxiety. By believing that we can trace the phenomena of these disciplines to a source does not so much solve the problem as it does settle an anxiety. That the ultimate source is in the subjective factor, in the enigma of the human spirit, is disguised by the fantasy of objective origins.

Reductionism of the later to the earlier and of the complex to the simple presupposes a growth or evolution fantasy. Moreover, this mental process of reductionism seems to become less and less exigent as it nears its goal: an explanation in terms of origins. The origins fantasy is mimetic to much of the child archetype's *simplicity,* where simple means single — being satisfied with a single answer or a single source for multiple complexities; and where simple means fool — a foolishness of weak-minded and windy thinking.

Reductionism is so easily satisfied. Its contentment with naive explanations for complex problems — for instance, its unsophisticated idea of causality — indicates that a subjective factor is influencing the objective rationality of the hypothesis. We should not let pass unobserved this psychological oddity. The sophistication, and even intelligence, of scholars give way as they move from the immediate complexity of a problem at hand to an account of its remote origins. Their fantasy shows that, in their search for beginnings, they become guided by the child archetype. They seem to lose sight as they move from known to unknown, their evidence ever slimmer, that a hypothesis is truly hypothetical, a supposing, a conjecturing about an unknown lying behind the known, and that they have moved from one level of discussion to another where fantasy plays a more vital role. So they become like the child described in Plato (*Rep.* 378D) who "cannot

32

judge what is allegorical and what is literal".

Research comes to a stop when it has formulated a fantasy of beginnings into a hypothesis of origins, when an allegory can be presented as a literal reality. Since the dominant of beginnings governs the research, the real origin searched for is the child archetype and the real prompter of the endeavour is the lost child. Under the influence of this archetype the research, psychologically, is itself an allegory: the search for an *imaginary childhood,* whether of language, of mankind, of neurosis, supposedly buried in a prior condition, whether in primitives, myths, archaeological digs, subconscious mental structures, root syllables.

Because these origins are imaginary we could also say that the origins lie in the imaginal, implying that the beginnings of every deep human question formulated into an academic, scholarly discipline lie in the *mundus imaginalis.* This provides the archetypal background or *causa formalis* of the matter under investigation. Hence, investigation is satisfied only when it reaches an extensively fantastic reconstruction of beginnings whether in the pre-history of the individual or of a field. When the imaginal is reached, the archetypal urge in the research is satisfied. The anxiety is quelled. The child, as it were, has come home.

The Fantasy of Creativity

The topic of this *Tagung,* creativity, also belongs partly among the fantasies constellated around the child archetype. There are many notions of creativity, and we have already examined them and grouped them in an earlier lecture ("On Psychological Creativity", *Eranos Jahrbuch* 35, 1966) which spares us now from more than merely noting in passing the relevance of this theme.

In the literature of psychology one of the notions of creativity — originality, imagination, eros, novelty, play, spontaneity, naiveté — expresses the child. George Boas has gathered quotations mainly from critics and painters in which the creative vision and the vision of the child are identified. When we identify the creative with this set of connotations we have taken our perspective from the child archetype. Consequently, when we speak of the unconscious as the "creative unconscious", we are seeing it mainly in its guise of the child and our simplifications of its processes are childish. The cult of childhood continues in the awe with which we hold "creativity", the attention we pay the "creative man" and the "creative impulse". We should not be surprised that psychology's research into creativity frequently yields silly results, especially noticeable when play is given a disproportionate place, as if imagination were not a discipline or art, not a work. The last ideas of Winnicott are case in point. His prolonged devotion to the psychiatry of children resulted in a theory of play which extends the word to a metapsychology of creativity, the archetypal background to which is the child.

Concentration upon the child aspect of creativity makes us miss its other faces: the destruction and aggression of the shadow, the work of the ego, the renewing periodicity of the mother, the moodiness of the anima, and the ordering limits and inevitable failure given by the senex — all of which too enter psychological descriptions of creativity and which have their part in the formation of any *œuvre*.

The Fantasy of Futurity

There is yet a fifth fantasy belonging to the child. This fantasy too seizes us from behind when the child is not held in consciousness. The child archetype speaks also in the language of goals. One of its essentials is futurity.

A goal, from the psychological point of view, is a final cause in Aristotle's sense of "that for the sake of which". Inasmuch as a final cause enters every complex as one of its four grounds, the child is never absent; we feel him in our hoping. But then he gets abandoned by throwing himself forward into goal fantasies, hopes literalized. Each complex projects a teleology about itself: how it will evolve, what purpose it has, how it can be resolved or brought to an end.

Therapeutic psychology too has a *telos* and speaks of goals which language it assumes it has taken "empirically" from the psyche. Thus it speaks of the synthesis of personality, individuation, conjunction of the opposites, self. It has as well an elaborated goal imagery — lapis, mandala, tree, child — which again is the result of "clinical findings". But the spontaneous imagery of completion and its literalization into goals are better kept distinct. Otherwise we place the *telos* inherent within the complex outside, at the end of the line. Then we move the *telos* from an internal component to an external image; then we take it literally, placing futurity in the future, a mistake as naive as taking the efficient cause literally and placing it in the past.

Predictions about the future of a complex and reduction to its past are both fantasies within it. Efficient cause and final cause are movements within every psychic complexity giving belief that the troubling question at hand has come from somewhere and is going somewhere, reflecting a genealogy myth and an eschatology myth. But psychologically, past and future function *now* so that a goal is a dynamism *now* at work in a complex. To separate out the *telos* is to separate way and goal. We could hardly cripple the movement of a complex more than by speaking literally of its goal which aborts it of its teleological impulse, robs it of its child. The more we fix on the goals, like wholeness and self and individuation, the less likely it is that they are actually working. The more literal is our description, the more we are possessed by the fantasy of futurity, enacting the child even though disguised in the wisdom-language of highest and last things.

Mothering and Nursing

When the child returns through mimesis and we return to its condition, enacting childish behaviour and experiencing childish emotions, there also returns the problem of "how to deal with it".

Here we shall note an essential contrast between mothering and nursing. In their early discoveries, Freudian and Jungian psychologies both were dominated by parental archetypes, especially the mother, so that behaviour and imagery were mainly interpreted through this maternal perspective: the oedipal mother, the positive and negative mother, the castrating and devouring mother, the battle with the mother and the incestuous return. The unconscious and the realm of "The Mothers" were often an identity. Through this one archetypal hermeneutic, female figures and receptive passive objects were indiscriminately made into mother symbols. What was not mother! Mountains, trees, oceans, animals, the body and time cycles, receptacles and containers, wisdom and love, cities and fields, witches and death — and a great deal more lost specificity during this period of psychology so devoted to the Great Mother and her son, the Hero. Jung took us a step forward by elaborating other archetypal feminine forms, the anima, and I have tried in several lectures here to continue in Jung's direction by remembering that breasts and milk do not belong only to mothers, that other divine figures besides Maria, Demeter and Kybele have equally important things to say to the psyche, and, that the women

35

attendant on Dionysos were not turned into mothers but nurses. Like those frescoes of the madonna Church which conceals a congregation under her billowed blue skirts, the Great Mother has hidden a pantheon of other feminine modes for enacting life.

Mother and nurse are separated in the abandoned child motif. In myth they are two distinct figures. Similarly, in our reactions to the abandoned child's return — sudden spontaneous affects of the heart, weakness and longing, narcissistic demands and complaints, playfulness, fantasies of conquest, invincibility, specialness — we too might distinguish the taking up the child by the nurse and by the mother.

For the mothering attitude, it is always a matter of life and death; we are obsessed with how things will turn out; we ask what happened and what will happen. The mother makes things "great", exaggerates, enthuses, infuses the power of life and death into each detail, because the mother's relation to the child is personal, not personal as related and particular, but *archetypally personal* in the sense that the child's fate is delivered through the personal matrix of her fate, becoming fate in general which she then is called. The mother archetype gives the personalistic illusion to fate. Whatever she has to do with takes on overwhelming personal importance which actually is general and altogether impersonal: the desires and loathing of the mother-son relation so intimately personal become suprapersonal enormities, just as the experiences of despair, renewal, continuity and mystery of the mother-daughter relation that seem so fatefully personal become impersonal eternal events.

The growth she furthers is all-out and passionate, the death overwhelming, *mater dolorosa,* for the mother is always too much: goodness and support, concern for weakness, or interest in ambition. Her too-muchness makes the child into hero and rebel, into princess and prostitute, for her passion converts our hurt derelict conditions into archetypal importance.

As Jung spontaneously remarks in that famous passage in his essay on the mother archetype (CW 9, 1, §172): "Mother is mother-love, *my* experience and *my* secret". Although the mother experience is archetypal, "strange like nature", "cruel like fate", yet it is so acutely personal that, as Jung observes, we tend to "load that enormous burden of meaning, responsibility, duty, heaven and hell, on to the shoulders of one frail and fallible human being...who was our mother" (ibid). "This figure of the personal mother looms so large in all personalistic psychologies that, as we know, they never got beyond it..." (§159). In other words, the mother archetype itself is responsible for personalistic psychology and for loading the burdens of the archetypal upon personal figures, personal relations and personal solutions, and for taking oneself so personally, one's problems and fate always as "mine". Consequently the mother-complex does show in the too-much and too-little of personal life, flight into impersonal distance coupled with personal fascination and intensity.

Here mother and nurse divide even though, as Jung points out, the term mother-complex having been borrowed from psychopathology always has associated ideas of injury and illness, and so intrudes into the domain of the nurse. And though Maria seems to be both (Jesus not having had a distinct nurse figure in his abandoned moments) so that our Western consciousness still has difficulty separating the two psychological attitudes, the division is necessary. The nurse is not personally connected with the child; it is not hers, nor is her history carried forward into the child; its life and death are not hers; her love for it is not incest and taboo. The constellation is not personal in the same way, so we should not assume that the nurse is a foster-parent, a substitute or "second" mother. Nor should we reduce these archetypal distinctions to psychodynamic notions of a "good" and "bad" breast, which ultimately return the configuration of the nurse to that of the mother.

The nurse is a figure in her own right which connects to the plight of abandonment in a different way. Primarily, the injury, illness and exposure is met with the nursing instinct, binding up, repairing, protection, the aims of which do not go beyond these matter-of-fact needs; in the acts there is no fateful projection, no dream of what has happened and what will happen. There is care with little hoping.

The nursing attitude would allow the child to remain abandoned for that is where the nurse appears. She nourishes it in its weakness or nourishes the weakness. The mothering attitude expects something – growth, a personal fate to emerge, specialness. Caring and hoping flow as one. But the nurse is obliged to accept the child as it is, and, since this attitude can only appear out of a wound, in connection with woundedness, for nursing to be constellated there must first be dereliction. Thus, the converse also occurs: the nurse can make us feel injured and abandoned. It seems that neither mothering nor nursing alone is enough. The child needs both, as we need a personal and impersonal relation to fate.

37

I believe we might look at "hypochondria", complaints, and the narcissistic appeal for help, as a peculiar constellation occasioned through the imaginal world, less a mother-complex than attempts to constellate the nurse. The hopeless fits of Picasso in bed in the mornings unable to draw, unable to paint; the bottles of pills and packages of powders of Stravinsky on every nearby table and shelf; Coleridge unable; Carlyle's stomach, he and his wife alternatingly nursing each other; Voltaire "dying" for forty years; Michelangelo and Dürer complaining; Elizabeth Barrett Browning languishing on a couch, Emily Dickinson confined to her room, Charlotte Bronte and George Eliot with sick headaches and upset stomachs; Scott Fitzgerald meeting Hemingway to talk about health; Proust in bed; Rossini in bed; Darwin in bed...here is the child and the nurse, a combination not yet examined adequately by psychology in its attempts to get at the constellations of creativity and genius, nor in its attempts to understand the psychopathology of hypochondria and neurasthenia, nor in its analyses of families and the battle between its members as to who will be ill and who the nurse.

Psychotherapy has taken all nursing phenomena into the mother archetype, confusing weakness with sickness (confounding the wet-nurse and the sick-nurse and then both with mother). In the heroic attempt to be free of the mother complex we turn mistakenly against our weakness and sickness. Whether an infantile content becomes a Hero or a Dionysos or a Zeus, or whether it remains a pathologized area of insights or a childish area of reveries, depends upon the style of nursing it receives. And we cannot begin to differentiate the faculty of nursing until we have distinguished nursing from mothering.

The Dead Child

A motif tangent to our theme but separable is the dead child. The motif occurs in dreams, sometimes as an unborn child that never came into the world; as well, the dead child worries our lives in various ways: the fear of a child dying, over-protectiveness towards children and its reverse child-cruelty, and the question of abortion. This last is usually discussed in the language of expediencies – population control, moral sin and legal wrong about the taking of life, women's rights. However, the return of the abortion theme in dreams and its power in the emotions attest to an internal importance deserving psychological attention.

Abortion echoes the older practise of child exposure (*apothesis*), abandon-

38

ing the unwanted child to its death. As an interior drama the aborted child is the miscarriage of the archetypal qualities we have presented: hope for the future, the sense of conquest, the new start and fulfilled end. The dead child is our lost hope and failed spark, our creative disappointment and stricken imagination that can point no way forward, spontaneity, openness, movement gone. No wonder that grief and mourning may continue many years after an actual abortion since the abortion theme expresses the psychic condition of dead childhood.

The mother wishes to make the child last forever in the realm of making, doing, loving — Demeter with Persephone and Demophoon is case in point. But its death evidences her limits. It has a fate separate from her, showing again that the child component is separable from the mother. If we remain within the perspective of the mother, then the dead child yields only lamentation, and we overlook whatever else this archetypal theme might be indicating.

For the dead child is also the child belonging to death, alluding not only to the death of life but the life of death (cf. Riklin, 1970). Then, death does not mean end as finish of life, but end as purpose of life, signifying the invisible, only psychic existence of Hades whose place is "below" and "beyond" life and whose time is "after" life with its visibility, its making and doing and loving. The child aborted then signifies life aborted, for the sake of Hades.

The dead child may also be an image for the soul's child, performing the role of *psychopompos* which, like the image and emotion of a classical funerary stele leads the psyche to reflections about all that belongs to the child archetype but from a wholly psychic viewpoint. The dead child then makes possible an interiorization of the futurity and growth fantasies, and independence reverses its meaning to express independence from the values of life. Death itself then is no longer viewed through the eyes of life, but, in being led by the dead child, one may regard death in its own terms as a specifically psychic condition, i.e., the condition where there is nothing else but psyche. Although this motif has been saccharinely sentimentalized — but walk through a Victorian graveyard for its statuary of dead angelic children as emissaries of the beyond — the psychic content concretized in the marble is nonetheless valid. This image uniquely unites Eros and Thanatos whose conjunction, although understood in Neoplatonism (Wind, 1967), was conceptually riven by Freud's rationalism. The dead child may offer healing to what the mind has torn apart and placed in opposition.

39

Childishness – Childlikeness

The deepest dilemma concerning the return of the child is that conundrum inherent to any archetype, its supposedly good and bad sides, the digestible and indigestible portions, according to whatever model of integration we are serving. In the case of the child these poles become childishness and childlikeness. On the one hand, one works to become mature, to put all childish things away, to develop out of infantilisms and *avidya* of ignorance. On the other hand, one is to become a child, for only into the child enters the kingdom of heaven, and the child should lead the psyche and be its "end". How does one then reconcile the two contradictory instructions: to overcome the child and to become the child?

The poles appear already in Plato for the child of the *Meno* is not the same as the child of the *Lysis,* the *Republic* and the *Laws.* And the poles appear in Paul (I Cor. 14:20) who appeals for childlikeness of heart but will not have childishness of mind. Or, as Augustine put the dilemma: "Childhood is proposed to us as a model of humility which we should imitate, but it is equally proposed as a type of folly to be avoided" (*Enar. in Ps.* XLVI, 2). The division in the archetype also appears in what Philippe Ariès calls "the two concepts of childhood", on the one hand the indulgent coddling provided by the family, on the other, the rational disciplining provided by society, church, and education. The division finally appears in education theory today, between the tender-minded who take their lead from Rousseau, Froebel and the Romantics and their vision from "childlikeness", and the tough-minded who follow a pattern more Classical, more Medieval, seeing in the child a miniature adult whose waxlike impressionable "childishness" requires moulding by disciplined *Bildung.*

Jung suggests a choice between the opposites and an end to the ambivalence inherent in any archetypal pattern. He offers childhood recaptured without its childishness. The solution he suggests is that by sacrificing childishness, one creates a new childlikeness. Innocence, play and spontaneity are regained by giving up ignorance, games and unruliness. We move from false liberty to true freedom; only a childishness abandoned can be refound as childlikeness; clinging to silliness and innocence never makes the wise and holy fool. Surely this suggestion I have elaborated from Jung (CW 11, §742) seems right, for what place is there in the reborn man of individuation for childish petulance and incapacity, foibles and single-minded desires, and for the magical wishful hopes so subjective and so un-conditioned by past experience. What else is consciousness but putting away all childish things?

Nevertheless, the distinction between the child and his childishness is diffi-cult to maintain. In actuality is separation possible; can we choose one pole? Is not the child this very complex of opposites whose psychic impact derives precise-ly from the tension of its "good" and "bad", its static and changing, sides. Extract the childishness from the child and we are left not with an angel (which are anyway demons of might and terror), but with an idealized image of how one thinks one ought to be, the innocence of repression, again constellating an abandoned child who willynilly must return. We cannot advance psychology, or the psyche in the throes of its complexes, one jot by attempting to separate out even through sacri-fice or for the sake of eschatology the pathological elements.

Perhaps this is what to become as a child now means psychologically. It means what it says: the state as a whole with its pathological childishness, to think as a child and to speak as a child, still babes in wisdom of perfected praise (Ps. 8:2; Matt. 21:16) whose reminiscences do indeed transcend experience.

Without the shadow of childishness how do we enter truly the consciousness of the child? Is there another way to innocence and humility than through ignor-ance and humiliation, by being made simple, small, fearing? To be led by the little child then psychologically implies to be led not only by one's spontaneous surprise and frank wonder where something is new and we are innocent, but also by one's childishness: by the sense of loneliness and abandonment and vulnerability, by the idealizations of Greatness upon outer authorities and the inner powers of our com-plexes who give us parentage, by the intoxications of magical invincibility, by the peculiar sexuality which is both hermaphroditic and incapable of being actualized, and by the unadapted pitiless feelings, the child's cruelty, the short memory, stupid-ity, which too form the stuff of innocence.

Especially Freud's discoveries concerning the child need to be recollected in relation with the idea of rebirth that is so representative of the child archetype. Because the resurrection of the whole man includes the body, its sinful, weak, lust-ful members (Rom. 6:12-13), we cannot neglect the child in the body which Freud re-affirmed. If we are anywhere most the victim of childishness, or more at war with it, it is in the body, treated as an enemy, as an inferior to be disciplined or in-dulgently coddled. Yet if the child — even Freud's — is at least partly a reminiscing imaginal factor, then the body impulses which we associate with the child also must at least partly refer to an imaginal body. Then even our polymorphous perversions and our longings of childishness would provide entry to the childlikeness of resurrection, where the work of rebirth would proceed through infantile sexuality, a discipline of perversion. We could no longer insist upon distinction between childlike and childish.

But must so much be given over to this one archetype so that it personifies not only body and the concrete mode of direct experience but almost all of our subjectivity as well? Must the child carry our bodily delights and our imaginal reminiscing, our wholeness and our creative liberation, our play and our eros, our past and our future? If we give all these aspects of existence to the child, then of course these areas of experience become childish. Then eros is loaded with childish longings, the body a childish complaint, the revolution a childish enactment, imagination a childish fantasy and concrete play an inferior activity. Then too we can never be satisfied with any of these areas as they are; they must be "developed" — our fantasy by means of active imagination or art therapy, and our bodies, our eros, our fun, and the revolution too, must go through a process of becoming more conscious, more "mature", to lose "primitivity".

Even childhood does not have to remain a province of the child. For childhood is mainly a word we use to cover modes of experience and perception, imaginal modes which we abandon every moment for the sake of more adult behaviour, that is, more conceptual and more willed. If we abandon "childhood" as a cover for what is most valuable to human life, then the dilemma of childish and childlike may be resolved. Because we do not need to be fresh, naive and simple "to become as a child", we could abandon the idealization of play as the path to the imaginal. We would no longer believe that we must be innocent to be new, simple to be whole. The restoration of the childish shadow to the ideal of childlikeness would return to wholeness its affliction and weakness, and to the imaginal both its psychopathological distortions and the hard work of actualization.

Bearing the Child

Because abandoning the child is a mythological motif, it stands as a permanent psychological reality, not to be cured but to be enacted. But how? Mythology may give theme and pattern, but depth psychology with its practical aim "to alter something" (Freud) leaves to the subject the manner of enactment. We have no simple answer, and what has gone before has deliberately complicated a rather uncomplicated motif. Thomas Mann wrote that only the exhaustive is truly interesting; in psychology, only the complicated is truly representative.

The pattern we have been exposing shows a vicious circle. Abandoning *of* the child in order to become mature and then abandonment *to* the child when it returns. Either we repress or we coddle this face of our subjectivity. In both cases the child is unbearable: first we cannot support it at all, then we give way to it altogether. We follow a pattern contained in the word "abandon" itself, alternating between the opposite meanings of "losing" and of "releasing". On the one hand we free ourselves of a condition by letting it go from us, and on the other hand, we free ourselves by letting go to it.

One of the ways we abandon ourselves to the child has been in the form of fantasies, called ideas, by means of which the child in sublimated form captures our consciousness. It is a psychological axiom that the more we move away from the repressed child the more vulnerable we are to possession of this abandoned part (CW 9, 1, §277). The more unbearable we find the childish emotionalisms in our subjectivity, the more are we prey to childlike simplifications in our ideas that attempt to reflect objectivity, maturity and responsible unemotionality. Then the child dominates our theory-forming with naive concepts of psyche and therapy, of growth and wholeness, of revolution and freedom, of love and genius. Then we choose, or are chosen by, sentimental philosophies of feeling that deny value to intellect — only connect, relate, believe, encounter — for the child represents the good, innocent heart. And this child is the primary anti-intellectual, who knows without learning things which are hidden from the learned but revealed unto babes (Luke 10:21-22).

Indirectly we have also been examining the way in which we constellate this mythical motif in our individual subjectivities. The relation between psyche and myth goes in two directions; the mythemes govern the soul, but at the same time as it lives they are drawn into enactment. Of these enactments, the heroic model of consciousness always refers back to the child for its origins. We can never perform the ego's tasks, coping, struggling, advancing into light and knowledge, without also regressing to the child. The concept of ego so permeated by hero mythemes is based also upon the abandoned child as its pre-condition. (CW 9, 1,

§281-84; Neumann, p. 45.) The child returns hidden in the hero's boots, to swagger and control his naively literal notion of reality.

But the child does not have to return only as hero. In fact he does not have to "return" at all, if he is never repressed, never abandoned. Dionysian consciousness keeps the child with it as a permanent aspect of its archetypal structure: at the oldest Dionysian Spring festival in honour of the God in the new wine, the second day belonged to the child; small children took part in the ritual and the children's drinking jugs show them with toys and crowns.

Because myths are always true, they are always happening; we abandon the child daily in our attitudes and acts. Whatever we do not acknowledge as having begotten, whatever we disown, to whatever we refuse historical lineage becomes one more orphan. The orphan has no history, everything lies ahead, complete futurity. History provides parentage to psychic events, giving them background in race, culture, tradition. When we refuse the historical aspect in our complexes, how history reaches us through our complexes — for it is in them that my race, my ancestors and my historical culture affect me most closely — then we create orphans: we abandon our complexes to the power of the child archetype. They go to the orphanage, the breeding ground of renegade psychopathy.

Thus, as a psychologist I must refuse the attack upon history now coming from two sides: from the mystics of religion who would make way for spiritual rebirth by breaking through the historical, and from the heralds of political change who would start anew, the past "a bucket of ashes" (Carl Sandburg). The cults of immediacy, of relevance, of transcendence, of revolution, whether in mind expansion or in social liberation are the cult of childhood in a new form (but read Marcuse!), negating the historical roots of the complexes turning them into orphans with nothing behind them. Then history, as to Oedipus, comes out of a void. Oedipus' delusion about his history was material to his tragedy.

It may seem odd for an American psychologist speaking to European intellectuals to stress history, since for Europe, as Joyce — I believe — said, "History is a nightmare from which I am trying to awaken". Yet, psychological reality is only partly separable from historical reality. Our subjectivity is complicated throughout with our Western history, and we can never awaken from it unless we recognize it in our complexes. If psychotherapy conceives its task in altering and in correcting "the one-sided extravagances of consciousness" (Jung), then psychotherapy is an attempt also to re-vision history and its work in the complexes.

Change in psyche is change in history, and that is why psychic change is so difficult, for it means moving history. Yet, nothing moves in ourselves or in the world if history be not borne. A revolution that neglects taking history with it will change nothing; it will leave the psyche untouched, and thus become a new repression.

The child archetype, because of its a-historical and pre-historical tendencies, by moulding consciousness after itself would have us lose history producing a generation of abandoned children who see all things in their beginnings and ends, an existence of omnipotent hope and catastrophic dread. The obsession with this archetype also has its other side, the parental other pole to the child, which gives us a burdening sense of parentage, of worldwide responsibility, the parental inflation compensatory to the child. Then we become all *Sorge* amidst the existential *Geworfenheit.*

History gives a sense for what is authentic; it limits the possible. Without this historical sense everything is new and anything can happen. Any delusional course of salvation lies open — and the confusion in subjectivity about "how to be" and what the soul wants is matched with a myriad of liberation programs, including the turn Eastwards as a way out of Western History. Psychology itself tends to be just one more "trip", owing to the child's influence.

But Jung's psychology is altogether a reflection of the historical psyche and is not a program for its transcendence. Jung's vision of a complex polyvalent wholeness, pregnant with innumerable possibilities and individually different, is too precious, too fertile to become but another delusional omnipotence fantasy with goals of stalwart independence achieved through naive growth to oneness, where becoming self and becoming God conflate.

Surely psychology can be more critical and less childlike in its use of "wholeness" and "self"; surely psychology can abandon in its theory its fantasies of growth, creativity, independence and futurity, so that change might be left as change and its kinds more accurately noted — not always newness and development — and the unchanging may be viewed less sadly. Then individuation may be separated from development so as to reflect more precisely the actualities of experience. For is not psychology's task to reflect the psyche *as it is* rather than to structure it with a hermeneutic system or inculcate through therapy a psychological dogma?

Reflecting the psyche as it is has been the concern of this essay. And I do mean "essay" — an attempt to articulate and thereby constellate that level of archetypal subjectivity which is the child. But our attempt must inevitably fail in order to correspond with the subject itself. Our inadequacy reflects its helplessness. So, we may not expect that what the psyche says through the word "childhood" can be translated into the mature and intellectual speech of science or scholarship. Psychology, it seems to me, has too long laboured in this mistake. Our essay rather follows some lines from T. S. Eliot (*East Coker,* V): "every attempt / Is a wholly new start, and a different kind of failure ... And so each venture / Is a new beginning, a raid on the inarticulate ...". In this way the failure and the venture belong together. They are each part of instigating the new start in regard to the child by stimulating our imagination about archetypal childhood.

The dominance of the child archetype in our psychological thinking, besides softening our intellect, has deprived the adult of his imagination. This "inferior" activity has been relegated to childhood, like so much else unreal, autoerotic and primitive. The adult must go back to childhood to re-find imagination — feeling it unreal, autoerotic, primitive — for lost childhood has meant lost imaginal power, amnesia as lost *memoria,* an abandoned capacity for reminiscence in the Neoplatonic sense. Thus "adult" and "mature" have come to signify demythologized existence whose underlying mythemes return to possess the adult and his psychology in the sentimental and simplified ways we have suggested. We might condense this psychological process into a formula: *the less the child is borne as an emotional vulnerability and imaginal reality, the more we shall be abandoned to it in our rationalized fantasies.*

Preferable to the division into child and adult and the consequent patterns of abandonment which we have been sketching, would be a psychology less given over to the child, its woes and romanticism. We might then have a psychology descriptive of man, an aspect of whom is perennially child, carrying his incurable weakness and nurse to it, enacting the child neither by development nor by abandonment, but bearing the child, the child contained. Our subjective experience might then be mirrored by a psychology both more exact in its description and more sophisticatedly classical, where the child is contained within the man who carries in his face and mien the shame of the childish, its unchanging psychopathology — untranscended, untransformed — and the invincible high hopes together with the vulnerability of these hopes, who bears his abandonment in dignity, and whose freedom comes from the imaginal redeemed from the amnesia of childhood.

REFERENCES

P. Ariès, *Centuries of Childhood* [transl. R. Baldrick from *L'Enfant et la vie familiale sous l'ancien régime,* Paris: Plon, 1960], New York (Knopf) and London (Cape), 1962.

G. Bachelard, "Reveries toward Childhood", Chapter Three in his *The Poetics of Reverie* (transl. D. Russell), Boston (Beacon), 1971.

G. Boas, *The Cult of Childhood,* London (Warburg Inst.), 1966.

J. Bowlby, *Child Care and the Growth of Love,* Harmondsworth (Penguin), 1965, Part I.

M. W. Bundy, "The Theory of Imagination in Classical and Mediaeval Thought", *Univ. Illinois Stud. Lang.,* XII, Urbana, 1927.

P. Collins, *Dickens and Education,* London (MacMillan), 1963, Chap. VIII "The Rights of Childhood".

R. F. Deardon, *The Philosophy of Primary Education,* London (Routledge), 1968, Chapter III, "Growth".

M. Delcourt, *Stérilités mystérieuses et naissances maléfiques dans l'antiquité classique,* Liège, 1938.

T. S. Eliot, "East Coker", V, and "The Dry Salvages", II, in *Four Quartets,* London (Faber), 1944.

E. H. Erikson, *Childhood and Society,* New York (Norton), 1950.

E. H. Erikson, "Human Strength and the Cycle of Generations", in *Insight and Responsibility,* New York (Norton), 1964.

E. H. Erikson, "Growth and Crises of the Healthy Personality", in *Identity and the Life Cycle,* New York (Internat. Univ. Press), 1959.

M. Foucault, *Madness and Civilization* [transl. R. Howard from *Histoire de la Folie,* Paris: Plon, 1961], New York (Pantheon), 1965.

S. Freud, *Collected Papers,* Volumes II and III, London (Hogarth), 1924, 1925. (CP)

S. Freud, *New Introductory Lectures on Psycho-Analysis* (Sprott transl.), London (Hogarth), 1933 (1957). (NIL)

A. Gesell, F. L. Ilg and L. B. Ames, *Youth – The Years from Ten to Sixteen,* London (H. Hamilton), 1956.

S. Isaacs, *The Nursery Years,* London (Routledge), 1932/68, Chap. IV, "The Norms of Development".

C. G. Jung, *Collected Works,* Volumes: 9,1 (2nd ed. 1968), 12 (2nd ed. 1968), 13 (1967), London (Routledge). (CW)

M. L. W. Laistner, *Christianity and Pagan Culture in the Later Roman Empire,* Ithaca (Cornell), 1951, pp. 31f.

J. Laplanche et J.-B. Pontalis, "Fantasme originaire, fantasmes des origines, origine du fantasme", *Les Temps Modernes* (Paris) 215/19, 1964, pp. 1833-68.

S. Légasse, *Jésus et l'enfant – "Enfants", "petits" et "simples" dans la tradition synoptique,* Paris (Gabalda), 1969.

H. Marcuse, *An Essay on Liberation,* Boston (Beacon), 1969.

E. Neumann, *The Origins and History of Consciousness,* London (Routledge), 1954, p. 45 fn.

J. Piaget, *The Psychology of Intelligence,* London (Routledge), 1950.

J. Piaget, *Structuralism,* London (Routledge), 1971.

P. Picasso, *Worte des Malers,* (ausg. J. Haase), Zürich (Sanssouci), 1970. (Unfortunately I have not been able to locate the originals of these passages.)

G. Poulet, *The Metamorphosis of the Circle* [transl. C. Dawson and E. Coleman, Paris: Plon, 1961], Baltimore (Johns Hopkins), 1966, Chap. VI, "Romanticism".

D. B. Redford, "The Literary Motif of the Exposed Child (cf. Exodus ii, 1-10)", *Numen,* XIV/3, 1967, pp. 209-228.

F. Riklin, "The Crisis of Middle Life", *Spring 1970,* New York (Spring Publications), 1970.

C. Rogers, *On Becoming a Person,* Boston, 1961, Chap. 9.

R. M. Stein, *Incest and Human Love,* New York (The Third Press), 1974.

H. Stoffer, *Die Bedeutung der Kindlichkeit in der modernen Welt,* München/Basel (Reinhardt), 1964.

L. L. Whyte, (ed.) *Aspects of Form,* Bloomington (Indiana Univ. Press), 1961.

L. L. Whyte, *Accent on Form,* London (Routledge), 1955.

E. Wind, *Pagan Mysteries in the Renaissance,* Harmondsworth (Penguin), 1967, Chap. X, "Amor as a God of Death".

D. W. Winnicott, *Playing and Reality,* London (Tavistock), 1971.

From *The Stages of Life in Creative Process: Eranos Yearbook 40 - 1971* (ed. Adolf Portmann and Rudolf Ritsema), Leiden: E. J. Brill, 1973, pp. 358-406. Lecture delivered August 25, 1971 at the Eranos Tagung, Ascona.

III

POTHOS:

THE NOSTALGIA OF THE PUER ETERNUS

The question which shall be engaging us in our wanderings this morning is the psychological one of nostalgia.

We must, however, before setting forth, distinguish between the principal and profound experience of nostalgia — an archetypal nostalgia which may itself be a "nostalgia for the archetype" — and all recent manifestations of nostalgia: the attractions for the 30's and 40's in the film, the longings for Romantic sexuality or for pure unpolluted nature, the nostalgia for the mud (*boue*) of the honest peasant, or for gypsy clothes and antiques. This is a temporalization of nostalgia into *autre fois* (another time), or a secularisation and commercialisation of nostalgic values. Such is sociological nostalgia whereas our eye is on archetypal nostalgia.

I hope we can arrive at a third perspective towards our phenomenon: one that is neither the *dernier cri* of a commercial vogue nor the *premier cri* of primal

49

scream therapy (Janov), a cry for the mother and the past pains in our souls, but a *cri imaginaire,* a cri for the imaginal, the C. R. I. of Chambéry.

To go in this third direction, away from both social and personalistic explanations, we must follow a fundamental principle upon which archetypal psychology is based — the principle of *epistrophé* or reversion. *Epistrophé* is a Neoplatonic idea: we find it elaborated best in Proclus' *Elements of Theology,* especially Proposition 29. Briefly, this idea considers all phenomena to have an archetypal likeness to which they can be led back, reverted, returned. All events in the realm of soul, that is all psychological events and behaviours, have a similarity, correspondence, likeness with an archetypal pattern. Our lives follow mythical figures: we act, think, feel, only as permitted by primary patterns established in the imaginal world. Our psychological lives are mimetic to myths. As Proclus notes, secondary phenomena (our personal experiences) can be reverted to a primary or primordial background against which they resonate and to which they belong. The task of archetypal psychology, and its therapy, is to discover the archetypal pattern for forms of behaviour. The assumption is always that *everything belongs somewhere:* all forms of psychopathology have their mythical substrate and belong or have their home in myths. Moreover, psychopathology is itself a means of reverting to myth, a means of being affected by myth and entering into myth. Or, as Jung said: "The gods have become diseases" (CW 13, §54), so that today it is to our pathologies we must look for finding the Gods.

The particular psychopathological events that attract us this morning are those of restlessness and wandering, homelessness and homesickness together, the suffering of nostalgia which is at the same time an impetus for search and quest.

Our method has been partly described by Henry Corbin when writing of *ta' wĩl,* which he says means: "reconduire, ramener une chose à son origine et principe, a son archetype". As he says further: "In *ta'wĩl* one must carry sensible forms back to imaginative forms and then rise to still higher meanings; to proceed in the opposite direction (to carry imaginative forms back to the sensible forms in which they originate) is to destroy the virtualities of the imagination". For us, it is the conservation and exploration and vivification of the imagination and the insights derived therefrom, rather than the analysis of the unconscious, that is the main work of therapy.

I

Turning now directly to our theme, we find that Jung describes the phenomenology of wandering and longing as follows: "The heroes are usually wanderers (Gilgamesh, Dionysos, Heracles, Mithras, etc.), and wandering is a symbol of longing, of the restless urge which never finds its object, of nostalgia for the lost mother" (CW 5, §299). The secret goal of wandering, said Jung in 1912, is the lost mother. There is a piece of libido, which he calls the renegade libido, that turns away from the heroic tasks and incestuously wishes to go back and down to mother. Blocked by the incest taboo, the libido never finds its goal and so wanders and longs eternally. This dynamic explanation is the early and classical Jungian account of the archetypal figure of the *puer aeternus:* the eternally youthful component of each human psyche, man or woman, old or young, that is eternally wandering, eternally longing, and is ultimately attached to the archetypal mother.

We shall not, let me insist, be following this account. And one of our main deviations with the classical Jungian school is just here. For to place all the spiritual phenomenology of the puer eternus motif with the mother archetype is a psychological materialism: a view which attributes spirit to an appendage of maternal matter. To our archetypal view, puer eternus psychology — the wounded hands and feet and bleeding, the high flights and verticality, the aestheticism and amorality, the peculiar relation with Artemesian and Amazonian women, the timelessness which does not age, the penchant for failure, destruction and collapse (*la chute*) — all these events belong to a series of mythical figures of young God-like men or divine youths and are not to be imagined only through a psychologistic language of mother-complex. Rather, as we are working out, these puer events pertain to the phenomenology of spirit. By not grasping this fact as it appears in young men and women today, and in the puer eternus figures in our dreams and fantasies, we miss the epiphanies of the spirit archetype, judging them as something "too young", too weak, sick or wounded, or not yet grown up. Thus does the perspective of the mother archetype prevent the possibilities of spirit as it emerges in our lives. Therefore, we shall be especially wary of attributing wandering and nostalgia to the mother archetype.

However, to go on with the classical position. Norman O. Brown elaborates the same view from the Freudian perspective: "The wandering heroes are phallic heroes ...All walking, or wandering, is from mother, to mother, in mother; it gets us nowhere. Movement is in space; and space, as Plato says in the *Timaeus* is a receptacle...as it were, a mother...". Space eventually becomes the female genital, the mother's "yawning pit", or the night-like pit, as Hegel called the imagination. This position asserts that longing is ultimately for the mother, and when the mother is lost or tabooed the wandering begins, for example Orestes and Alcmaeon slew their mothers after which they wandered, unable to return to their home lands. And Apollo, after slaying Python, suffered nine years in exile.

If we accept this classical position then we must see the journey of the sailor, wanderer, adventurer, neither as a mode of Hermes with a spiritual occult mission, nor as an activity of spiritual quest, but as a prolonged coition with the mother; this world, a double movement of union with her and escape from her. The polytheistic archetypal possibilities of wandering are reduced to one single meaning. The restless urge of puer psychology has been turned into the psychopathology of mother-son incest.

Let us begin again. We may accept the first part of Jung's proposition that wandering is a symbol of longing, but the second we may hold in suspension. Nostalgic longing may not be incestuous at all.

For this new beginning, we follow Ulysses. He is a primordial wanderer — and he detests it. Sitting on the shore of Calypso's island, staring disconsolately, he is filled with nostalgia. "There is nothing worse for mortal man than wandering". Ulysses longs for home. And others long for Ulysses: Antikleia (Bk. 11.202), Telemachos (Bk. 4, 596), Eumaeos (Bk. 14, 144). They pine, long, age, die out of a deep *pothos* or longing for the missing beloved wanderer Ulysses.

Ulysses' longing is not for mother, but for his home and native island. Calypso and Ogygia, after all, could fulfill all the incestuous renegade libidinal longings that a wandering sailor might ever imagine! But Ulysses still pines and suffers for home, the great round bed with Penelope. Nostalgia arises from a separation of halves, a missing conjunction. Our question of wandering has shifted to one of Eros.

I I

The Greek word for this specific erotic feeling of nostalgic desire was *pothos*. Plato defines it in the *Cratylus* (420a) as a yearning desire for a distant object. Its associations in the Classical corpus are with longings for *that which cannot be obtained:* yearning for a lost child, or a beloved (the swineherd, the son, or the mother longing for Ulysses), longing for sleep and for death. *Pothos* also applies to a kind of flower placed on graves (blue delphinium or larkspur), to a white asphodel or hyacinth-like flower, and also to a clambering travelling plant that never stays in one place and is always seeking new attachments. As late as the Church Father, Gregory of Nazianzus, *pothos* was described as a striving power in plants. It is the "vegetable love", a *vis naturalis* of which Andrew Marvell has written, or "the force that through the green fuse drives the flower drives my blood" of Dylan Thomas.

The greatest exemplary of pothos in antiquity was Alexander the Great. He is said to have himself invented the phrase "seized by pothos" to account for his indescribable longing for something beyond, a longing that carried him beyond all borders in a horizontal conquest of space, a true "space man" of ancient times. Alexander had merely to sit upon a river bank or before his tent and look into the distance when he would be seized by pothos and urged to go further. Space and distance became the visual image that released his yearning. (I cannot here go into the other puer eternus characteristics of Alexander the Great: early death, mythical divine father, wounded foot, intoxication, etc.)

Pothos was not only a concept and a feeling; he was also a divine personification, an actual figure, for example sculpted by Skopas (395-350 B.C.), which has been described as a "youngly ripened boy's body". This figure has been brought into association with Dionysos, Apollo, Attis and Hippolytos, and with phallic Hermes. According to Pliny, the main cult figures on Samothrace were Aphrodite and Pothos.

Let us look for a moment at this Aphrodite-Pothos relationship before setting forth to Samothrace. There are three portions or persons of Eros that have been classically differentiated: *himeros* or physical desire for the immediately present to be grasped in the heat of the moment; *anteros* or answering love; and *pothos,* the longing towards the unattainable, the ungraspable, the incomprehensible, that idealization which is attendant upon all love and which is always beyond capture. If *himeros* is the material and physical desire of eros, and *anteros* the relational mutuality and exchange, *pothos* is love's spiritual portion. *Pothos* here would refer to the spiritual component of love or the erotic component of spirit. When *pothos* is presented on a vase painting (fifth century, British Museum) as drawing Aphrodite's chariot, we see that *pothos* is the motive force that drives desire ever onward, as the portion of love that is never satisfied by actual loving and actual possession of the object. It is the fantasy factor that pulls the chariot beyond immediacy, like the seizures that took Alexander and like Ulysses' desire for "home".

Pothos here is the blue romantic flower of love that idealizes and drives our wandering; or as the Romantics put it: we are defined not by what we are or what we do, but by our *Sehnsucht:* Tell me for what you yearn and I shall tell you who you are. We are what we reach for, the idealized image that drives our wandering. Pothos, as the wider factor in eros, drives the sailor-wanderer to quest for what cannot be fulfilled and what must be impossible. It is the source of "impossible love", producing the Tristan complex that refuses *himeros* and *anteros* in order to maintain the transcendence of *pothos.* This side of eros makes possible living in the world as a scene of impossible mythical action, mythologizing life. This component of eros is the factor, or the divine figure, within all our senseless individuation adventures, the phallic foolishness that sends us chasing, the mind's mad wanderings after impossibilities, our forever being at sea, and the fictive goals we must set ourselves — all so that we may go on loving.

III

We come to another island — and our Greek topology is a topology of islands, of sailors and travelers, of nostalgia for Ithaca, and of winds and wind-Gods that blow one off course, a topology that is like that of the individuation adventure through unconscious waters — Samothrace (Samothraki). The cult of the Kabiroi on Samothraki was perhaps the most important, after Eleusis, of all mystery initiations of the ancient world. A series of rituals there took place. The acts and the mythic contents are understood even less than those of Eleusis. We have only conjectures by Bengt Hemberg, Karl Lehmann, and Karl Kerényi. Legends say that wandering heroes stopped on this island for initiation: Jason and the Argonauts, Hercules, Ulysses. Prometheus — who was also a wanderer — is associated with the Kabiroi cult; and Alexander indirectly, for legends say that his parents, Olympias and Philip, fell in love there while they were undergoing the initiations — as if Alexander was conceived in the place of *pothos,* his life becoming its embodiment and a demonstration of its power. The heiron of Samothraki was sacred to the Dioskuri because of shipwrecks and for the protection of sailors. It was, in other words, a haven for wanderers; if one could enter into some relation with *pothos,* there was protection against "shipwreck".

Let us look at a few of the other relevant phenomena conjectured by classical scholars and archeologists about Samothraki, the Dioskuri, and the Kabiroi mysteries, in order to understand something more about wandering in relationship with nostalgia, and about pothos in relationship with the archetype of the puer eternus. But let us at the same time bear in mind how speculative and fantasy-full all scholarship must be in this area. As Farnell has written about the Dioskuri: "The study of these twin-personalities of cult presents more perplexing problems than perhaps any other chapter of Greek religion".

First, there is the perplexing mystery of the Mighty Ones or *Megalo Theoi.* The Kabiroi were called The Mighty Ones. The initiation seemed to have involved a ritual activity in regard to a *pair of unequal male figures,* perhaps a male parallel to the mother-maiden pair at Eleusis. Who were this pair of Gods? Perhaps a brother pair: Prometheus-Hephaistos? Perhaps the Dioskuri Twins? Or was it, as Kerényi seems to believe, a bearded God-figure together with a *pais* or younger boy-figure: Pothos, perhaps?

The pair of unequal male figures is one of those archetypal themes that releases extraordinary speculations. They have been imagined to be mortal and immortal, or divine and human, or age and youth, or initiated and uninitiated, or cultural and natural. This unequal pair even appears in the recently published letters of Freud and Jung, where Freud (Letter 274F) considers the theme to refer back to primal memories: the mortal brother of the Dioskuri pair is nothing else in Freud's letter than the placenta, the short-lived afterbirth, the twin companion with which each human is born.

The pair on Samothraki — where our interest centers because there the Skopas' statue of Pothos held such prominence and because there the cult was for wanderers, sailors and adventurers — are further complicated by the discovery of a statue of a blind old man. It has been suggested that this old man was Teiresias, which fits in with Lehmann's theory that part of the Kabiroi cult was a journey through the underworld. Others have imagined the statue to be of Homer; others, Aristotle. As Teiresias was Ulysses' teacher, Aristotle played old man to Alexander *pais*. Kerényi believes the older male figure to be central to the entire mystery and that this older figure was Dionysos-Hades. So much for the unequal male figures and who they might have been: a boy and an older man, puer and senex.

Second, there is an erotic and phallic aspect of the Kabiroi world. On Samothraki a phallic Hermes was identified with Pothos; the Kabiroi themselves were phallic figures such as are familiar from vase paintings. Moreover, Pliny says that Skopas' statue of Pothos together with Aphrodite were the main cult figures on Samothraki. There is the later association of Priapos (son of Aphrodite) with wanderers, sailors and fishermen. Again, Aphrodite, in her form as Helen, has a special relation with the twin Dioskuri.

This collection of erotic and phallic motives seems to give mythological depth to Jung's and Norman Brown's vision of wandering as a renegade phallic activity in nostalgic search of mother. Pothos would then be the figure of the boyish urge to come home and be safe in the harbour of Aphrodite. Aphrodite would be image of what the puer in us each longs for, the Helen-Paris conjunction arranged by Aphrodite, the face that launches a thousand ships daily in our erotic fantasies. Kerényi interprets the Kabiroi mysteries similarly: according to his fantasy, the renegade or primordial phallic force was tamed by bird-like women and placed in service of civilized generation.

Beyond these two major fantasies of Samothraki (which I have condensed and abstracted), the one about unequal male figures and the underworld, the other about sexual initiation and Aphrodite, scholarship can penetrate no further. The secret of the mystery still remains closed.

I V

If we know so little of what the place of Pothos is within the Kabiroi mysteries, perhaps our ignorance is due to a psychological lack and not only to historiographical lacunae. Archeological digs cannot help us if our psychological awareness cannot penetrate to equal depths. Sometimes we can refine this awareness through reflection upon comparative psychological events. What the texts don't tell us, we may be able to reconstruct through the context of archetypal experience. At the level of myth and archetype, time does not matter. Samothraki is also an eternal island of the imaginal psyche, of psychological geography.

Therefore at this point in our discussion we shall return to the psychological, even psychopathological, face of the archetype. Just as we can illumine psychology through mythology, so we can substantiate mythology through psychopathology. The double movement between mythology and pathology is the basis of our archetypal work. Just as myths move our pathologies into a wider field and deeper background, away from personalistic and literalistic reductions, so pathologies are the means by which myths enter our lives and become corporal. Then they are no longer stories in an illustrated book; the story is taking place in our lives and we are its illustration.

The idea we follow here is that each archetype has its style of pathology. The *pathos* of the archetype, our being moved by it, is as essential to it as its *logos,* its significance. Myths tell us not only about archetypal psychodynamics but also about archetypal psychopathology. In our pathologies we enter myths and myths enter us; pathologies are ways we imitate, are mimetic to, divine patterns.

The particular archetype we are concerned with is the *puer aeternus.* This figure appears early in Jung's writings (1912) and has been worked out in some detail by members of the Zürich school since then, especially by Marie-Louise von Franz. The term comes from Latin epithets for heroic and divine figures. Some mythic figures bearing typical puer traits are Attis, Adonis, Hippolytus, Bellerophon, Icarus, Jason. But there are puer aspects as well in Horus, in Dionysos, in Hermes, in Jesus. Students of literature would find the puer perhaps in St. Exupery, in Shelley, Rimbaud, in Rousseau; Shakespeare's Hotspur is an example; Herman Melville has at least five such beautiful sailor-wanderers.

In our pathological lives the puer eternus appears as a specific style of prolonged adolescence, lasting sometimes until forty — and sometimes ending with sudden violent death. The puer would be the figure within Sartre's remark: "La jeunesse? C'est une maladie bourgeoise" — no, not a social reflection but the archetypal background to it, an archetypal reflection: *une maladie archetypique,* as are all pathologies.

In Part I above I sketched a few characteristics of this figure. Let me review them again: woundedness (hypochondria, wounds of hands and feet, lungs, bleeding); ascensionism (verticality); proclivity for fire and water (Icarus); aestheticism (flower-people, Hyacinthus, Narcissus); timelessness (unable to enter time or to grow old, or a curious antiquarianism); self-destructiveness (desire to fail, to fall, to die in cataclysm); amorality or super-morality; exaggerated parental constellation (the divine figure's inability to live in a human situation without divinizing or demonizing the actual parents). Finally, for our purposes here, the puer eternus is that structure of consciousness and pattern of behaviour that (a) refuses and struggles with the senex — time, work, order, limits, learning, history, continuity, survival and endurance — and that (b) is driven by a phallicism to inquire, quest, travel, chase, search, to transgress all limits. It is a restless spirit that has no "home" on earth, is always coming from somewhere or going to somewhere in transition. Its eros is driven by longing; psychologists condemn this spirit as unrelated, autoerotic, Don Juanistic, even psychopathic.

It is these last two traits — erotic phallicism and the puer-senex division — which are particularly focussed, and *focussed together,* on Samothraki. There we found the concatenation of puer motifs: wanderers, sailors and adventurers; old man and young boy; beautiful youthful body of Skopas' statue of Pothos; phallicism.

Let us imagine: perhaps the Mighty Ones initiated the wanderer into the archetypal source and significance of his restlessness, revealed to him the *telos,* "that for the sake of which" we are so driven. Perhaps the cult was a mythic enactment for the sake of teaching *pothos* about itself, giving a ritual account of the psychopathological drivenness of the renegade libido that eventually leads to "shipwreck" (the *scheitern* of Jaspers) unless some transformation of awareness brings sight to our blindness. Blind Teiresias and blind Homer bring insight, by taking the boy in the man into the underworld, into psychic reality, leading to a consciousness of depths about one's driven windblown wandering across surfaces. The unequal male pair tell us that at Samothraki puer and senex rejoin, as they do in the person of Ulysses. Young spirit finds its cautionary counterpart that teaches survival; bearded man finds the *pothos* of eros again, the awakened heart. He can set sail again, go on journeying. If there Hermes was identified with Pothos, then the signs of *pothos* in us — the nostalgic longing to move, the erotic yearning, the driven urge to transgress — have a hermetic quality. These feelings are from Hermes, Guide of Souls. These movements refer to the relationship between *soul and space,* offering psychological possibilities to the horizontal puer, and possibilities to a psychology of space other than Cartesian materialism. It was space, we remember, that released Alexander's pothos; and *pothos* is the emotion equivalent to the experience of space as a spiritual phenomenon, such as described by Plato in the *Timaeus*: the formless, incomprehensible, existential condition that is the ground of all becoming, the space and spaced-outness in which all humans are puer wanderers, guided by the goals of our longing.

V

The initiation which we imagine taking place at Samothraki brings puer consciousness to an awareness of its *essentially double nature.* It is this double nature that we imagine to be at the root of its pothos, its nostalgic longing and wandering in search of the lost or missing other. The pair of Mighty Ones and the Dioskuri and all the other couplings point directly at a *double structure of consciousness.* We do not need to qualify the doubleness as this or that pair of opposites — old-young, mortal-immortal, male-female. Nor must we make a grand philosophy, a senex principle, of binarism (Lévi-Strauss) as the fundamental mode of all myth. Nor is it necessary to concentrate our focus only on the pair as witness to the spiritual aspect of all erotic longing and the erotic aspect of all spiritual quests.

These precisions of the pair tend to literalize too narrowly the fundamental idea: *puer consciousness is a twin consciousness and awareness of this doubleness of individuality is precisely the initiation.* Unlike Eleusis, the Samothraki cult was for individuals. One went through it alone. It was for freeman and slave, for Greek and barbarian, for man and woman. It had therefore to do with transformation of consciousness in regard to one's individuality, one's individual daimon spirit or angel and one's destiny in relation to it. The initiation transmits an awareness that individuality is not essentially unity but a doubleness, even a duplicity, and our being is metaphorical, always on two levels at once. Only this twofold truth, *gloria duplex,* can offer protection against shipwreck by teaching us to avoid foundering upon the great monolithic rocks of literal realities. Eleusis told much the same thing: Mother and Daughter are always each other. Wherever one is, there is always an "other" by means of whom we reflect existence and because of whom we are always "more", "other" and "beyond" what is here-and-now.

In our lives the presence of otherness feels like self-estrangement, self-alienation. I am always somehow a stranger to myself and can never know myself except through discovering the other which I fantasy to be somewhere else — so I

59

wander in search of him or her. In my life this is felt as an valence, dissatisfaction, restlessness. Self-division, or the divided self of modern psychiatry is the *primary condition* and not a result, mistake or accident. Self-division is not to be joined or healed, but to be reflected through an archetype which initiates consciousness into the significance of the pathology. The unequal, the asymmetrical, pair of Samothraki states that no individual is whole-hearted and single-minded, at one with himself and in at-one-ment with the Gods. This initiation does not make us whole; rather it makes us aware of always being in a syzygy with another figure, always in a dance, always a reflection of an invisible other. Whether the other be senex to puer, female to male, mother to child, death to life — in whatever form the other is constellated from moment to moment — *it is beyond reach,* though we travel to Ogygia or with Alexander beyond the Indus. The other is an *unattainable image,* referring not to *himeros* and *anteros,* but to *pothos.* Or rather, the other is an image that is attainable only through imagination.

Moreover, singlemindedness, or the onesidedness of unity of personality is the condition *before* initiation. Oneness is not the goal, but the pre-condition. Jung has considered "onesidedness" to be the widest definition of neurosis, that is, pathos without logos. The initiation through the Mighty Ones (*Megalo Theoi*) is an initiation by the *two*. And an *asymmetrical* two! The mighty image of necessary doubleness and asymmetry teaches us about both the driven compulsions of onesidedness (uninitiated condition of literal-mindedness) and about the significance of our eternal sense of disbalance. The Mighty Ones are an epiphany of *ontological inequality* which gives an archetypal image to the disharmonies we feel as longings. Metaphorical man, unlike literal man fixed in his certainties, is always at sea, always en route between, always in two places at once. The Samothraki mystery as we have imaginally reconstructed it in the soul does not resolve tension and assuage longing; but it does provide their archetypal context.

Thus we are left at the end with a source of nostalgia other than the mother and other than eros. The only response which is as limitless as the limitlessness of pothos is the imaginal itself. Our wandering and our longing is for the very archetypal imaginal figure that instigates the longing, the *puer aeternus* in his personification as *Pothos.* Our desire is towards the image that initiates the desire; it is an *epistrophé,* a desire that would return desire to its source in the archetype. And this archetype of the puer eternus is, as Henry Corbin has often said, the figure of the angel, the wholly imaginal reflection of ourselves — an image who makes us realize that we are metaphors of him. Not Freud's placenta was lost at birth, but Corbin's twin likeness, our sense of doubleness. Not Jung's renegade libido that would go "back" home to mother, unless home is the womb as metaphor (the Receptacle of the *Timaeus*) for the "place" where our original doubleness is imagined to be "originally" located and contained. Ultimately, then, our pothos refers to our angelic nature, and our longings and sea-borne wanderings are the effects in our personal lives of the transpersonal images that urge us, carry us, and force us to imitate mythical destinies.

====

REFERENCES

C. G. Jung, *Collected Works*, 5.

Norman O. Brown, *Love's Body*, New York, 1966, p. 50.

Henry Corbin, *Avicenne et le récit visionnaire*, Paris, 1954.

Henry Corbin, *L'Imagination créatrice dans le Soufisme d'Ibn Arabi*, Paris, 1958.

Karl Kerényi, "The Mysteries of the Kabiroi" (from *Eranos-Jahrbuch 1944*), transl. R. Manheim in *The Mysteries*. Bollingen Series, New York, 1955.

Karl Kerényi, *Prometheus*, New York (Pantheon), 1963.

Karl Kerényi, "Das *Theta* von Samothrake" in *Geist und Werk: Zum 75. Geburtstag Daniel Brody*, Zürich, 1958.

Karl Kerényi, *Symbolae Osloenses* 31, 1955, pp. 141-52.

Karl Kerényi, "Theos und Mythos" in *Griechische Grundbegriffe*, Zürich, 1964.

V. Ehrenberg, "Pothos" in *Alexander the Great: The Main Problems* (ed. G. T. Griffith), Cambridge, 1966.

Pauly-Wissowa, "Pothos", 1953.

W. H. Roscher, *Lexikon* (1909/1965), "Pothos".

Liddell and Scott, *A Greek-English Lexicon* (1968), "Pothos".

Bengt Hemberg, *Die Kabiren*, Uppsala, 1950.

Karl Lehmann, *Samothrace*, Bollingen Series, New York, 1958.

L. R. Farnell, *Greek Hero Cults and Ideas of Immortality,* Oxford, 1921.

W. B. Stanford, *The Ulysses Theme,* Oxford, 1968, Chap. 14, "The Wanderer".

M.-L. von Franz, *The Problem of the Puer Aeternus,* Zürich/New York (Spring Publications), 1970.

J. Hillman, "Senex and Puer: An Aspect of the Historical and Psychological Present" in *Eranos-Jahrbuch 36,* 1967.

J. Hillman, "On Senex Consciousness", *Spring 1970,* Zürich/New York (Spring Publications), 1970.

J. Hillman, "The Great Mother, her Son, her Hero, and the Puer" in *Fathers and Mothers,* Zürich/New York (Spring Publications), 1973.

Unpublished Lecture delivered originally in French at the Centre Universitaire de Savoie (Chambéry, France), Annual Meeting of the Centre de Recherche sur l'Imaginaire (C.R.I.), May 18, 1974.

I V

BETRAYAL

There is a Jewish story, an ordinary Jewish joke. It runs like this: A father was teaching his little son to be less afraid, to have more courage, by having him jump down the stairs. He placed his boy on the second stair and said, "Jump, and I'll catch you". And the boy jumped. Then the father placed him on the third stair, saying, "Jump, and I'll catch you". Though the boy was afraid, he trusted his father, did what he was told, and jumped into his father's arms. Then the father put him on the next step, and then the next step, each time telling him, "Jump, and I'll catch you", and each time the boy jumped and was caught by his father. And so this went on. Then the boy jumped from a very high step, just as before; but this time the father stepped back, and the boy fell flat on his face. As he picked himself up, bleeding and crying, the father said to him, "That will teach you: never trust a Jew, even if it's your own father".

This story — for all its questionable anti-Semitism — has more to it than that, especially since it is more likely a Jewish story. I believe it has something to say to our theme — betrayal. For example: Why must a boy be taught not to trust? And not to trust a Jew? And not to trust his own father? What does it mean to be betrayed by one's father, or to be betrayed by someone close? What does it mean to a father, to a man, to betray someone who trusts him? To what end betrayal at all in psychological life? These are our questions.

I

We must try to make a beginning somewhere. I prefer in this case to make this beginning "In the beginning", with the Bible, even though as a psychologist I may be trespassing on the grounds of theology. But even though a psychologist, I do not want to begin at the usual beginnings of psychologists, with that other theology, that other Eden: the infant and its mother.

Trust and betrayal were no issues for Adam, walking with God in the evenings. The image of the garden as the beginning of the human condition shows what we might call "primal trust", or what Santayana has called "animal faith", a fundamental belief — despite worry, fear, and doubt — that the ground underfoot is really there, that it will not give way at the next step, that the sun will rise tomorrow and the sky not fall on our heads, and that God did truly make the world for man. This situation of primal trust, presented as the archetypal image of Eden, is repeated in individual lives of child and parent. As Adam in animal faith at the beginning trusts God, so does the boy at the beginning trust his father. In both, God and Father is the paternal image: reliable, firm, stable, just, that Rock of Ages whose word is binding. This paternal image can also be expressed by the Logos concept, by the immutable power and sacredness of the masculine word.

But we are no longer in that Garden. Eve put an end to that naked dignity. Since the expulsion, the Bible records a history of betrayals of many sorts: Cain and Abel, Jacob and Esau, Laban, Joseph sold by his brothers and their father deceived, Pharaoh's broken promises, calf-worship behind Moses' back, Saul, Samson, Job, God's rages and the creation almost annulled — on and on, culminating in the central myth of our culture: the betrayal of Jesus.

Although we are no longer in that Garden, we can return to it through any close relationship, for instance, love, friendship, analysis, where a situation of primal trust is reconstituted. This has been variously called the *temenos,* the analyti-

64

cal vessel, the mother-child symbiosis. Here, there is again the security of Eden. But this security — or at least the kind of *temenos* to which I refer — is masculine, given by the Logos, through the promise, the covenant, the word. It is not a primal trust of breasts, milk and skin-warmth; it is similar but different, and I believe the point worth taking that we do not always have to go to Mother for our models of the basics in human life.

In this security, based not on flesh but on word, primal trust has been re-established and so the primal world can be exposed in safety — the weakness and darkness, the naked helplessness of Adam, the earliest man in ourselves. Here, we are somehow delivered over to our simplest nature, which contains the best and least in us, the million-year-old past and the seed ideas of the future.

The need for security within which one can expose one's primal world, where one can deliver oneself up and not be destroyed, is basic and evident in analysis. This need for security may reflect needs for mothering, but from the paternal pattern within which we are talking, the need is for closeness with God, as Adam, Abraham, Moses, and the patriarchs knew.

What one longs for is not only to be contained in perfection by another who can never let one down. It goes beyond trust and betrayal by the other in a relationship. What one longs for is a situation where one is *protected from one's OWN* treachery and ambivalence, one's own Eve. In other words, primal trust in the paternal world means being in that Garden with God and all things *but Eve.* The primeval world is pre-Eve'l, as it is also pre-evil. To be one with God in primal trust offers protection from one's own ambivalence. One cannot ruin things, desire, deceive, seduce, tempt, cheat, blame, confuse, hide, flee, steal, lie, spoil the creation oneself through one's own feminine nature, betray through one's own left-handed unconsciousness in the treachery of the anima who is that source of evil in Eden and of ambivalence in every Adam since. We want a Logos security where the word is Truth and it cannot be shaken.

Of course, a longing for primal trust, a longing to be at one with the old wise Self, where I and the Father are one, without interference of the anima, is easily recognized as typical of the *puer aeternus* who stands behind all boyishness. He never wants to be sent down from Eden, for there he knows the name of everything in creation, there fruit grows on the trees and can be had for the picking, there is no toil, and long interesting discussions can be carried on in the cool of the evening.

Not only does he know; he expects to be known, totally, as if God's omniscience is focussed all upon him. This perfect knowledge, this sense of being wholly understood, affirmed, recognized, blessed for what one is, discovered to oneself and known to God, by God, in God repeats itself in every situation of primal trust, so that one feels only my best friend, my wife, my analyst truly understands me through and through. That they do not, that they misperceive and fail to recognize one's essence (which must anyway be revealed through living and not concealed and turned in on itself), feels a bitter betrayal.

It would seem from the Biblical tale that God recognized that He is not help enough for man, that something other was needed more meet for man than God Himself. Eve had to be created, evoked, pulled out of man himself, which then led to the break of primal trust by betrayal. Eden was over; life began.

This way of understanding the tale implies that the situation of primal trust is not viable for life. God and the creation were not enough for Adam; Eve was required, which means that betrayal is required. It would seem that the only way out of that Garden was through betrayal and expulsion, as if the vessel of trust cannot be altered in any way except through betrayal. We are led to an essential truth about both trust and betrayal: they contain each other. You cannot have trust without the possibility of betrayal. It is the wife who betrays her husband, and the husband who cheats his wife; partners and friends deceive, the mistress uses her lover for power, the analyst discloses his patient's secrets, the father lets his son fall. The promise made is not kept, the word given is broken, trust becomes treachery.

We are betrayed in the very same close relationships where primal trust is possible. We can be truly betrayed only where we truly trust — by brothers, lovers, wives, husbands, not by enemies, not by strangers. The greater the love and loyalty, the involvement and commitment, the greater the betrayal. Trust has in it the seed of betrayal; the serpent was in the garden from the beginning, just as Eve was pre-formed in the structure around Adam's heart. Trust and the possibility of betrayal come into the world at the same moment. Wherever there is trust in a union, the risk of betrayal becomes a real possibility. And betrayal, as a continual possibility to be lived with, belongs to trust just as doubt belongs to a living faith.

If we take this tale as a model for the advance in life from the "beginning of things", then it may be expected that primal trust will be broken if relationships are to advance; and, moreover, that the primal trust will not just be outgrown.

There will be a crisis, a break characterized by betrayal, which according to the tale is the *sine qua non* for the expulsion from Eden into the 'real' world of human consciousness and responsibility.

For we must be clear that to live or love only where one can trust, where there is security and containment, where one cannot be hurt or let down, where what is pledged in words is forever binding, means really to be out of harm's way and so to be out of real life. And it does not matter what is this vessel of trust — analysis, marriage, church or law, any human relationship. Yes, I would even say relationship with the divine. Even here primal trust would not seem to be what God wants. Look at Eden, look at Job, at Moses denied entrance to the Holy Land, look at the newest destruction of His "Chosen People" whose complete and only trust was in Him. [I am implying that Jewish primal trust in God was betrayed by the Nazi experience, requiring a thoroughgoing reorientation of the Jewish attitude, of Jewish theology, in terms of anima, a recognition of the ambivalent feminine side of both God and of man.]

If one can give oneself assured that one will come out intact, maybe even enhanced, then what has been given? If one leaps where there are always arms to take one up, there is no real leap. All risk of the ascent is annulled — but for the thrill of flying through the air, there is no difference between the second step, the seventh or the tenth, or ten thousand metres up. Primal trust lets the puer fly so high. Father and son are one. And all masculine virtues of skill, of calculated risk, of courage, are of no account: God or Dad will catch you at the bottom of the stairs. Above all, one cannot know beforehand. One cannot be told ahead of time, "This time I won't catch you". To be forewarned is to be forearmed, and either one won't jump, or one will jump half-heartedly, a pseudo-risk. There comes that one time where in spite of a promise, life simply intervenes, the accident happens and one falls flat. The broken promise is a breakthrough of life in the world of Logos security, where the order of everything can be depended upon and the past guarantees the future. The broken promise or broken trust is at the same time a breakthrough onto another level of consciousness, and we shall turn to that next.

But first let us return to our story and our questions. The father has awakened consciousness, thrown the boy out of the garden, brutally, with pain. He has initiated his son. This initiation into a new consciousness of reality comes through betrayal, through the father's failure and broken promise. The father wilfully shifts

67

from the ego's essential commitment to stand by his word, not to bear false witness by lying to his son, to be responsible and reliable come what come may. He shifts position deliberately allowing the dark side to manifest itself in and through him. So it is a betrayal with a moral. For our story is a moral tale, as are all good Jewish stories. It is not an existentialist fable describing an *acte gratuit;* nor is it a Zen legend leading to liberating enlightenment. It is a homily, a lesson, an instructive piece of life. The father demonstrates in his own person the possibility of betrayal in even the closest trust. He reveals his own treacherousness, stands before his son in naked humanity, presenting a truth about fatherhood and manhood: I, a father, a man, cannot be trusted. Man is treacherous. The word is not stronger than life.

And he also says, "Never trust a Jew", so that the lesson goes yet one step further. He is implying that his fatherhood is patterned after Jahweh's fatherhood, that a *Jewish* initiation means as well an initiation into an awareness of God's nature, that most untrustworthy Lord who must be continually praised by psalm and prayer as patient, reliable, just, and propitiated with epithets of stability — because he is so arbitrary, emotional, unpredictable. The father says, in short, I have betrayed you as all are betrayed in the treachery of life created by God. The boy's initiation into life is the initiation into adult tragedy.

I I

The experience of betrayal is for some as overwhelming as is jealousy or failure. For Gabriel Marcel, betrayal is evil itself.[1] For Jean Genet, according to Sartre, betrayal is the greatest evil, as "the evil which does evil to itself".[2] When experiences have this bite to them, we assume an archetypal background, something all-too-human. We assume that we are likely to find a fundamental myth and pattern of behaviour by which the experience can be amplified. I believe the betrayal of Jesus to be such an archetypal background, which may give us further understanding of the experience from the point of view of the betrayed one.

I am hesitant to talk about the betrayal of Jesus. So many lessons may be drawn. But that is just the value of a living symbol: from it can be drawn an endless flow of meanings. And it is as psychologist in search of psychological meanings that I again trespass on theological grounds.

In the story of Jesus we are immediately struck by the motif of betrayal. Its occurrence in threes (by Judas, by the sleeping disciples, by Peter) — repeated by Peter's betrayal thrice — tells us of something fateful, that betrayal is essential to the dynamics of the climax of the Jesus story and thus betrayal is at the heart of the Christian mystery. The sorrow at the supper, the agony in the garden, and the cry on the cross seem repetitious of a same pattern, restatements of a same theme, each on a higher key, that a destiny is being realized, that a transformation is being brought home to Jesus. In each of these betrayals he is forced to the terrible awareness of having been let down, failed, and left alone. His love has been refused, his message mistaken, his call unattended, and his fate announced.

I find that our simple Jewish joke and that great symbol have things in common. The first step of betrayal by Judas was already known beforehand. Forearmed, Jesus could accept this sacrifice for the glorification of God. The impact must not yet have fully hurt Jesus, but Judas went and hanged himself. Peter's denial was also foreknown, and again it was Peter who went and wept bitterly. Through the last week, the trust of Jesus was in the Lord. "Man of sorrows", yes, but his primal trust was not shaken. Like the boy on the stairs, Jesus could count on his Father — and even ask His forgiveness for his tormentors — up until the last step; he and the Father were one, until that moment of truth when he was betrayed, denied and left alone by his followers, delivered into the hands of his enemies, the primal trust between himself and God broken, nailed to the irredeemable situation; then he felt in his own human flesh the reality of betrayal and the brutality of Jahweh and His creation, and then he cried the twenty-second Psalm, that long lament about trust in God the Father:

> My God, my God, why hast thou forsaken me? Why art thou so far from helping me, and from the words of my roaring? O my God, I cry in the daytime and thou answerest not; and in the night... Yet thou art holy... Our fathers trusted in thee: they trusted, and thou didst deliver them... They trusted in thee, and were not confounded... Thou art He that took me out of the womb: thou didst make me trust when I was upon my mother's breasts. I was cast upon thee from my birth: thou art my God from my mother's belly. Be not far from me; for trouble is near; for there is none to help...

And then come these images of being set upon by *brutal* bestial forces:

Many bulls have compassed me, strong bulls have beset me
round. They open wide their mouth against me as a lion...
the dogs have compassed me. The company of evil-doers
have inclosed me: they pierced my hands and feet...

This extraordinary passage affirms that primal trust is in the paternal power, that the cry for rescue is not a cry for mothering, but that the experience of betrayal is part of a masculine mystery.

One cannot help but remark upon the *accumulation of anima symbolism constellated with the betrayal motif.* As the drama of betrayal unfolds and intensifies, the feminine becomes more and more apparent. Briefly, may I refer to the washing of the feet at the supper and the commandment to love; to the kiss and the silver; to the agony of Gethsemane – a garden, at night, the cup and the salty sweat pouring like drops of blood; to the wounded ear; to the image of the barren women on the way to Golgotha; to the warning from the dream of Pilate's wife; to the degradation and suffering, the gall and bitter sop, the nakedness and weakness; the ninth-hour darkness and the abundance of Marys; and I refer especially to the wound in the side at the helpless moment of death, as Eve was torn from Adam's side. And finally, the discovery of the risen Christ, in white, by women.

It would seem that the message of love, the Eros mission of Jesus, carries its final force only through the betrayal and crucifixion. For at the moment when God lets him down, Jesus becomes truly human, suffering the human tragedy, with his pierced and wounded side from which flows the water and blood, the released fountain of life, feeling, and emotion. (This blood symbolism has been amplified extensively in the work of Emma Jung and M.-L. von Franz on the Grail.[3]) The puer quality, the position of fearless safety of the miracle preacher, is gone. The puer God dies when the primal trust is broken, and the man is born. And the man is born only when the feminine in him is born. God and man, father and son no longer are one. This is a radical change in the masculine cosmos. After Eve was born from sleeping Adam's side, evil becomes possible; after the side of the betrayed and dying Jesus was pierced, love becomes possible.

III

The critical moment of the "great let down", when one is crucified by one's own trust, is a most dangerous moment of what Frances Wickes would call "choice".[4] Matters may go either way for the boy who picks himself up from the floor; his resurrection hangs in the balance. He may be unable to forgive and so remain fixated in the trauma, revengeful, resentful, blind to any understanding and cut off from love. Or he may turn in the direction which I hope to sketch in the rest of my remarks.

But before we turn to the possible fruitful outcome of betrayal, let us stay awhile with the sterile choices, with the dangers which appear after betrayal.

The first of these dangers is *revenge*. An eye for an eye; evil for evil; pain for pain. Revenge is natural for some, coming immediately without question. If performed directly as an act of emotional truth, it may be cleansing. It may settle the score without, of course, producing any new results. Revenge does not lead to anything further, but counter-revenge and feuding. It is not psychologically productive because it merely abreacts tension. When revenge is delayed and turns into plotting, lying low and waiting your chances, it begins to smell of evil, breeding fantasies of cruelty and vindictiveness. Revenge delayed, revenge refined into indirect methods can become obsessional, narrowing the focus from the event of betrayal and its meaning to the person of the betrayer and his shadow. Therefore, St. Thomas Aquinas justifies revenge only when it is against the larger evil and not against the perpetrator of that evil. The worst of revenge, psychologically, is its mean and petty focus, its shrinking effect on consciousness.

The next of these dangers, these wrong though natural turns, is the defence mechanism of *denial*. If one has been let down in a relationship, one is tempted to deny the value of the other person; to see, sudden and at once, the other's shadow, a vast panoply of vicious demons which were of course simply not there in primal trust. These ugly sides of the other suddenly revealed are all compensations for, an enantiodromia of, previous idealisations. The grossness of the sudden revelations indicates the previous gross unconsciousness of the anima. For we must assume that wherever there is bitter complaint over betrayal, there was a background of primal trust, of childhood's unconscious innocence where ambivalence was repressed. Eve had not yet come on the scene, was not recognized as part of the situa-

71

tion, was repressed.

I mean by this that the emotional aspects of the involvement, especially the feeling judgments – that continuous stream of evaluations running within every connection – were just not admitted. Before betrayal the relationship denied the anima aspect; after betrayal the relationship is denied by the anima resentments. An involvement that is unconscious of the anima is either mostly projected, as in a love affair, or mostly repressed, as in an all-too-masculine friendship of ideas and "working together". Then the anima can call attention to herself only by making trouble. Gross unconsciousness of the anima is simply taking the emotional part of a relationship for granted, in animal faith, a primal trust that there is no problem, that what one believes and says and "has in mind" about it is enough, that it works all by itself, *ça va tout seul*. Because one failed to bring overtly into a relationship the hope one had for it, the need for growing together in mutuality and with duration – all of which are constellated as ultimate possibilities in any close relationship – one turns the other way and denies hopes and expectations altogether.

But the sudden shift from gross unconsciousness to gross consciousness belongs to any moment of truth and is rather evident. And so it is not the main danger.

More dangerous is *cynicism*. Disappointment in love, with a political cause, an organisation, a friend, superior, or analyst often leads to a change of attitude in the betrayed one which not only denies the value of the particular person and the relationship, but all love becomes a Cheat, causes are for Saps, organisations Traps, hierarchies Evil, and analysis nothing but prostitution, brainwashing, and fraud. Keep sharp; watch out. Get the other before he gets you. Go it alone. I'm all right, Jack – the veneer to hide the scars of broken trust. From broken idealism is patched together a tough philosophy of cynicism.

It is well possible that we encounter this cynicism – especially in younger people – because enough attention has not been paid to the meaning of betrayal, especially in the transformation of the puer eternus. As analysts we have not worked it through to its significance in the development of feeling life, as if it were a dead end in itself out of which no phoenix could arise. So, the betrayed one vows never to go so high again on the stairs. He remains grounded in the world of the dog, *Kynis,* cynical. This cynical view, because it prevents working through to a positive meaning of betrayal, forms a vicious circle, and the dog chases his own tail. Cynicism, that sneer against one's own star, is a betrayal of one's own ideals, a betrayal of one's own highest ambitions as carried by the puer archetype. When he crashes, everything to do with him is rejected. This leads to the fourth, and I believe main, danger: self-betrayal.

Self-betrayal is perhaps what we are really most worried about. And one of the ways it may come about is as a consequence of having been betrayed. In the situation of trust, in the embrace of love, or to a friend, or with a parent, partner, analyst, one lets something open. Something comes out that had been held in: "I never told this before in my whole life". A confession, a poem, a love-letter, a fantastic invention or scheme, a secret, a childhood dream or fear — which holds one's deepest values. At the moment of betrayal, these delicate and very sensitive seed-pearls become merely grit, grains of dust. The love-letter becomes silly sentimental stuff, and the poem, the fear, the dream, the ambition, all reduced to something ridiculous, laughed at boorishly, explained in barnyard language as *merde,* just so much crap. The alchemical process is reversed: the gold turned back into faeces, one's pearls cast before swine. For the swine are not others from whom one must keep back one's secret values, but the boorish materialistic explanations, the reductions to dumb simplicities of sex-drive and milk-hunger, which gobble everything up indiscriminately; one's own pig-headed insistence that the best was really the worst, the dirt into which one casts away one's precious values.

It is a strange experience to find oneself betraying oneself, turning against one's own experiences by giving them the negative values of the shadow and by acting against one's own intentions and value system. In the break-up of a friendship, partnership, marriage, love-affair, or analysis, suddenly the nastiest and dirtiest appears and one finds oneself acting in the same blind and sordid way that one attributes to the other, and justifying one's own actions with an alien value system. One is truly betrayed, handed over to an enemy within. And the swine turn and rend you.

The alienation from one's self after betrayal is largely protective. One doesn't want to be hurt again, and since this hurt came about through revealing just what one is, one begins not to live from that place again. So one avoids, betrays oneself, by not living one's stage of life (a middle-aged divorcee with no one to love) or one's sex (I'm through with men and will be just as ruthless as they) or one's type (my feeling, or intuition, or whatever, was all wrong) or one's vocation (psychotherapy is really a dirty business). For it was just through this trust in these funda-

73

mentals of one's own nature that one was betrayed. So we refuse to be what we are, begin to cheat ourselves with excuses and escapes, and self-betrayal becomes nothing other than Jung's definition of neurosis *uneigentlich leiden,* inauthentic suffering. One no longer lives one's own form of suffering, but through *mauvaise foi,* through lack of courage to be, one betrays oneself.

This is ultimately, I suppose, a religious problem, and we are rather like Judas or Peter in *letting down the essential thing,* the essential important demand to take on and carry one's own suffering and be what one is no matter how it hurts.

Besides revenge, denial, cynicism, and self-betrayal, there is yet one other negative turn, one other danger, which let us call *paranoid.* Again, it is a way of protecting oneself against ever being betrayed again, by building the perfect relationship. Such relationships demand a loyalty oath; they tolerate no security risks. "You must never let me down" is the motto. Treachery must be kept out by affirmations of trust, declarations of everlasting fidelity, proofs of devotion, sworn secrecy. There must be no flaw; betrayal must be excluded.

But if betrayal is given with trust, as the opposite seed buried within it, then this paranoid demand for a relationship without the possibility of betrayal cannot really be based on trust. Rather it is a convention devised to exclude risk. As such it belongs less to love than to power. It is a retreat to a logos relationship, enforced by word, not held by love.

One cannot re-establish primal trust once one has left Eden. One now knows that promises hold only to a certain point. Life takes care of vows, fulfilling them or breaking them. And new relationships after the experience of betrayal must start from an altogether different place. The paranoid distortion of human affairs is serious indeed. When an analyst (or husband, lover, disciple, or friend) attempts to meet the requirements of a paranoid relationship, by giving assurances of loyalty, by ruling out treachery, he is moving surely away from love. For as we have seen and shall come to again, love and treachery come from the same left side.

I V

I would like now to leave the question of what betrayal means to the son, the one betrayed, in order to return to another of our earlier questions: What might betrayal mean to the father? What it meant to God to let His son die on the cross we are not told. What it meant to Abraham to lead his son to sacrifice we are also not told. But they performed these actions. They were able to betray, just as Jacob the patriarch entered into his estate by betraying his brother. Could it be that the capacity to betray belongs to the state of fatherhood? Let us look further at this question.

The father in our story does not merely show his human imperfection, that is, he does not merely fail in catching his son. It is not merely weakness or error. He consciously designs to let him fall and cause him pain and humiliation. He shows his brutality. The same brutality is shown in the treatment of Jesus from his capture to his crucifixion, and in the preparations of Abraham. What happens to Esau and to Job are nothing else than brutal. The brutality comes out again in the animal skin Jacob wears to betray Esau, and the great beasts God reveals to Job as the rationale for his torment. Also, in the images of Psalm XXII as we saw above.

The paternal image — that just, wise, merciful figure — refuses to intervene in any way to ameliorate the suffering which he himself has brought about. *He also refuses to give an account of himself.* The refusal to explain means that the explanation must come, if it comes at all, from the injured party. After a betrayal one is in no position to listen to the explanations of the other anyway! This is, I believe, a creative stimulus in betrayal. It is the betrayed one who must somehow resurrect himself, take a step forward, through his own interpretation of what happened. But it can be creative providing he doesn't fall into and stay in the dangers we have sketched above.

In our story, the father does explain. Our story is after all a lesson, and the action itself is educative as an initiation, whereas in the archetypal tales and in much of daily life betrayal is not explained by the betrayer to the betrayed, because it happens through the autonomous left side, unconsciously. In spite of the explanations, our story still shows brutality. *The conscious use of brutality would seem a mark common to the paternal figures.* The unjust father reflects unfair life. Where he is impervious to the cry for help and the need of the other, where he can admit that his promise is fallible, he acknowledges that the power of the word can be transcended by the forces of life. This awareness of his masculine limitations and this hardheartedness imply a high degree of differentiation of the weak left side. Differentiation of the left side would mean the ability to carry tension without action, going wrong without trying to set things right, letting events determine principles. It means further that one has to some extent overcome that sense of uneasy guilt which holds one back from carrying out in full consciousness necessary though brutal acts. (By conscious brutality, I do not mean either deliberately perverse brutality aimed to ruin another, or sentimental brutality as found sometimes in literature and films and the code of soldiers.)

Uneasy guilt, tendermindedness, makes acts double-binding. The anima is not quite up to the task. But the father's hard heart is not double-binding. He is not cruel on the one hand and pious on the other. He does not betray and then pick up his son in his arms, saying, "Poor boy; this hurt me worse than it hurt you".

In analysis, as in all positions of trust, we are sometimes led into situations where something happens that requires a consciously brutal action, a betrayal of the other's trust. We break a promise, we are not there when needed, we let the other down, we alienate an affection, betray a secret. We neither explain what we do, nor pull the other off his cross, nor even pick him up at the bottom of the stairs. These are brutalities — and we do them, with more or less consciousness. And we must stand for them and stand through them, else the anima renders our acts thin, listless and cruel.

This hardheartedness shows an integration of brutality, thereby bringing one closer to nature — which gives no explanations of itself. They must be wrested from it. This willingness to be a betrayer brings us closer to the brutish condition where we are not so much minions of a supposedly moral God and immoral Devil, but of an amoral nature. And so we are led back to our theme of anima-integration, where one's cold-heartedness and sealed lips are as Eve and the serpent whose wisdom is also close to nature's treachery. This leads me to ask whether anima-integration might not show itself not only in the various ways we might expect — vitality, relatedness, love, imagination, subtlety, and so on — but whether anima-integration might not also show itself in becoming nature-like: less reliable, flowing like water in the paths of least resistance, turning answers with the wind, speaking with a double tongue — conscious ambiguity rather than unconscious ambivalence. Supposedly, the sage or master, in order to be the psychopompos who guides souls through the confusion of creation where there is a fault in every rock and the paths are not straight, shows hermetic cunning and a coldness that is as impersonal as nature itself.[5]

In other words, our conclusion to the question: "What does betrayal mean to the father?" results in this — *the capacity to betray others is akin to the capac-*

ity to lead others. Full fatherhood is both. In so far as psychological leading has for its aim the other's self-help and self-reliance, the other will in some way at some point be led down or let down to his own level, that is, turned back from human help, betrayed into himself where he is alone.

As Jung says in *Psychology and Alchemy* (pp. 27-8):

> I know from experience that all coercion — be it suggestion, insinuation, or any other method of persuasion — ultimately proves to be nothing but an obstacle to the highest and most decisive experience of all, which is to be alone with his own self, or whatever one chooses to call the objectivity of the psyche. The patient must be alone if he is to find out what it is that supports him when he can no longer support himself. Only this experience can give him an indestructible foundation.

V

What then is trustworthy in the good father or psychopompos? What in this regard is the difference between the white magician and the black? What separates the sage from the brute? Could we not, by means of what I have been presenting, justify every brutality and betrayal that a man might commit as a sign of his "anima-integration", as a sign of his attainment to "full fatherhood"?

I do not know how to answer this question other than by referring to the same stories. We find in all of them two things: the motif of love and/or the sense of necessity. The Christian interpretation of God's forsaking Jesus on the cross says that God so loved the world that He gave His only Son for its redemption. His betrayal was necessary, fulfilling his fate. Abraham so loved God that he prepared to put the knife to Isaac in offering. Jacob's betrayal of Esau was a necessity already announced in the womb. The father in our story must have so loved his son that he could risk the broken bones and broken trust, and the broken image of himself in his son's eyes.

This wider context of necessity or love leads me to believe that betrayal — going back on a promise, refusing to help, breaking a secret, deceiving in love — is too tragic an experience to be justified in personal terms of psychological mechanisms and motives. Personal psychology is not enough; analysis and explanations will not do. One must look to the wider context of love and fate. But who can be certain when love is present? And who can state that this betrayal was necessary, fate, a call of the Self?

Certainly a part of love is responsibility; so too is concern, involvement, identification — but perhaps a surer way of telling whether one is closer to the brute or the sage is by looking for love's opposite: power. If betrayal is perpetuated mainly for personal advantage (to get out of a tight spot, to hurt or use, to save one's skin, to gain pleasure, to still a desire or slake a need, to take care of Number One), then one can be sure that love had less the upper hand than did the brute, power.

The wider context of love and necessity is given by the archetypes of myth. When the event is placed in this perspective, the pattern may become meaningful again. The very act of attempting to view it from this wider context is therapeutic. Unfortunately, the event may not disclose its meaning for a long, long time, during which it lies sealed in absurdity or festers in resentment. But the struggle for putting it within the wider context, the struggle with interpretation and integration, is the way of moving further. It seems to me that only this can lead through the steps of anima differentiation sketched so far, and even to one further step, towards one of the highest of religious feelings: *forgiveness.*

We must be quite clear that forgiveness is no easy matter. If the ego has been wronged, the ego cannot forgive just because it "should", notwithstanding all the wider context of love and destiny. The ego is kept vital by its *amour-propre,* its pride and honour. Even where one wants to forgive, one finds one simply can't, because forgiveness doesn't come from the ego. I cannot directly forgive, I can only ask, or pray, that these sins be forgiven. Wanting forgiveness to come and waiting for it may be all that one can do.

Forgiveness, like humility, is only a term unless one has been fully humiliated or fully wronged. Forgiveness is meaningful only when one can neither forget nor forgive. And our dreams do not let us forget. Anyone can forget a petty matter of insult, a personal affront. But if one has been led step by step into an involvement where the substance was trust itself, bared one's soul, and then been deeply betrayed in the sense of handed over to one's enemies, outer or inner (those shadow values described above where chances for a new loving trust have been permanently injured by paranoid defences, self-betrayal, and cynicism), then forgiveness takes on great meaning. It may well be that betrayal has no other positive outcome but forgiveness, and that the experience of forgiveness is possible only if one has been betrayed. Such forgiveness is a forgiving which is not a forgetting, but *the remembrance of wrong transformed within a wider context,* or as Jung has put it, the salt of bitterness transformed to the salt of wisdom.

This wisdom, as Sophia, is again a feminine contribution to masculinity, and would give the wider context which the will cannot achieve for itself. Wisdom I would here take to be that union of love with necessity where feeling finally flows freely into one's fate, reconciling us with an event.

Just as trust had within it the seed of betrayal, so betrayal has within it the seed of forgiveness. This would be the answer to the last of our original questions: "What place has betrayal in psychological life at all"? *Neither trust nor forgiveness could be fully realized without betrayal.* Betrayal is the dark side of both, giving them both meaning, making them both possible. Perhaps this tells us something about why betrayal is such a strong theme in our religions. It is perhaps the human gate to such higher religious experiences as forgiveness and reconcilication with this silent labyrinth, the creation.

But forgiveness is so difficult that it probably needs some help from the other person. I mean by this that the wrong, if not remembered by both parties — and remembered as a wrong — falls all on the betrayed. The wider context within which the tragedy occurred would seem to call for parallel feelings from both parties. They are still both in a relationship, now as betrayer and betrayed. If only the betrayed senses a wrong, while the other passes it over with rationalisations, then the betrayal is still going on — even increased. This dodging of what has really happened is, of all the sores, the most galling to the betrayed. Forgiveness comes harder; resentments grow because the betrayer is not carrying his guilt and the act is not honestly conscious. Jung has said that the meaning of our sins is that we carry them, which means not that we unload them onto others to carry for us. To carry one's sins, one has first to recognize them, and recognize their brutality.

Psychologically, carrying a sin means simply recognizing it, remembering it. All the emotions connected with the betrayal experience in both parties — remorse and repentance in the betrayer, resentment and revenge in the betrayed — press towards the same psychological point: remembering. Resentment especially is an emotional affliction of memory which forgetting can never fully repress. So is it not better to remember a wrong than to surge between forgetting and resenting? These emotions would seem to have as their aim keeping an experience from dissolving into the unconscious. They are the salt preserving the event from decomposing. Bitterly, they force us to keep faith with sin. In other words, a paradox of betrayal is the *fidelity* which both betrayed and betrayer keep, after the event, to its bitterness.

And this fidelity is kept as well by the betrayer. For if I am unable to admit that I have betrayed someone, or I try to forget it, I remain stuck in unconscious brutality. Then the wider context of love and the wider context of fatefulness of my action and of the whole event is missed. Not only do I go on wronging the other, but I wrong myself, for I have cut myself off from self-forgiveness. I can become no wiser, nor have I anything with which to become reconciled.

For these reasons I believe that forgiveness by the one probably requires atonement by the other. Atonement is in keeping with the silent behaviour of the father as we have been describing him. He carries his guilt and his suffering. Though he realizes fully what he has done, he does not give account of it to the other, implying that he atones, that is, self-relates it. Atonement also implies a submission to betrayal as such, its transpersonal fateful reality. By bowing before the shame of my inability to keep my word, I am forced to admit humbly both my own personal weakness and the reality of impersonal powers.

However, let us take care that such atonement is not for one's own peace of mind, not even for the situation. *Must it not somehow recognize the other person?* I believe that this point cannot be overstated, for we live in a human world even if victims of cosmic themes like tragedy, betrayal, and fate. Betrayal may belong within a wider context and be a cosmic theme, but it is always within individual relationships, through another close person, in immediate intimacy, that these things reach us. If others are instruments of the Gods in bringing us tragedy, so too are they the way we atone to the Gods. Conditions are transformed within the same sort of close personal situation in which they occurred. Is it enough to atone just to the Gods alone? Is one then done with it? Does not tradition couple wisdom with *humility*? Atonement, as repentance, may not have to be *expressis verbis,* but it probably is more effective if it comes out in some form of contact with the other, in full recognition of the other. And, after all, isn't just this full recognition of the other, love?

V I

May I sum up? The unfolding through the various stages from trust through betrayal to forgiveness presents a movement of consciousness. The first condition of primal trust is largely unconscious and pre-anima. It is followed by betrayal, where the word is broken by life. For all its negativity, betrayal is yet an advance over primal trust because it leads to the 'death' of the puer through the anima experience of suffering. This may then lead, if not blocked by the negative vicissitudes of revenge, denial, cynicism, self-betrayal and paranoid defences, to a firmer fatherhood where the betrayed can in turn betray others less unconsciously, implying an integration of a man's untrustworthy nature. The final integration of the experience may result in forgiveness by the betrayed, atonement by the betrayer, and a reconciliation — not necessarily with each other — but a reconciliation by each to the event. Each of these phases of bitterly fought and suffered experiences which may take long years of fidelity to the dark side of the psyche, is also a phase in the development of the anima, and that has been, despite my emphasis upon the masculine, the main theme of this paper.

===

NOTES

1. *Being and Having*, (Fontana edition), London, 1965, p. 47.
2. *Saint Genet: Actor and Martyr*, (Mentor edition), New York, 1964, p. 191.
3. *The Grail Legend*, New York, 1971.
4. *The Inner World of Choice*, New York, 1963.
5. "Heaven and Earth are not humane
    They regard all things as strawdogs
    The Sage is not humane
    He regards all people as strawdogs."
    — Tao-Te King, No. 5.

From The Guild of Pastoral Psychology: Guild Lecture No. 128, 1964, 1966, 1971, London, and also *Spring 1965*, pp. 57-76. Lecture delivered October 2, 1964, London.

V

SCHISM

As Differing Visions

You may recall as I do from school-days the sad sweet passages towards the end of *The Merchant of Venice* (v. 1) where Lorenzo and Jessica tell each other of mythical lovers from the Classics, Lorenzo saying:

> "In such a night
> Stood Dido with a willow in her hand
> Upon the wild sea-banks, and waft her love
> To come again to Carthage."

"Parting at the seas' edge", says Gaston Bachelard, "is at once the most tearing and most literary of good-byes". It is a perennial image — to be found again at the opening of John Fowles' *The French Lieutenant's Woman,* the heroine roaming melancholy on the wild sea-bank — perennial image because it is a perennial experience. Between us two lies now an ocean, depths of salt, cold and darkness. Though easily bridged today by phone-cable and jet-plane, still, out of one world there are now two, continents far-flung, oneself now an island, apart.

Such is parting; yet this is not quite schism which means a special kind of parting, the worst perhaps: splitting. An ugly word that, something we ought not do, split or be split, or split things and people off. Schism means cleaving, cutting like a cleaver, the knife, severing. Consequently, it is bad for integration, for it is hardly a whole-making thing, favouring growth and synthesis and those other goals at which we work. Thus schism is one of those phenomena that requires a fresh look to see what it is all about and whether anything might be redeemed from it; it is another of those phenomena in need of some saving by means of the usual psychological question that differs from the moral question — and let us keep those two approaches quite distinct. The moralist asks what can we *do* with the will about schism, while the psychologist asks reflectingly, what *place* has it in psychic life at all; what is its necessity?

Reflections

When we think of schism — especially those of us here with theological interests — our minds reverberate with the great schisms of Christianity. Our first thought of schism is in terms of religion, and that is how the word has come into usage. "Schizoid" and "schizophrenia" are much later, and weaker, terms. Here, the notion of the general, of common sense is not so far off. We may appeal to that figure so dear to British lecturers, the "plain man" of "common sense" who understands schism as having to do with *doctrinal splits;* and for once the "plain man" is right on. For, as we proceed into this question of psychological necessity, we shall come to recognize that indeed the theological metaphor and framework is psychologically fundamental.

But first something of the emotions. You notice that the Conference is entitled "Relationship — Parting", and I have all along assumed that the topic dealt me is the dirty one, the radical unambiguous parting, irrevocable, the most tearing and the most literary, that is, passionately intellectual, a position at the sea's edge, the "drear and naked shingles of the world" (Matthew Arnold), out of earshot, excommunication. Schismatic parting is filled with rancour, bitterness: I hate you and your position, your thoughts, and above all, your blindness. What splits us now is not a higher fate and necessity, but evil; onto you falls the darkness because you no longer share my vision and cannot see where you have fallen. In your parting from my position you have brought me doubt, *zweifel,* devil. No wonder that one tradition holds that all divisions are the work of the Devil, and that devilry enters religion mainly through schism and heresy.

A schism may have to do with one God or three, with Protest or Popery, with Christ as Man or Christ as God, with national or international communism, with kinds and times of baptism, or theories of the libido, of art, cosmology, education, economics. . . whatever the contents, the stuff over which the split occurs, these are not themselves, psychologically, the cause of the cleavage. As psychologists, we are not taken in by the relative value of the arguments, on which side truth lies, or deviation, or evil; nor are we taken in by the strength or weakness of the people, their merits, their personalities. Our interest lies, as psychologists, in the phenomenon itself — schism — the extra-ordinary passion with which it is charged, and the specific quality of this passion, so tearing and so intellectual. Such exorbitant pledges — like Freud and his circle and their common signet rings — the megalomanic thunderous curses, anathema, the tortured heretics, the detailed doctrinal defenses and programmed revenge, promulgations of positions, intellectual gyrations to assure one's rightness, the other's wrongness: these intensities indicate something more at work than either the struggle of personalities or a contest of ideas.

In searching for the place to put schism and the affects it generates, we shall avoid the rubric of *growth.* Indeed it would be comfortable to place it there: growth is such a generous, warm notion, taking care of everything as "natural", as belonging to the development of personality. Psychology does so enjoy this new conceptual device of the Great Mother and her Child, who sees all psychic change as development and every process a sign of growth. This philosophy turns us all into infants again, and, though supposedly a good condition for Christians and for Romantics, the philosophy or fantasy of growth makes psychology both maternally materialistic and childish. Growth is indeed an appropriate vision and necessary metaphor for children, but in an adult growth also means aggrandizement, overweight, over-population, over-kill, cancer, escalation, proliferation. So that growth has become the foolish metapsychology of fat men in a declining culture. For let us be reminded squarely, that we in this room are not growing like plants and children, but, as the Buddha said, we are decaying, and our brains, like a deciduous forest of flaking cells, are paralleled in psychic process by narrowing of horizons and shrinking of possibilities, even as we change; the rule of Saturn extends daily in the psyche, bringing narrowing limitations in many senses, including the inevitable symptoms and irreversible signs of physical and psychological decay. Change, yes, schism brings, but change is not necessarily growth. To ignore the limitations and insist on growth (as with Teilhard de Chardin, for instance), to speak of the expansion of consciousness, of growth towards individuation, of development towards larger synthesis of wholeness, is to deceive ourselves by placing events that have to do with the soul of mature men and women and their deaths against an unfitting archetypal background of growth and life.

So, to see schism as a biological process — the schizocarp splitting for seeds, ground splitting as grasses push up, cells splitting for new generation — would indeed place the fracturing affects of schism against an unfittingly optimistic background. The Great Mother who favours biological metaphors, seeing things as "only natural" meaning "comfortable", takes out the sting, allays the sharpness of the knife, lulls us into assuming that the hatred is merely a reflection on the unwitting personal level of an impersonal necessary process in nature. So they deceive us, the psychologists of growth, when they say: things must divide in order to grow and the pain is of parturition, the destruction really a creation in disguise. Do not focus on the cleavage, they say, but on what is coming forth from the cleft, the child without history, without past, without any concern for what was split so that it might be born. Forward, onward, upward.

Similar to the delusional background of growth and just as inadequate is the background of *separation*. We are familiar — especially in England owing to the influence of John Bowlby, of Melanie Klein and the *kleine* Jungians — with the psychodynamic idea that the human begins in a state of fusion with mother, or collective unconscious, or self, and then separates; he cleaves apart from that which he had been cleaving to. First fusion, then separation in order to find identity and individuality. Schism would thus be a radical attempt at individual identity by means of parting and separation emotions. We must split from the original ground, whether this be actual mother and breast, or internal symbolic mother and breast, or dragon monster, darkness, collective unconscious, or self. Schism is taken to be a necessary step of ego development in the process of individuation.

Let us pause over this one; let us think, and feel, just what this psychodynamic fantasy of individuality means, for does it not imply that individuality is a separated, isolated, split-off condition in its origins? Does it not also tend to characterize the ego in its development as schizoid, that its strength partly depends on its separatedness, and that its reality principle is partly one of insular competitiveness, paying your own way, being your own man, a Hobbesian vision of all against all, of radical independence, dependency overcome. After all, the hero with his knife as a metaphor for a "strong" ego facing "hard" problems in a "tough" world also is a metaphor for an ego who cleaves and cuts, at whose very essence is separation and parting, the theme of this Conference.

Is it then a wonder that we are so obsessed with "relationship" and with fantasies of merging by falling: into love, into depression, into illness, into Self. And is it really surprising that there is today a movement towards communal togetherness, groups and the blurring of consciousness' sharp edges which classical analysis still diagnoses as "weak ego". If the new ego is blamed for its penchant toward fusion, was not the old ego schismatic, having for its metaphor the separated independence, the *opus contra naturam* of Prometheus and Hercules, of St. George and Christ — who, too, brought a sword.

No, we shall keep away from these two interpretative backgrounds to the questions of schism. Neither growth nor separation is satisfactory. The first makes schism too pleasant, the second, too much in keeping with the heroic — and cruelly schizoid — metaphor of individuality. These two ways of understanding schism would blunt its subjective pain.

The psychologist is obliged to be a phenomenologist, to take things as they appear as authentic and real, and to stick with them. Let us not associate away from the pain of schism, nor amplify it into something else, but remain, existentially if you will, in its presence. There is nothing more objective than its own intense subjectivity; when it hurts, it hurts, and we betray the hurt by moving away from it. All we can do is to let the archetypal background to the savagery, bitterness and tearing present itself.

Already we begin to see that *schism can present itself according to different visions:* from within the cosmos of the Great Mother it is a biological necessity, a manner of growing. Yet, if principally a doctrinal, intellectual matter, then maybe schism has little to do with maternal metaphors of botany and vegetables, and we must search for other visions of the cleaver, e.g., the Hero with the knife, or the Great Enemy and divider, or, another, the dismembered Dionysos, the divided/undivided as he was called. One phenomenon, in this case, schism, in an archetypal psychology will have various possible mythical perspectives.

Returning to the earlier question — what place has schism in psychological life, what is its necessity — we may note a similarity in the various schism metaphors, whether vegetative, psychiatric, parturitional, or even geological where a schist refers to crystalline rock that is easily split into layers. Common to the metaphors is the *one becoming many;* the one breaks into a dyad, a polarity, or a polycentric field. Doctrinal divisions can be taken in the same way: the single unitarian monotheistic vision resolves into several. Another God is born, the God of the Many.

If we continue within our *theological* fantasy, then the word "schism" does, as the dictionary says, appear mainly in contexts of Christian thought — and we know why. Schism reflects the inherent capacity of any unified doctrine reinforced by a monotheistic vision to fragment, to reveal the many that are potential in the one. Employing a *psychiatric* fantasy, schism means latent psychosis (schizophrenia), reflecting the psyche's potential for splitting into inherent components, losing its coherence and modes of communication between parts, ending the rule of a strongly ordered ego. Within a *mythological* fantasy schism refers to the absence of Hermes-Mercury, or his concretization. The interpenetration of archetypal perspectives ceases, or has become concretized into self-isolating units, each promulgating its own doctrine. The mutual entailment of the Gods breaks down, and when they can no longer speak with each other how can we?

The main writings on schism in the early Church were by Cyprian and then later by Augustine. Each wrote of the phenomenon in treatises called "On Unity of the Church" (*de Ecclesiae unitate*). *The idea of schism made sense only within the perspective of a prior unity.* In Augustine's words (*contra epist. Parmeniani,* ii, 8) schismatics are those who "have cut themselves off from Unity". Whereas heresy has to do with sacrilegious *teachings,* "you are schismatic by your sacrilegious *separation*" (*Ephes.* v. 27, italics mine).

Thus in Christianity the word schism received a value not usual in earlier Greek philosophers whose polytheistic psychology perhaps allowed them to take it as a fact of natural life, e.g. Plato (*Phaedo* 97A, 101C) as a parting of paths, and Aristotle (*History of Animals* 4, 7, 8) as a cleavage in a hoof. Schism is not a threat, not an abnormality when roads divide or hooves are cleft, but within the cosmos of unity schism is indeed a passionate dangerous issue, the very worst that can happen. And we note that in the history of the early Church the controversies of schism were all in regard to the *symbols of unity:* authority of the Bishop,

Eucharist and sacraments, role of Rome. These were not theological disputes only, only concerned with the relative value of certain dogmas; they were transposed at once into the question of unity, the unity of the Church and of God, because within that unity still lay the ghost of polytheistic paganism, the threat of the Gods of the many, monotheism's "latent psychosis".

Thus Henry the Eighth's refusal to comply with the rule of Rome, symbol of unity, had to lead to the schismatic reaction of the Pope (*"schisma patimus, non fecimus"*, the English were fond of saying). Although there were economic and political reasons for Henry's actions, his "case" provides a notorious paradigm for the curious intermixture of personal anima psychology and doctrinal schism. The unified doctrine of the Church did not have room for all the requirements of Henry's soul. Nor would Anne Boleyn comply: she would not become a mistress to the throne, but of it. Something had to give; something had to split. Henry held together, so what gave was the unity of marriage and the unity of the Church. The *causa efficiens,* the immediate impetus which carried Henry into his perilous theological course was his passion for Anne Boleyn.

We may suspect that the anima has much to do with schism. As envoy of life, whenever situations become too principled — monolithic, monotheistic, monogamous — spiritually *one*-sided in other words, this archetypal factor will appear to cause correction through trouble-making, by awakening passions. And these passions must appear also in the spiritual, doctrinal realm, for it is there that she is particularly enclosed. Were it merely a matter of emotion versus reason, love versus duty, or anima versus spirit, we would not be involved with schism, because a schism must split intellectual principles, creeds and codes, by envisioning doctrine differently, by meeting doctrine with doctrine in its own area of spirit. Henry did not fight Rome only in the name of the heart, for love, but in doctrinal language of theological dispute involving the best minds of Western scholarship; hence, a schism.

So, when you or I get into those tearing conflicts over ideas and we are then judged by perceptive colleagues in terms of the anima — he gets into such anima rages; his anima does all his thinking; it's all because of the women in his life; he loves the vanity of scandal — these perceptions will not do. Certainly the anima has put emotion into the ideas, filling them with life; but surely, too, the passion has been transposed to an intellectual realm where the conflict of people has become the schism of ideas with transpersonal, historical significance.

In recognizing the archetypal factor of the anima in these splits we do her a service by adding to our knowledge of her. Besides the anima as mediatrix between what we understand and what we do not understand, as representative of life, as carrier of nature, beauty, tradition and psyche, we may add the further essential function of *the anima as troublemaker,* as cause of dissent between man and man, man and woman, man and himself. Moreover, since this is the manner in which anima mainly appears – in the messes we get into, the moods, arguments and foolishness – we are again obliged as psychologists, before condemning and setting out to correct with therapy, to enquire what point to this trouble, what intention this division. If the anima is an archetypal factor, then the trouble she is making is not merely emotional, but also theological, that is, archetypal.

Henry's conflict was focussed upon divorce and divorce is indeed one of the ways that schism today reaches us as a vivid, threatening experience. Where there was one, joined in marriage, held in a golden ring, all others forsaken (neglected, abandoned), there shall be divorce into two. Marriage is split, and split marriage, like a split Church, is an impossibility. The monogamous view of marriage corresponds with the monotheistic view of God; it is therefore not surprising that so much theological writing so concerned with unity was on this theme of marriage. Divorce in human life alludes to the possibility of schism in God. Polygamous and promiscuous are Old Testament metaphors for polytheistic.

Marriage — even secular by registrar — has a theological background. It too is formulated by law and into a credo of words, and in this formulation divorce is psychologically inherent. For, if my thesis is correct, the more we rigidly insist upon unity the more will diversity constellate. The forsaken "other" must inevitably appear: the repressed return.

The situation that then occurs is called a *triangle,* but the triangle is after the event. First the unity of marriage has constellated the "other", and only after the other has had his or her effect does the triangle appear. Until then, the marriage conjunction has served as a defensive or transformative mandala, keeping out all others, providing a set of habits, a delusional or transformative system in which the force of love could be contained. The third releases love from this psychic structure. The mandala breaks. For a while everyone seems crazy, and also is crazily searching for new systems and justifications to encompass the energy. We study theories of love, use novels and films as models, put it all into the money complex, talk to friends and analysts and ministers, turn even to the Bible to build for ourselves new defenses, new structures.

The triangle necessarily releases a host of demons, because it breaks up unity of psychic structure and its pairings of balance and compensation. The "other" represents "all others", reminding us of the latently split nature of the psyche into multiples.

Psychology has said a great deal about individuation *alone* — the one to the One — and of individuation in the *dyad* (or *quaternio*) — relating, pairs, conjunction — but the triangle is where the demons are: immense psychological energy in rage, jealousy, anxiety, delusions. We might look again at all triangle relationships — of couples and the child, of couples and the affair, of couples and the analyst, of mother-daughter-son-in-law, etc., — through a model that does more justice to the passions displayed. Why do mother and father manage all right until the son enters the room, or why must a patient in analysis spend so much fantasy-energy upon the analyst's wife or previous patient? Freud's original metaphor (Oedipus) was triangular. And this remains the only metaphor psychology has had for matters of extraordinary importance. Something archetypal is taking place that has an intensely separating effect on a prior unity, yet seems to increase the flow of energy through the parts. One vision no longer holds things together, yet there is a holding together with intense differentiation through so-called negative affects.

The questions raised by the schism of divorce need new ways of reflection. The triangle provides one, but it too needs a perspective freed from our former models of unity, models which do not leave enough space for understanding polyvalent multiplicities.

———

Returning to Dido and Aeneas, this time Virgil's, we find an episode — indeed tearing and literary — bearing directly on our theme. You may recall that Dido was the Queen of Carthage, who fell in love with Aeneas. Now Aeneas was a child of Venus, and was afflicted and persecuted by Juno. The conflict in Aeneas, and between him and Dido, begins in heaven as a conflict between Juno and Venus. Dido's love grows while Aeneas and his men, beaten in war, fatigued from travel, rest in Carthage. Venus fears that he may not be received well there and then that he will dally there, which could mean forsaking his goal, Italy and the founding of Rome. Juno, however, is quite pleased with the development (Dido's passion) originated by Venus in order to assure Aeneas a safe haven.

Juno wants to make political capital out of it, saying to Venus: "Where is our rivalry taking us? Would it not be far better, by arranging a marriage, to seal a lasting peace? You have got the thing you had set your heart on: Dido's afire with love, wholly infatuated. Well then, let us unite these nations and rule them with equal authority." So, she arranges that during a storm the lovers shall meet in a cave where Juno will unite them in lasting marriage. "Venus", says Virgil, "made no opposition to Juno's request, though she smiled at the ingenuity of it".

All happens as Juno plans. The lovers meet in the cave, each coming with his own vision from his own Goddess. "Dido recked nothing for appearance or reputation: the love she brooded on now was a secret love no longer; Marriage she called it, drawing the word to veil her sin". You know how it ends, as echoed in *The Merchant of Venice:* Aeneas never saw *his* love and union with Dido as marriage for he was a son of Venus, and Jove and Mercury reminded him of his destiny, so that he says to Dido when they divide: "His orders: I saw the god, as clear as day, with my own eyes, entering the city, and these ears drank in the words he uttered. No more reproaches, then — they only torture us both. God's will, not mine, says 'Italy'."* Dido, having seen another vision prepared by another God, rightfully rages in despair, curses, and finally kills herself. "We make our destinies by our choice of Gods" (Virgil). That schism, so literary, so rending and at the water's edge, represented the entire complex of hatred and rivalry between Rome and Carthage, Europe and Africa. The legendary Dido, her face on Carthaginian coins, had become the archetypal image of the troublemaking anima, inspirer of war.

Thus when people fall in love, not only eyes, lips and hearts meet, but theologies. We come to the encounter not only with love but also with an *idea* of love. Juno and Venus are two ways of loving and also two *philosophies* of love stemming from different archetypal perspectives which do not agree — partly because, by the way, Aeneas did not give Juno enough recognition (Bk. III, 11, 430). We bring into a situation a subjective factor "made in heaven", that is, we bring with us a

---

*Passages quoted from Book IV of *The Aeneid of Virgil,* translated by C. Day Lewis, London (Hogarth Press), 1961.

perspective archetypally governed by a suprapersonal dominant which forms our ideas in accordance with the logos of that theos. We come with a theology.

In Classical theology (what we call mythology) one of the divinities who gives most trouble of the sort we today call "anima" is Aphrodite (Venus). In her way she governs several schisms. Due to her, Paris chooses against Athene and Hera, a choice among archetypal perspectives resulting in that epic account of splittings, the Iliad, upon which much in our culture rests. Aphrodite also gives Hippolytos hell (by means of Phaedra) dividing him from his comrades and his one-sided pursuit of Artemis; and she gives the women of Lemnos hell by visiting them with a bad smell, dividing them from their men and turning them into Amazons. In each case Aphrodite insists upon her portion of human attention that a Goddess deserves. Helen, Aphrodite's human incarnation, is an instrument that launches a thousand ships, and, through the affects she constellates — like the anima troubles (as psychologists would call them, had they Henry Tudor in analysis) between Rome and England — a historical schism is prepared, forcing the Gods apart. Aphrodite and Ares (Venus and Mars) are secret lovers, i.e., they merge with each other, so that love's honey and war's gall are tastes not as distinct as we might suppose.

When Jung writes that the anima and the old wise man archetypes have a close, sometimes indiscernable relation, we see this working itself out in theological disputes. They begin as anima contention and rivalries, with scheming, pique, insult, revenge. (The Donatist schism, so important during the fourth century, began partly owing to the intrigues of Lucilla, a historically obscure, enigmatic woman friend of the rebelling Bishops.) Issues of personal vanity and desire turn finally into doctrinal positions about the nature of man, God and the universe for which men kill and will die. But the ideas are present at the beginning as are the affects to the end.

———

If I were to attempt a fundamental statement about the intention of the anima in this trouble-making, it would be in terms of Jung's description of her (together with the animus):

> They are quite literally the father and mother of all the
> disastrous entanglements of fate and have long been recog-
> nized as such by the whole world. Together they form a

divine pair. . .the anima wears the features of Aphrodite, Helen (Selene), Persephone, and Hecate. Both of them are unconscious powers, "gods" in fact, as the ancient world quite rightly conceived them to be. To call them by this name is to give them that central position in the scale of values which has always been theirs whether consciously acknowledged or not . . . (CW 9, ii, §41).

In the same work (*Aion*, §427) he correlates the anima/animus with polytheism, the self with monotheism (cf. *Spring 1971* for a discussion of this theme: "Psychology: Monotheistic or Polytheistic").

In other words, the conflict brought by the anima has as its background the *multiplicity of the psyche.* Multiplicity is absolutely basic in Jung's description of the psyche. Psychic structure is polycentric. It is a field of many lights, sparks, eyes; its energy is scattered into constellations, like a starry sky. Jung does not depart from this description though at times he worries over plurality (CW 12, §105, 156), his introverted temperament, I suppose, preferring the monistic tendency (CW 6, §536). Because the anima is mediatrix between the discrete personality and its collective, archetypal background, *she becomes the representative of multiplicity,* who splits us up by sowing divisions, thereby reminding us how complex is totality.

The reality of our wholeness is therefore not to be confused with singleness, or unity, or a monotheistic description of totality, because as Jung says: "Reality consists of a multiplicity of things", while the unity of the *unus mundus* must remain "a metaphysical speculation", a "hypothesis" (CW 14, §659-60). The polycentricity of the psyche, its many constellations with their many foci, were represented once by a polytheistic pantheon and by the animation of nature through the personification of nymphs, heroes, spirits, daimons, and the like.

Should we take a standpoint exclusively from any single one of these configurations and behave mimetically to only one archetypal pattern, that is, should we act monotheistically, we have already performed an excommunication by cleaving ourselves off from communion with the many forms. Then the Goddesses in their variety, epitomised by the promiscuity of Aphrodite, insisting on plurality, embroil us in situations in which other standpoints must be recognized, creating those doctrinal divisions we refer to, after the event, as schisms. Schism seems hardly possible in a polycentric universe. The quarrel of the Gods is not schism. But in any system whose stress is on unity, as the Church with its one creed and one God (even in three persons), schism is inevitable, as if the monolith, Petrus, on whom it stands is potentially a geological schist.

When I say "forcing the Gods apart", I refer to a human fault. By insisting on clarity of borders, proper definitions, we make divisions. In a sense we bring about the quarrel of the Gods through our one-sidedness which we ennoble by calling choice and free-will. When we insist upon concrete, literalistic enactment of the myth to which we happen to stand closest, then, by choosing one pattern in our enactments, we become one-sided. We become psychologically monotheistic. This one-sided choice can occur even in a polytheistic religion where it is called henotheism.

There is a difference between monotheistic *religion* and monotheistic *psychology*. The first is a belief, and the second an attitude. We may have one without the other. Judaism, for instance, seems more monotheistic in religion than in psychology. In Judaism God is not defined and the Torah may have 600,000 faces, one for each Jew in Exile. The content of belief is left suspended, uncodified, and the psyche is free to fantasy. The volumes of Jewish commentaries exhibit the endless fantasies. None are heretical. Although the religion remains monotheistic, the psychological attitude within it displays all the variety of multiplicity. Schism is rare (except for that major one, Christianity).

By psychological monotheism I refer to the literal attitude toward psychic events which tends to exclude their speculative, mythical play, their 600,000 faces. One vision dominates, attempts to extend its system to make "unity"; the one converts, integrates and swallows the many. Like Dido, we see only the constellation that we are in, the vision that both makes us see and blinds us. In contrast, the polytheistic attitude recognizes from the outset the polyvalence of psychic structure. Borders are ill-defined, so that flow and interconnection between archetypes and imagery stay open. "The fact is that the single archetypes are not isolated from each other in the unconscious, but are in a state of contamination, of the most complete, mutual interpenetration and interfusion".* One cannot say that this activity or image always belongs to this or that God, for the Gods are not so clearly defined. We are not sure that it is an "anima mood" or an "animus attack". One cannot really be certain where love and hatred separate because Mars

---

*C. G. Jung, "Archetypes of the Collective Unconscious", (S. Dell translation) *The Integration of the Personality,* London, 1940, p. 91.

and Venus do intertwine. Imagination speculates rather than fixes into concepts; borders dissolve. The Gods imply each other. Thus, we have such difficulties with the Greek religion: the Gods blend into each other, not keeping to distinct spheres which we, with our literal monotheistic consciousness, expect from them. We want irreconcilable opposites that require transcendent functions, grace, and synchronistic magic to synthesize. We do force the Gods apart.

The Gods are forced apart by our strong ego stands. They create between the Gods a no-man's-land marked out by psychiatric diagnoses. To take a position between and among the Gods, where they interpenetrate and interfuse, is to be in a "borderline state", the possibilities of which have been denied by the heroic ego's insistence on well-defined positions.

Conclusion

The psychological significance of the polycentric structure of the psyche, and its reflection in pagan polytheism, goes perhaps further than we are able to realize. If there are truly differing visions of one and the same event, and if these visions are given by differing archetypal perspectives, we have to reconcile ourselves to differences more profound, and to separations more divisive, than those of sex and age, of nation, culture and class, of attitude and type — all these are social, historical, or biological givens, but they are not made in heaven. Inasmuch as man is created in the image of God, we are created in the image of this or that face of God, or this or that God, and our createdness is not only a one time historical event but also a continuing metaphorical event offering possibilities of interpretation and enactment.

As we are made according to a divine image, so our images are divine. In our imagination we reflect the different divinities of the imaginal realm. In our subjectivity we are governed by a multiplicity of factors, each with its eye shining through ours. And, as the Gods demand that they be not neglected and forgotten, they insist stubbornly upon their being seen according to their own eyes, each according to his or her own light. To look at Aphrodite only from the viewpoint of Artemis may bring us disaster, as to Hippolytos. What is Hermes to his brother's vision but a cattlethief, and what is the Dionysian perspective to the Apollonic but a hysterical rout without distance, form or proportion. I may not analyze anima behaviour only from the viewpoint of the heroic ego on its career, nor may I look at the exhilarations of spirit only from the perspective of the mother who will condemn it as a puer inflation to escape from her complications she calls "the mother-complex".

Each of the archetypes will be seen, even if they, like the Gods, drive us to rupture, madness and suicide in order that we give them their due. We see them though but darkly, in the mirror of our subjectivity which is limited to only this or that face, knowing only in part, restricted by the mytheme in which we are and the God we have chosen or that has chosen us.

I cannot change my vision as a matter of opinion, nor be proved wrong, nor be argued out of a position. I can at best not excommunicate, giving recognition to a reality that consists of a multiplicity of things. I can at best recognize that our visions, like those of Dido and of Aeneas, are archetypally given, and that our personal tragedy is partly because we have not seen the other's God since we worship at different altars. Once the shift of vision from one myth to another, once I have been created through the vision of another God, in that God's image, there is no return and I shall see phenomena differently, now by means of the logos of another theos.

Though the visions may be incompatible, they do *not require the animosity of schism.* We may after all stay together in hatred, just as we may separate in love. Psychology usually puts hatred with parting, love with union, but is this not too easy? It is easy to leave you in hatred, and easy to stay with you in love. But the reverse of these pairings is that psychological art we call "consciousness". It is a consciousness that inhabits borders, at the seas' edge.

So, you and I cannot agree and neither of us is right or wrong since each archetypal perspective has its justice. We can but strive against each other, parted, agreed to disagree, without the luxury of knowing that one of us is closer to the truth. There are many mansions and a house divided does indeed stand, even in hatred. The necessity of schism? *To end the illusion of unity,* of any delusional system that does not give place to the distinctive multiplicity of the archetypal powers affecting our lives.

Finally, then, to resolve the question of schism by placing it within this cosmos of multiplicity, let me quote a passage from "Sermon IV" of Jung's *Seven Sermons to the Dead.*

For me, to whom knowledge hath been given of the multiplicity and diversity of the gods, it is well. But woe unto you, who replace these incompatible many by a single god. For in so doing ye beget the torment which is bred from not understanding, and ye mutilate the creature whose nature and aim is distinctiveness. How can ye be true to your nature when ye try to change the many into one? What ye do unto the gods is done likewise unto you. Ye all become equal and thus is nature maimed . . . The multiplicity of the gods correspondeth to the multiplicity of man.

From The Guild of Pastoral Psychology: Guild Lecture No. 162, 1972, London. Lecture delivered September 24, 1971 at the Annual Guild Conference, Oxford.

V I

THREE WAYS OF FAILURE
AND ANALYSIS

I Failure in Analysis

We are each familiar with the failure of certain kinds of cases in analysis.
Particularly difficult and unresponsive to "successful" therapy are people with
styles of life in which homosexuality, alcoholism, or chronic depression are the
major presenting "problems". To these can be added those with paranoid obses-
sions, the severe so-called character neuroses and people who have been diagnosed
as sociopaths and psychopaths. That so many and so varied kinds of cases for
which analysis may have been considered the preferred method of treatment turn
out to be failures, gives cause for considering analysis afresh and in the light of
these failures.

We are also familiar with another sort of failed cases, those in which a morbid
cancer develops during the analysis, or which end in suicide, or where the counter-
transference reactions constellate such exorbitant fantasy and massive affect, or

98

psychopathological lacunae, in the analyst that the case must be transferred or the analysis abandoned. Smaller failures perhaps go unrecognized — analyses that have as by-products estrangements within families, loss of extraverted adaptation, splintered friendships.

Through *clinical reflection* upon these various sorts of failures we may examine the kinds of cases which fail, or for which analysis fails, and we may bring our own failures as analysts to other analysts for scrutiny — all of which reflection attempts to correct present failures and minimize future ones. This manner of clinically reflecting is a function of the dominant empirical and moral theme of our culture: learning through mistakes, trial and error, getting better through working at it, if at first you don't succeed try, try again, in which the model is one of improvement away from mistakes, error, and failure, towards competence.

Failure in this metaphor is linked in a polarity with success, and we tend to measure failures normatively, that is as a privation of success. Failure is the obverse of successful treatment; success equals the minimum of failure. A successful analysis would then mean success with those areas of failure in the case — the dominating presenting complaints of homosexuality, alcoholism, delusions — and a failure would mean their continuation despite the personality development and insight gained through the analysis.

This model of failure, simple though it might seem, has nonetheless encouraged some sophisticated discussions of analysis. Existential analysis would do away with normative criteria of success and failure altogether. On the other hand, behaviour therapy would consider failure wholly in terms of the normative criteria of positive functioning, making suspect the belief in analysis as a method of personality growth and increase of consciousness unless there is positive evidence of symptom elimination and relief of distress.

By what we define analysis will also define its success and failure: an analysis that aims for increase of consciousness or individuation cannot be judged a failure if it does not cure symptoms, and vice versa, an analysis that aims at removing a crippling phobia cannot be called a failure if it never goes into the patient's dreams, or integrates the phobia into meaningfulness.

Of course this simple, normative model of success (as optimum health, psychic order or wholeness) neglects that success and failure may be conceived not as opposites or poles of a continuum, but as an identity, so that *every analysis is both a failure and a success at the same time,* and every part of every analysis is both

99

right and wrong, leading and misleading, constructively growing and destructively killing, implying that for analysis to succeed at all it must always fail.

II Failure of Analysis

The inevitability of the first kind of failure opèns a larger perspective, and we may move the question from specific failures in analysis to the general failure of analysis. Since analysis always shows certain sorts of failures, is there not something general about analysis which brings about failure, so that analysis itself may be considered a failure?

The literature shows that as there are discussions about the failure *in* analysis in certain kinds of cases, there are also discussions on the failure *of* analysis as a whole. Freud's late reflections on "Analysis terminable or interminable" is the *locus classicus* for this kind of pessimistic consideration.

Does analysis ever reach its end, in time or fulfillment; is transference ever resolved, individuation ever achieved? Even if analysis does not satisfy the goal of cure, does it indeed yield enlargement of consciousness, depth of personality, finer love, better adaptation, significant life? If we look at the analysts, ourselves, as the paradigms for the process in which we sit for many years, what effect has analysis had upon our adaptation, our consciousness, our loving?

From another perspective, where are the validating statistics in regard to kinds of cases and kinds of improvement within such classes, and how may we ever formulate such statistics since nosological classifications into which we might class our cases are today all in doubt? Is "paranoiac" a valid term with an actual referent? Where are the "manics" and "hysterics" of yesteryear? How can we assess success and failure of a treatment without agreed criteria for what we are treating, i.e., what is psychic illness and psychic health which gives meaning in general to an idea of "treatment".

The view that analysis in general has failed comes from critics from many sides. Experimentalists ask for public evidence of achievement; clinicians ask for evidence of improvement through analytical treatment; societal critics see analysis as the establishment's tool for maintaining our notions of sickness, of exclusive individuality, and of professionalism, perpetuating a system of bourgeois capitalism. Theologians and philosophers consider its failure more profoundly, regarding analysis to have an inadequate ideational critique and a suspect method that is more like brain-washing, or initiation into a religious sect, than either a therapeutic treatment or an empirical science of personality exploration which it claims to be. It fails because its subliminal premises differ from its overt intentions. Finally historians (of ideas, social movements, and medicine) see analysis within its setting of the twentieth century, as a response to a specific failure within that civilization, and that what was right for early twentieth century men is insufficient for us today.

Through just such *historical reflection* upon the failure of analysis we may recall that analysis did arise out of failure, in that it was a specific method for dealing with those peculiar kinds of cases that had failed to be understood, or even find a hearing by the prevailing system, e.g., the hysterics of Freud and Breuer and the schizophrenics of Jung and Bleuler. These were the medically and socially failed, and psychotherapy was invented as a specific response to these specific failures. If analysis arises from the maladapted, the peculiar neurotic discontents of our civilization who hitherto could find no meaningful place, the failed so to speak, then a third perspective opens in regard to the relationship between analysis and failure.

III *Failure as Analysis*

Despite the critique of the first kind (that analysis fails in many specific instances) and the critiques of the second kind (that analysis as such is a failure), for me, and I shall assume for us preponderantly, the merits of classical analysis are so obvious that one need not dwell upon them. A panegyric here, or even an apology, is hardly in place, so let us turn instead to the defects of the merits. Let us take the clinical and historical reflection upon the failure of classical analysis one step further into an *archetypal reflection.*

By classical analysis I mean a course of treatment in an atmosphere of sympathy and confidence of one person by another person for a fee, which treatment may be conceived as educative (in various senses) or therapeutic (in various senses) and which proceeds principally through the joint interpretative exploration of habitual behaviour and of classes of mental events that have been traditionally called fantasies, feelings, memories, dreams, and ideas, and where the exploration follows a coherent set of methods, concepts and beliefs stemming mainly from

101

Freud and from Jung, where focus is preferably upon the unanticipated and affectively charged, and whose goal is the improvement (subjectively and/or objectively determined) of the analysand and the termination of the treatment. This description leaves room for many versions of improvement — from alleviation of symptoms to individuation and mystical revelation. This description also leaves room for various aspects of Freud's and Jung's methods, concepts and beliefs as they receive differing emphasis according to place, time and practitioner.

An archetypal reflection upon the failure in and of analysis would leave untouched its definition, that is, we would not attempt to improve analysis in specific instances, nor redefine (update) it in general so that it becomes a more adequate response to contemporary psychic ills. Rather I would suggest — and this shall be my final point — that analysis may continue as before even where it conceives itself not only as having failed historically and clinically, but as *being failure archetypally;* as being concerned with failure in the dictionary sense of failure: weakness, defectiveness, absence of victory, bankruptcy, deception, lack and incompletion.

Failure would be regarded as one fundamental psychic factor in terms of which every man lives his life. Existentialism calls this category "scheitern", or the consciousness that arises from shipwreck. Alchemy has considered it under the rubrics of dissolutio, mortificatio, putrefactio. Buddhism speaks of inherent decay; D. H. Lawrence of the "ship of death".

Were analysis to be imagined in terms of its inherent failure (which merely parallels the inherent failure of every life) emphasis would no longer be placed too onesidedly upon the integrative, increasing, enlarging and upward-striving metaphor, the eros aspect of ever more unions, a metaphor which may be condensed into the key-word "growth" (which already has taken on overtones of escalation, proliferation, and cancer). Instead we would return to that tradition of the analysis of the soul which recognizes "two opposite propensities in the human frame; one constantly and uniformly tending to corruption and decay, the other to life and health" — a sentence from Ernst Stahl, the eighteenth-century German physician-philosopher who placed the soul at the center of his concerns. But the sentence might as well have come from Freud's contrast of Eros and Thanatos. Thanatos provides the archetypal reflection to our theme of failure.

When analysis follows the models of thought of nineteenth-century medical philosophy, its heroic and Great-Mother-Nature determined consciousness, then it will tend, as with Bichat, to define life as "the sum of forces which oppose death", and then it will consider the unconscious — as did Schopenhauer, von Hartmann, Carus and even Bergson, as an organic life force that develops and has, as Freud said, no negation. I believe we still tend to view the unconscious in this nineteenth-century model, as the creative will of life slumbering in the soul, which unfurls into time and which if read rightly can keep us from failing.

Were analysis to take its historical origins (as a response to failure) also as its archetypal base, then its perspective might derive more from Thanatos and the statement of Bichat could be reversed. Analysis explores failure in terms of death, and it is called into existence as the psyche's preferred instrument to explore failure in terms of all the forces which oppose life, i.e., to look for Thanatos and its related archetypal dominants wherever life is blocked, defeated, bankrupt, and failed.

This approach investigates (analyzes) failure less to remove it for new growth, than to lead each mistake, error, and weakness into failure (be "psychopompos" to it) by leading it to its final consequences, its psychic goal in death. Then every mistake of life, every weakness and error in and of analysis, instead of being set straight in repentance or wrung for its drop of consciousness or transformed and integrated, becomes rather the entrance to failure, an opening into the reversal of all values. Rather than as a block in Eros and the flow of life, we might consider failures as constellated, intended, even finally caused, by the underworld which wants life to fail in order that other attitudes governed by other archetypal principles be recognized.

The Gods then which we would consider to be the dominants of analysis would particularly be those who govern what the Romantics called the "nightside of the soul". Analysis would derive its attitudes from those archetypal dominants personified in the Gods who have a special relationship with the invisible, underground night-time world of death, terror, and tragedy, such as Hermes, Hades, Saturn, Persephone, Dionysos (Lord of Souls and source of tragedy), and especially the Children of Night described by Hesiod (Theogony): doom, old age, death, murder, destiny, fate, deception, sleep, dreams, quarrels, grievances, misery, nemesis. These personifications of Hesiod are the main content of analysis and they are partly what we today call failures since we have placed analysis among the healing, helping professions of positivism with its emphasis upon the Gods and Heroes of above, visible in Apollonic light, Gods and Goddesses of city, field, life, and deed.

Even love we tend to conceive in the concrete manner of Aphrodite, forgetting the subtle intimacy of Eros and Thanatos, even their identity in Renaissance Neoplatonism.

We may do more justice with the failures in analysis and the failure of analysis when we consider analysis as a process in failure, and even individuation as a movement in the realm of Hades, invisibly, where the literalisms of life are reflected in the metaphors of death. Then individuation, the uniqueness of individual personality, will be recognized as Unamuno characterized it in the tragic sense of life, which has its own joy, its own comedy.

When I am in despair, I do not want to be told of re-birth; when I am aging and decaying and the civilization around me collapsing from its over-growth that is over-kill, I cannot tolerate that word "growth", and when I am falling to bits in my complexities, I cannot abide the defensive simplistics of mandalas, nor the sentimentalities of individuation as unity and wholeness. These are formulae presented through a fantasy of opposites – the disintegration shall be compensated by integration. But what of cure through likeness where like takes care of like? I want the right background to the failure of life; I want to hear with precision of those Gods who are served by and thrive upon and can hence provide an archetypal background to and even an eros connection with the defeat, decay, and dismemberment, because these dominants would reflect the *experienced* psyche (not in its Aristotelian conceptualization as belonging to life), but in the actuality of its only known goal which is also both its way and its substance, death.

Delivered in London as a Paper at the Fifth International Congress for Analytical Psychology, September 1971, and printed in the Proceedings of that Congress, *Success and Failure in Analysis,* G. Adler ed. (New York: Putnam's, 1974), and in *The Journal of Analytical Psychology* 17/1, 1972, pp. 1-6.

VII

TOWARDS THE ARCHETYPAL MODEL
FOR THE MASTURBATION INHIBITION

I

Just down this lake where we are gathered for our Congress, in Lausanne, a Swiss physician, inventor of the term *Nervenkrankheit* or *maladie des nerfs,* M. Samuel Auguste André David Tissot, Professor of medicine at Lausanne and Pavia, Member of the Royal Societies of London, Paris, Milan, and Stockholm, published in the year 1758, his thirtieth year, a work in Latin which in his own French translation in 1764 is called *L'Onanisme: Dissertation sur les maladies produites par la masturbation.* This work appeared within a few years in all major European languages, and more than thirty editions were published within a century.

Tissot was a knowledgeable writer on nearly every aspect of medicine, and in the latter half of the eighteenth century enjoyed an international reputation. He has been recognized as one of the most famous physicians of his time. His word became a household authority – an eighteenth-century Dr. Spock – and his book on masturbation the standard work on the subject. Since its publication, it has been a main influence on Western attitudes, and therefore still influences our psychotherapeutic work today.

II

Before we turn to Tissot's arguments against masturbation and the theoretical model of his physiology on which those arguments are based, let us review briefly the modern and contemporary view of the "masturbation question".

Jewish and Roman Catholic traditions rigorously condemn masturbation. It is rarely mentioned, however, in writings on medicine, on the *ars amatoria,* or on education in Western society until the eighteenth century, i.e., the period of Tissot. Anthropological evidence from other "uncivilized" societies shows that masturbation is one of the *least* punished of sexual practices. It is generally held to be a private or family affair, not a clan or society matter. In our society, however, partly owing to the influence of Tissot, masturbation became not only a religious sin and a social crime, but a medical disease. For Kant, self-abuse was worse than suicide; Voltaire and Rousseau condemned it; Goethe and Lavater wrote of spiritual masturbation in their correspondence.

By the early nineteenth century "masturbatory insanity" had entered psychiatry (Hare, 1962). Eminent alienists – Benjamin Rush in the United States, Esquirol in France, Ellis and Yellowlees in England, Flemming and Griesinger in Germany – considered masturbation a cause of mental derangement. Clitoridectomy was practised, mainly in England and the USA, for the relief of "masturbation-caused epilepsy" (Duffy, 1963). Fantastic metal contraptions similar to medieval chastity belts were applied to prevent the act. Around 1900, in a Kansas reform school for boys, castration was performed to prevent masturbation (Hawke). One of the "general disqualifications" of a candidate to the U.S. Naval Academy (1940) was masturbation, which was considered a moral infirmity. The Boy Scout manual (before Kinsey's personal intervention), of which some ten million copies have been issued in the United States, warned against masturbation. Campbell's textbook of urology as late as the 1959 edition recommended mechanical restraints to prevent it. Although Taylor (1933) had empirically challenged the seed-conservation idea by showing a group of cases where superior athletic performances were achieved directly following masturbation, the idea that masturbation was dangerous and could drive one crazy continued to linger in our cultural attitudes.

The first reaction against the repressive, prohibitory attitudes came in 1912 — a revolutionary year in psychology in many other areas as well (Hillman, 1972, pp. 164-65n). In that year the psychoanalysts held their first symposium on *Onanie* and the major paper in that symposium was written by Victor Tausk. For the first time a serious attempt was made to *understand* masturbation and to place it within the wider context of psychosexual development. The symposium members noted and considered two psychological facts of first importance in connection with masturbation: *fantasy* and *guilt*. Furthermore, the view of the conference was more tolerant of masturbation. Freud's earlier hypothesis that masturbation, like *coitus reservatus* and *interruptus,* was a cause of anxiety and neurasthenic neurosis because it provided insufficient discharge, did not find full support (Reich, 1951). (All of Freud's reflections on masturbation have been collected by Nagera, 1974, pp. 520-38.) The 1912 Symposium tended toward accepting masturbation as a usual widely practiced activity of childhood and adolescence, and hence it was normal. This led to the position of Stekel, which is, in short, that "Neurosis is a consequent of abstinence, not the result of the habit" (Stekel, 1951), that is, the disturbance in sexuality is not masturbation, but the guilt feelings arising from the prohibition of masturbation in connection with oedipal conflicts and superego formation. And so the enemy is not masturbation, but rather the prohibition and the unnecessary guilt.

In Krauss' *Anthropophyteia* (1910, 1911, 1912), an encyclopedia of anthropological esoterica, we can find sections on "Onanie als Heilmittel" for drying the gut in the hot period of the year, or for ridding a person of "Krankheitstoff", or as a sacrificial religious act (sacred masturbation) — all of which "evidence" lent further support to the psychoanalytic direction inaugurated mainly by Stekel.

Since 1912 — and despite certain reservations expressed by the second psychoanalytic symposium in 1928 on *Onanie* — the pendulum has been swinging further and further away from Tissot, towards the unrestricted approval of masturbation, so that at a modern White House Conference on Mental Hygiene the consensus fought with flying banners for adolescent masturbation (Reich, 1951). The two Kinsey reports (1948, 1953) once and for all statistically whitewashed masturbation. Even the notion that masturbation could be excessive was shown

107

as an absurdity, since the sexual impulse does not respond when sated. The only bogey left was the old-fashioned folklorish moralism — that cause of guilt, of bad conscience — traceable to Tissot.

Yet, for all this approval of masturbation, a curious disapproval remained. The disapproval was disguised, displaced. For example, "excessive" masturbation was condemned; or "masturbation fantasies" led one to "introverted schizoid withdrawal" and away from "real life and love"; or, although masturbation is normal for adolescence, it is not "mature" behaviour, or it prevents, in women, "vaginal orgasm".

However, the Kinsey reports note a high frequency of masturbation throughout adult life and among adults who enjoy other forms of sexual activity: "Many adults who are not immature in any realistic sense do masturbate, and there is no sense in refusing to recognize this fact". This outstanding fact, that masturbatory activity precedes, runs parallel with, and succeeds heterosexual activity in human life, that it goes on from infancy into very old age and is — in those about whom we have some reliable statistics, the Americans — after heterosexual intercourse the next most frequent form of sexual activity, raises basic questions. It can no longer be considered a substitute form of behaviour but a sexual activity *sui generis.* (As such, the activity continues even in men who have been castrated for "persevering masturbation" [Bremer, 1959, pp. 86-8]. For example, eleven "schizophrenic" males, castrated between ages 23 and 49 went on masturbating, even when the penis was flaccid.) As psychologists we have a task to understand the fact of adult masturbation which the Kinsey reports note, even stress, but leave unexplained.

III

We must first return to Tissot. In his view masturbation was catastrophically harmful. To it he attributed a host of *maladies des nerfs* — *tabes dorsalis,* weak eyes, pimples, consumption, epilepsy, weakness of the intellectual faculties, sexual and genital disorders, and a full range of hypochondriacal and hysterical symptoms in what is an early description of the neurasthenic syndrome. Tissot's principal argument against masturbation was that seed loss is physiologically harmful. Tissot's ideas on "loss of seed" were confirmed by another Montpellier physician in three volumes with scores of case reports (Lallemand, 1836-42).

The physiological model which Tissot uses to base his argument is so wide-spread and recurrent that we may with justification call it archetypal. This model of psycho-physiology appears early and forcefully in Hippocrates, whom Tissot relies upon and quotes at length. On the Hippocratic model, the nervous system is a set of very fine tubes or pipes through which circulate the *somata hormonta* or *corps excitant* (Bucher, 1958). This circulating essence is a psycho-physical vital fluidum described in many ways and given many names in subsequent centuries. It was linked by Galen to his theory of the four humours and their nourishment and replenishment. This "animal" or "vital spirit" has always been ambiguously psycho-physical, at times described as an actual fluid, at times as an immaterial flow (Hillman, 1960, pp. 75-7).

The hydrodynamic model of circulation goes back to the dawn of thought in China and foretells the discovery of the circulation of the blood (Boenheim, 1957). Similar expressions are the "circular thrust" (*periousis*) in Plato's *Timaeus* (79-80), *prana* in Indian psycho-physiology, the notion of breath in Avicenna, the essence of which is the moist element yet which is a luminous substance like the "light" which circulates in *The Secret of the Golden Flower* (Jung and Wilhelm, 1929). Freud's notion of the libido, of its damming by repression and channelling by the ego, of its special connection with the sexual instinct — even sexual fluids — is a modern restatement of the same archetypal hydrodynamic model of the psyche.

Of particular importance here is the encephalomylogenetic theory of semen held by Hippocrates, by Plato, and by many other authoritative figures who influenced Tissot. This theory conceived a direct anatomical line from the brain through the spine to the testicles (Lesky, 1950). Similar ideas can be found in Tibetan anatomical drawings, in Kundalini yoga, and, more important for our Western ideas, in the early Greek ideas of life-stuff explained by Onians (1954). This life-stuff, called *aion*, was a fluid or liquid flowing through all parts of the body but especially associated with sexual liquids, the brain, the spinal fluid, the water of the eyes, knees, kidneys, etc.

Tissot held semen to be an example *par excellence* of this vital fluid. Semen is both vital and visible, yet contains a semi-material invisible life principle, a sort of homunculus within, for which the visible fluid serves as a vehicle. Semen for Tissot was "the essential oil of the animal liquors". He writes: "It is true that we are ignorant whether the animal spirits and the genital liquor are the same thing; but observation teaches us... that these two fluids have a very strict analogy, and that the loss of one or the other produces the same ills" (Tissot, 1772). Tissot restates in the language of his time the idea that *loss of semen is loss of soul-substance* which must circulate within the body to maintain life and not be spent.

Seed-loss in masturbation was harmful because the motions of masturbation were more violent than those of coitus, resulting in excessive excitation analogous to the epileptic attack, leaving the individual exhausted, dry, and empty. Again the idea is ancient: the vital spirit, or stuff of life, is to circulate in rhythmical, moderate, harmonious flow, in keeping with Greek ideas of the soul as a harmony and the soul fibres as a chord. Passion over-stimulates the flow, forcing it into wrong passages and leading to unremitting genital excitation and obsessive sexual preoccupations, i.e., the "bad habit".

Further, the seed lost in masturbation was not replenished. For Tissot there was an invisible torrent flowing between two people in intercourse, an exchange through the pores, a transmission of vital breath which restores vigour. Masturbation is solitary; there is no inhalation, exchange, or replenishment.

IV

We cannot be content to reject Tissot's arguments because of their outdated physiology. As psychologists — especially as Jungian psychologists — let us look at these long-held ideas as having in themselves some archaic psychological truth even if they be physiologically incorrect. Tissot's physiological model for the masturbation prohibition is faulty; but this model, rooted in an archetypal image, gave to Tissot's arguments their staggering collective influence. So, it is not that masturbation excites and expends some quasi "nerve fluid". Rather it is that masturbation stimulates and then releases psychic tension. We need only to translate the physiological "spending of fluid" into the psychological "leak in the circulation of psychic flow".

With this rediscovery of the archetypal model in Tissot's thought, we can now approach the problem of guilt and masturbation inhibition anew.

A main conclusion of the 1912 psychoanalytic symposium on Onanism, as I have already reported, was that guilt was fundamentally connected with masturbation. These guilt feelings prove unresolvable, irreducible. Fenichel (1945) writes: "In adolescence and later life, frequently not only fears and guilt feelings are still connected with masturbation, but there is even a distinct resistance on the part of the patients against enlightenment about the harmless nature of masturbation. They seem to have some unconscious interest in believing that masturbation is a dreadful thing".

In their comprehensive report on sexual offenders (Gebhard *et al.* 1965) the Kinsey researchers remark (p. 503): "A substantial proportion of the males we interviewed had worried despite their knowledge that masturbation is well-nigh universal and despite the fact that not one of them reported being physically harmed by it. It is amazing how few persons asked themselves why a loss of semen in masturbation should be harmful while a loss of semen in coitus should have no ill-effect; no one grasped the concept that if masturbation were harmful, marriage would by the same token be suicidal". Again – the archetypal model is stronger than facts and reason whether in Tissot or in these sexual offenders. It is a persuasive argument in support of our position that these men, jailed for sodomy, homosexuality, rape, incest, child-molesting, and other "sexual offenses", who for the most part have great difficulty admitting guilt in relation with their offense, nonetheless experience worry, anxiety, and guilt concerning their masturbation. This statement, of course, requires a more differentiated discussion since the mechanism of denial (pp. 804-07) may work more strongly in regard to the criminal offense. But the main conclusion still stands: masturbation is accompanied by worrying guilt – "anxiety is ordinarily concomitant with the masturbation (generally ceasing when masturbation ceases)" (p. 500) – even in those who fully act out sexuality in violation of prohibitory laws and inhibitory taboos (incest).

The *fundamental guilt* is brought out by writers on masturbation ranging from Catholic theologians (von Gagern, 1955) to D. H. Lawrence. The sin of Onan (Gen. 38:9), which has nothing explicitly to do with masturbation, nevertheless was taken up by the psyche as masturbation guilt. Anthropological data on masturbation are difficult to gather, for the act is practiced in secret, culturally disapproved, and widely ridiculed. Man is evidently uncomfortable about masturbation. Our own supposedly enlightened attitudes also express guilt; for it is usually the view in psychological literature that masturbation is either substitutive or regressive behaviour, authentic only in the extenuating circumstances of *faute*

de mieux or *Not-Onanie* (prisoners, sailors), or in connection with therapeutic regression to more juvenile levels.

What is the origin of this discomfort and disapproval, this widespread guilt
in conscience? Can we lay it entirely to the prohibition imposed by the parental
representatives of culture? Has masturbation become associated with an introjected restrictive authority, so that the two — impulse and prohibition — appear
ever after together? Or has masturbation a *sui generis* inhibitor, as part of the
drive itself? Prohibition or inhibition? The answer will depend in part upon how
we view the psyche. If we assume the psyche to be a goal-directed, relatively closed,
individuating system, a basic model of which is the self as a circulating flow of psychic life within the person, then this system is also self-steering, self-guided. Conscience is the experience of the *spiritus rector* function of the self-guidance system.
Guilt in conscience is inhibition of function: inhibition of function is felt as guilt
in conscience. *Inhibition is self-imposed by the self-regulatory activity of the
psyche.* This position appears already in Eugen Bleuler's discussion of *Onanie-
Hemmung* (1913). There Bleuler recognized the signal importance of masturbation in the sexual life of the individual and its particular relation with shame, guilt,
and the tendency to secrecy. Freud even went so far in a note written in 1938
(Nagera, 1974, p. 438) as to suggest that the basis of *all* inhibition in the spheres
of intellect and working activity seems to lie in the inhibition of childhood masturbation. The implication in both Bleuler and Freud is that masturbation and
inhibition are fundamentally connected and that inhibition in its widest sense is
derivative of masturbation. We cannot have the one without the other.

Jung (1958) says of conscience: "... the phenomenon of conscience does
not coincide with the moral code, but is anterior to it, transcends its contents ...".
Guilt from superego formation — the masturbation *prohibition* coming from outside — is possible only if the psyche has the fundamental possibility already given
to "feel guilty", and to find meaning in moral codes as part of its self-guiding system. The introjected prohibition works only because it echoes the prior self-regulatory inhibition. And the lifting of the prohibition — as when Freud speaks of
the "therapeutic return of masturbation" — does not remove the fundamental
unease and problematics of masturbation, as psychoanalysts agree, which remain
but get displaced upon such issues as "excessive", "compulsive", or "infantile-
fixated" masturbation.

The hypothesis of a masturbation *inhibition* finds support in clinical findings.

An adolescent patient at Burghölzli, a schizophrenic and compulsive masturbator, once told me he wanted to turn it around the other way so that it would go up into his head and make him well. (This was the impetus to the research leading to this paper.) Cases discussed in the 1928 *Onanie* symposium report anxiety over seed-loss. Boys find masturbation without orgasm, without ejaculation and seed-loss, evokes less guilt.

The anthropological fact that masturbation evokes the least punishment of all sexual activities implies a natural self-inhibition requiring little external prohibitory reinforcement. If it were a major danger to society or the species, as some have interpreted the reason for God's punishment of Onan, masturbation would be met with an even greater universal abhorrence than incest.

One further argument in favour of the inhibition hypothesis arises from attitudes towards female masturbation. Even after the ovum was discovered in 1827 thereby finally disproving the Galenic and medieval theory that the female had semen (Gerlach, 1937-38) and ending the controversy over the role of the female in reproduction, female masturbation continued to be condemned with the same rigour as male masturbation. The evil was as great, the consequences as disastrous, and the measures inflicted to prevent masturbation as drastic. *Physiological fact had no effect on the archetypal idea.* In female masturbation we are not dealing with an actual vital fluid or concrete seed-loss, but with the archetypal meaning given to this fluid leakage by the model of the circulating flow of the psyche.

Conceding that the inhibition experienced in conscience as guilt anxiety is *sui generis* and not a cultural prohibition, perhaps its origin is biological. In other words, does guilt arise because masturbation runs counter to "natural law" by refusing procreation, so that the voice of species preservation speaks through the self? This is the old idea that masturbation is a perversion of instinct. The masturbatory activity of animals, particularly primates — and *in their natural habitats* — shows that masturbation is a regularly occurring activity without inhibition (e.g., porcupines, too, masturbate — Wendt, 1965, p. 297). *It does not interfere with procreation but runs parallel to it.* The inhibition would on this analogy with animals have to find its origin elsewhere than in "instinctual perversion" or "biologically-generated guilt". Biologically, masturbation is "natural". We can no more base the inhibition upon a biological function than we could upon introjected cultural prohibitions.

I hope that by now the difference between "prohibition" and "inhibition" has become quite clear. A prohibition is a negative command, a forbidding by authority. An inhibition is the action of hindering, restraining, checking, preventing. A prohibition requires authority, and in the history of masturbation discussion, this authority has ranged from the God who smote Onan to the forbidding parental figure in Freudian superego formation. An inhibition, on the other hand, can be conceived as native to, as part of, a function itself, as a built-in check and balance necessary for self-regulation.

A prohibition is "anti-masturbation"; it is opposed to it. An inhibition hinders masturbation; it is a complication of it. Moreover, the inhibition can be conceived as *part of the masturbation function itself,* in the manner of a *partie inférieure* and *supérieure* of the same function − to use the language of Janet borrowed by Jung in his description of the archetype. Masturbation and its inhibition are aspects of the same activity. The lower end is the impulse to action, the upper end consists of fantasies and the *spiritus rector* of conscience.

The prohibition imposed by outer authority reinforces the inhibition, the upper end at the expense of the lower end, and splits instinct against itself. Then we find that familiar pattern of compulsive masturbation alternating with rigid superego restrictions, morbid guilt, and displaced erotic fantasies. The therapeutic return of masturbation means more than what Freud meant, i.e., discharge of id energies channelled by the ego now freed from intolerable superego restrictions. The therapeutic return of masturbation means the reunion of the two ends of the instinctual spectrum. It means *the return of the inhibition as well,* in the form of reawakened fantasy life, and a sense of one's own autonomy, one's own innate guiding conscience, rather than an imposed superego morality.

V

To recapitulate briefly: our examination of masturbation guilt led to the assumption of a masturbation inhibition. We have not been able to reduce this inhibition either to cultural or to biological sources. Rather, we have followed an insight of Freud's "that something in the nature of the sexual instinct itself is unfavourable to the achievement of absolute gratification" (1912, p. 214). This inhibitory factor is wholly of psychological origin and is an inherent component of masturbatory activity. The model for our theory, however, goes in another direction than Freud's, for we are assuming as basis for the inhibition the archetypal idea of the self as a circulation of the psyche within a containing system, i.e., the self-containment of the psyche.

We arrive at our concluding question. What might be the meaning and purpose of the masturbation inhibition in regard to adult masturbation? As Layard (1945) has shown concerning incest, a taboo has not only a negative preventive function. The incest taboo also fosters the extension of culture. Similarly, the masturbation inhibition not only acts negatively against instinctual release; it fosters as well subjective guilt feelings, introspective worry, psychological conflict, and erotic fantasy. Without the incest taboo, biological and social culture could mainly be satisfied within the immediate family. Without the masturbation inhibition, psychological tension could be directly discharged.

We might make the claim that two psychological functions are instinctually furthered by the masturbation inhibition. These functions are conscience and imagination. About guilt, unease, secrecy, moral worry in conscience accompanying masturbation we have already spoken; about the vivid fantasy accompanying masturbation, at times even necessary for it, we need not speak since it is so well known. "Males who have never had fantasies during masturbation are relatively uncommon", says Gebhard *et al.* (1965, p. 503). Without the inhibition accompanying masturbation would there be fantasy? Is not the fantasy a part of the sexual drive itself, as the *partie supérieure* of the activity? Indeed, recent experimental evidence (Fisher, Gross & Zuch, 1956) supports the hypothesis that sexual excitation and fantasy are parts of the same function. Cycles of penile erection during sleep are synchronous with cycles of dreaming. Sexual fantasy which is blocked by anxiety or censorship in dream content also seems to by synchronous with loss of penile erection. Where the incest taboo through exogamy furthers extraverted development, the masturbation inhibition, through fostering intrapsychic tension, moral conscience, and mental imagery, furthers introverted development. Masturbation particularly vivifies relationships with imaginary partners (Lukianowicz, 1960); it is a way of making figures of the imagination both convincing and satisfying.

The pioneer work of Spitz on the genital play of infants also points to a relation between masturbation inhibition and introversion. He writes: "I found that genital play in infancy (or its absence) is an indicator of the nature of the child's object relations" (Spitz, 1962). Infants with good object relations to mothers and their surrogates masturbate; those deprived or isolated masturbate less or not at all. Masturbatory activity of infants is directly correlated with outgoing instinctual relatedness. In infants it is not, as we usually think, compensatory auto-erotic behaviour activated by isolation. If we accept the view that has been put forward that all (non-autistic, "normal") babies are extraverted, that is, object-oriented, the uninhibited masturbatory activity of infants belongs to extraversion.

The *partie supérieure,* the inhibition, evidently unfolds ontogenetically later. The inhibition, reinforced by oedipal conflicts, would seem to increase with maturation and the development of subjectivity, introspection, introversion, and psychological containment. I would risk the proposition that the inhibition is reinforced more strongly around puberty than at the time of the oedipal conflicts of early childhood. On the basis of our fluid model of the soul, the appearance of genital secretions would be the determining factor. This is the critical physical experience which clicks with the archetypal model of the soul substance as a fluid, intensifying the inhibition, its conflicts and fantasies.

The words we use for masturbation — auto-erotism, solitary vice, secret vice, self-satisfaction, self-stimulation, self-abuse — draw attention to the subjectivity of the act — Bleuler's "tendency to secrecy". Because it is the only sexual activity performed alone, it has been given a negative value for biological and social culture. The meaninglessness of masturbation for the species and for society, i.e., external culture, has long associated masturbation with suicide. However, as the only sexual activity performed alone, it may very well have another sort of meaning: *a sexual impetus to psychological or internal culture.* Its connection with fire-making and its role in creation myths point to its psychological importance (cf. Jung, CW 5, p. 142f.; CW 9, ii, p. 207; Bachelard, 1938). Of interest here is the fact that a childhood sign of the prospective Shaman among the Mohave is frequent masturbation (cf. Devereux, 1936).

Although we have been showing masturbation to be "natural" (occurring throughout human life and in animals), it is at the same time an *opus contra naturam.* The contra naturam aspect is represented by the inhibitory concomitants of secrecy, guilt and fantasy. Hence, its shamanistic significance. And hence the denigration of masturbation by those who hold the naturalistic and literalistic views of sexuality, i.e., that it should serve biological procreation or social relationship.

The contra naturam aspect of masturbation is expressed by various mythical fantasies that bring the act into connection with a monster, with an unnatural image that is both negative and creative. The monster Golem in Jewish legend is the result of sperm not entering the woman; the monster Erichthonios is the result of Hephaistos' seed falling into Gaia (rather than Athene); Pan, who was said to have invented masturbation, is himself a goat-footed monster.

As Murray Stein (1973) has suggested, Hephaistos is a God of introverted libido, a structure of consciousness that is both contra naturam and at the same time intimately connected with nature; Hephaistos activates the production of individual symbolism, forging nature into images. But it is precisely this production of individual symbolism and conscience which is opposed by orthodox religions. And it is they who have most to say about the suppression of masturbation. For instance the *Kitzur Schulchan Aruch* (§151), a Jewish book of laws supposedly put together originally by Rabbi Caro, explicitly compares masturbation with murder (hence God's justification for smiting Onan). Another instance is the position taken by the Roman Catholic Church under Innocent III at the Fourth Lateran Council (1215). It was at that most important meeting that the Church established vigorous modes of repression against individualistic fantasies (Averroism, the Albigenses); inaugurated the Inquisition and a new Crusade; circumscribed with dogma the activities of angels and defined demons as those spirits who became evil of their own accord through their own acts; and strongly reconfirmed sacerdotal celibacy, giving new impetus to the scrutiny of all sexual activities including masturbation.

The "monstrousness" of masturbation and the fear of "excess" pertains to the enormity of fantasy which goes beyond nature. "It is known that sexual behaviour envisaged in daydreams or fantasy during masturbation will, in many cases, go far beyond any behaviour the individual actually has experienced or wishes to experience in real life. This is especially true of males..." (Duvall & Duvall, 1961). The exorbitance of fantasy in relation with masturbation appears also in the warnings against the activity, such as those to be found in Tissot. Horrifying images of the drooling idiot boy or the febrile wasted and wanton girl presented in nineteenth-century home medical books, religious counselling, or travelling freak exhibits have their psychological source in the contra naturam aspect of the archetype that presents the same idea in images of Pan and Hephaistos.

In other words, there is something profound in the old idea that "masturba-

tion drives one crazy". Nydes (1950) has interpreted the craziness that one fears
to be a loss of reality to magical omnipotence fantasies. The vivid tactile happening of masturbation, by giving body (concrete physical experience) to omnipotence
fantasies, "fortifies the hallucinatory quality of the experience" (p. 306). Masturbation indeed makes possible the experience of the utter reality of fantasy beyond,
in excess of, and in contradiction to "nature".

VI

We generally consider the capacity to contain excitation and the development of introversion as belonging to maturity rather than to youth. Perhaps now
we can understand why masturbation has been condoned — and even, in some societies, encouraged — for youth, but almost universally condemned for adults.

The reasons against adult masturbation — that it is physiologically harmful,
theologically evil, biologically threatening, sociologically criminal — can all be
found faulty. Condemnation of adult masturbation as juvenile and regressive expresses the psychological idea that personality development requires *tapas* (internal heat), and that it is "youthful" to be unable to contain the excitation needed
for this development.

Containing sexual excitation, including seed retention, for the purpose of
psychological development is fundamental to sexual mysticism (*Études Carmélitaines*, 1953; Evola, 1968). Chinese, especially Taoist, sexual beliefs have worked
out these practices in great detail. These have been authoritatively described by
Maspero (1937) in the *Journal Asiatique,* and further explained in relation to Tan-
tric yoga and alchemy by van Gulik (1961). These mystical ideas of self-nourish-
ment through sexuality have been reduced in a Freudian way to "orality" (Weakland, 1956), an approach which misses the archetypal model of self-regulatory
"flow" which we are trying to put forth here.

To summarize these Oriental ideas briefly: The immortal body is not born
spontaneously, nor is it given by the Gods. Salvation depends on making one's
own immortal body through human action. This is the basis of all gymnastics,
ethics, dietetics, alchemy, etc. In all, the main work is nourishing the vital spirit,
principally accomplished by "swallowing the breath", that is, by introverting the
life-force and developing psychic tension. The main *opus contra naturam* demands

118

mastery of the sexual instinct. Because "a single coitus diminishes the life of the immortal body by one year" (Maspero, 1937), abstinence is recommended. However, copulation is both natural and necessary. Therefore techniques are developed for introverting or "translating" the semen through suppression of ejaculation (*coitus reservatus*), thereby forcing it, as was the fantasy in the Burghölzli patient, through those miniscule tubes (of Tissot) and making it "flow upward" to the brain. The sage has intercourse with any number of women, preferably adolescent, because of their "vital exhalations", and without violent excitation in order to nourish his vital spirits without loss, either of precious seed or through violent motion. The prescriptions correspond strikingly with Tissot's main arguments. Ackerman further expands these Taoist ideas in terms of occult masturbation instructions and a mystique of excitation, tumescence, but seed retention for internalized dispersion of the vital fluid. Pre-forms of this exotic practice can be found in adolescents struggling with masturbation, who allow themselves genital stimulation but not ejaculation.

Western attitudes towards sexuality are largely extraverted. We have no more been able to give full value to masturbation than we have to introversion. Their undervaluation is a corollary of the wider undervaluation of psychic life *per se,* unless it shows itself clearly in biological or social culture, that is, in extraverted forms. Therefore, we continue to find the literature on masturbation in works devoted to childhood and adolescence as if it disappears from psychological life after maturity. Therefore, we have been blind to the anthropological and psychological evidence for the inhibition, always assuming that a prohibition is necessary — and prohibitions, coming from outer authorities, are also extraverted.

Moreover, our extraverted naturalistic prejudices have altogether cut masturbation off from significance for the soul and relation with religion. (There is no mention of "onanism" in any of these standard works bearing on religion: Frazer's *Golden Bough,* Seligman's *Encyclopedia of the Social Sciences,* Hastings' *Dictionary of the Bible,* or his *Encyclopedia of Religion and Ethics* (cf. Jeffreys, 1951).) But if, as the philosopher Whitehead has said, "religion is what a person does with his own solitariness", then masturbation may have profound implications beyond a mere psychotherapy of the sexual function. Individuation itself will show its omnipotence in the fantasy world of masturbation and in the secret introspective worry accompanying the act, forcing the individual to recognize the God in the "symptom", the soul in the body, the ritual in the sexual. In the complexities

119

inherent to masturbation we come upon roots of the introverted aspect of the religious instinct: separation and solitariness, shame, sense of sin, individual fantasy formation, and body magic. Our individual resistance to masturbation confession and awareness of masturbation fantasies belongs therefore to the most profound levels of the religious instinct. These secret feelings and fantasies present patterns of our individuation.

Even the newest "free" ideas on masturbation originating with Stekel are extraverted, in that they oppose the prohibition in the name of extraverted expression of psychosexuality. Extraverted prejudices appear as well in the usual discussions of masturbation and petting. Excitation which does not lead to discharge is regarded as an unhealthy practice, and — as with the early Freud on *coitus reservatus* — a source of neurosis. Whether this extraverted prejudice, supported by Western religions, has not itself had an unhealthy effect on the cultivation of eros and heightened *tapas,* I would leave for discussion.

Psychoanalysts today seem to agree with Spitz that masturbation and its inhibition belong together. Spitz (1962) writes: "From the viewpoint of our civilization, the consequences of masturbation without restriction are probably as undesirable as those of restriction without masturbation. Both lead to sterility, be it mental or reproductive". Unfortunately the argument is based on the old model of an unchecked instinctive impulse countered by a restrictive prohibition. Spitz, and all others I have read, miss the inhibition, the *self-governing of the instinct mainly through fantasy and conscience,* which Tissot's model affords us. Whether the instinct expresses itself mainly on the lower end or the upper end would depend on whether psychic tension is to be released or held and cultivated in accordance with what is beneficial at that moment for the psychological constellation.

It is the constellation that determines the masturbation experience. If puer, then masturbation is freedom and omnipotence; if heroic, then inhibition and control become dominant; if Dionysian, then relaxation and spending take on more importance. Much of the prejudice against masturbation, including Freud's association of it with neurasthenia, can be referred to the heroic ego's stance against Dionysian weakening. Although the archetypal constellation determines the experience, the fundamental ambivalence between compulsion and inhibition is not bypassed; this ambivalence merely takes different forms by following different mythical patterns. Thus the crucial psychological value of masturbation lies precisely in the experience of ambivalence, of psychic tension, which reflects the self-inhibition of even what seems most natural, simple, and pleasure-giving.

Two dreams illustrate the importance of masturbation for introversion and the development of psychic tension. A man about forty has lived out his sexuality with women since adolescence. At the time of the dream he has projected his creative talents into a woman artist who is his mistress. His own considerable artistic gifts he neglects. He dreams that he is instructed by an older woman to masturbate into a silver cup. The dream implied to me that he should turn some sexual energy towards his own anima, contain it there, rather than all outwards into the relationship.

Another man, in his late thirties, who is wrestling with his very active homosexuality — that is, whether to stay at home at night and masturbate, or go out in the street — dreams that he is in the power of a brutal hardened older homosexual. By masturbating this older man he diminishes his power and gets free. He understood this dream to mean that masturbation was now the answer to his sexual urge, otherwise he would be under the dominion of his callous shadow. In both instances, masturbation meant the frustration of extraverted object-oriented sexuality for the sake of the subjective factor. In both cases, masturbation had been looked down upon as a childish substitute. After the dreams, masturbation could be connected to inner life and the inhibition acknowledged as the fantasy-unease function of the activity itself.

Tissot's archetypal model connecting sexual liquids with the flow of psychic energy tells us what masturbation might truly mean to the psyche. It is just what the term says: self-stimulation, a stimulus to the circulation of the psyche, at first primarily by constellating a pole for the libido opposite to the head. *Sexual energy is given to introversion.* The inhibition prevents direct discharge of the heightened excitation, thereby prolonging the circulation or rotation of the psyche. The mystery of adult masturbation may now be seen in a new light. It is an aspect of adult introversion, a primitive attempt at self-centering and self-regulation — even more, of active imagination at its fundamental level.

Summary

This paper examines Tissot's arguments against masturbation and the theoretical model of physiology underlying these arguments. The author gives a brief review of the modern "masturbation question" and shows the connection between masturbation, sin, crime, and disease. To Tissot loss of semen was loss of soul substance: it could not be replenished. There seems to be an archaic psychological truth behind Tissot's physiologically incorrect arguments; his model of circulating special fluids in a self-contained circuit is rooted in an archetypal image. This rediscovered meaning of Tissot's model leads to a necessary review of the problem of guilt and of masturbatory inhibition. The unresolvable guilt feelings associated with masturbation have been acknowledged by psychoanalysts in 1912, and by many since then. Although the professional literature tends to regard masturbation as either substitutive or regressive behaviour, there is collateral evidence from clinical observations and from other fields that this is by no means all. A masturbatory inhibition *sui generis,* prior to either culturally or biologically motivated prohibition, is postulated. This fits in with Jung's view of conscience as anterior to the moral code, not necessarily identical with it and transcending it, as well as with psychoanalytical findings. Clarifying the difference between prohibition and inhibition the author makes use of Janet's concepts of *partie inférieure* and *supérieure* of the same function. Where prohibition reinforces inhibition, instinct may get split against itself. This split may heal in analytical treatment ("the return of the repressed") but the original inhibition returns too, manifest in such forms as a re-awakened fantasy life, a sense of autonomy, and conscience. Referring to Layard's view of the positive function of the incest taboo the author examines the meaning and purpose of masturbatory inhibition in relation to adult masturbation. He claims that conscience and imagination are furthered by this inhibition; this fosters intrapsychic tension which may lead to increasing introverted development. Spitz discusses the relationship between masturbatory inhibition and introversion, and finds that the masturbatory activity of infants is directly correlated with satisfactory object-relationship, and is not compensatory auto-erotic behaviour activated by isolation. The inhibition evidently unfolds ontogenetically later. The author ventures to submit that the inhibition is reinforced more strongly around puberty than at the time of the oedipal conflict of earlier childhood. This would fit in with Tissot's model of the soul fluid. From the standpoint of the preservation of the species and of culture, masturbation has long been associated with suicide. It may also be viewed as the sexual impetus to the *opus contra naturam* of psychological or internal culture (cf. fire-making and creation myths).

REFERENCES

P. Ackerman, "Erotic symbolism in Chinese literature", Unpublished manuscript, Institute for Sex Research, University of Indiana.

G. Bachelard, *Psychanalyse du feu,* Paris (Gallimard), 1938.

E. Bleuler, "Der Sexualwiderstand", *Jahrbuch für Psychoanalytische und Psychopathologische Forschungen* V/1 (1913), pp. 442-52.

F. Boenheim, *Von Huang-ti bis Harvey,* Jena (Fischer), 1957.

J. Bremer, *Asexualization: A Follow-up Study of 244 Cases,* Oslo, Norway (Oslo Univ. Press), 1959.

J. S. Brown, "A Comparative Study of Deviations from Sexual Mores", *Amer. Sociol. Rev.*

H. W. Bucher, *Tissot und sein Traité des Nerfs,* Zürich (Juris), 1958.

G. Devereux, "Sexual Life of the Mohave Indians", Dissertation, University of California, 1936.

J. Duffy, "Masturbation and clitoridectomy", *J.A.M.A.* 186 (1963), p. 246.

E. M. Duvall and S. M. Duvall, *Sex Ways in Fact and Faith,* (Chap. 10 by W. B. Pomeroy), New York (Association Press), 1961.

J. Evola, *Métaphysique du sexe,* Paris (Payot), 1968.

O. Fenichel, *The Psychoanalytic Theory of Neurosis,* New York (Norton), 1945, pp. 75ff.

C. Fisher, J. Gross, J. Zuch, "Cycle of penile erection synchronous with dreaming (REM) sleep", *Arch. Gen. Psychiat.* 12, pp. 29-45.

S. Freud, (1896), "Heredity and the Aetiology of the Neuroses", *Collected Papers* I, London (Hogarth), 1924.

S. Freud, (1912), "The Most Prevalent Form of Degradation in Erotic Life", *Collected Papers* IV, London (Hogarth), 1925.

F. von Gagern, *The Problem of Onanism* (with theological appendix), Cork (Mercier Press), 1955. Trans. M. Booth, *Die Zeit der Geschlechtlichen Reife,* Frankfurt a/M (Knecht).

P. Gebhard, J. H. Gagnon, W. B. Pomeroy, C. V. Christenson, *Sex Offenders,* New York (Harper and Row), 1965.

W. Gerlach, "Das Problem des 'weiblichen Samens' in der antiken und mittelalterlichen Medizin", *Sudhoffs Archiv f. Ges. d. Med. u. d. Naturwiss.* 30 (1937-38), pp. 177-93.

E. H. Hare, "Masturbatory insanity: the history of an idea", *J. ment. Sci.* 108 (1962), pp. 2-25.

G. C. Hawke, "Castration and sex crimes", Archives of Institute for Sex Research, University of Indiana.

J. Hillman, *Emotion,* London (Routledge & Kegan Paul), 1960.

J. Hillman, "An Essay on Pan" in *Pan and the Nightmare* (with W. H. Roscher), New York and Zürich (Spring Publications), 1972.

J. Hillman, *The Myth of Analysis,* Evanston (Northwestern), 1972.

M. D. W. Jeffreys, "Onanism: An Anthropological Survey", *Internat. Journ. Sexology* V/2 (1951), pp. 61-65.

C. G. Jung, *Aion,* Zürich (Rascher), 1951. Transl. "Aion", *Coll. Wks.* 9, ii.

C. G. Jung, *Symbole der Wandlung,* Zürich (Rascher), 1952. Transl. "Symbols of Transformation", *Coll. Wks.* 5.

C. G. Jung, "A Psychological View of Conscience", in *Civilization in Transition, Coll. Wks.* 10.

C. G. Jung & R. Wilhelm, *Das Geheimnis der goldenen Blüte* (1929). Transl. *The Secret of the Golden Flower,* revised edn., London (Routledge & Kegan Paul), 1962.

A. C. Kinsey *et al., Sexual behavior in the human male,* Philadelphia (Saunders), 1948.

A. C. Kinsey *et al., Sexual behavior in the human female,* Philadelphia (Saunders), 1953.

F. S. Krauss, *Anthropophyteia,* vols. 7, 8, 9 (1910, 1911, 1912); articles by K. Amrein and J. Heimpel ("Onanie als Heilmittel").

M. Lallemand, *Des pertes séminales involontaires,* 3 vols., Paris (Béchet), 1836-42.

J. Layard, "The incest taboo and the virgin archetype", *Eranos Jahrbuch* 12, Zürich, pp. 253-307.

E. Lesky, *Die Zeugungs- und Vererbungslehren der Antike und ihr Nachwirken, Abh. d. Geistes-u. Sozialwiss, Klasse* 19, Wiesbaden, pp. 1227-1425.

N. Lukianowicz, "Imaginary Sexual Partner: Visual Masturbatory Fantasies", *Archives General Psychiatry* 3, pp. 429-49.

H. Maspero, "Les procédés de 'Nourrir le principe vital' dans la religion Taoiste ancienne", *J. Asiatique* 229, pp. 177-252; 353-430.

H. Nagera, *Psychoanalytische Grundbegriffe,* transl. Fr. Herborth, Frankfurt a/M (S. Fischer), 1974.

J. Nydes, "The Magical Experience of the Masturbation Fantasy", *Amer. Journ. Psychotherapy* 1950 (April), pp. 303-310.

R. B. Onians, *The Origins of European Thought,* London (Cambridge University Press), 1954.

A. Reich, "The discussion of 1912 on masturbation and our present-day views", *Psychoanal. Stud. Child* 6, 1951, pp. 80-94.

R. A. Spitz, "Autoerotism re-examined", *Psychoanal. Stud. Child* 17, 1962, pp. 283-315.

M. Stein, "Hephaistos: A Pattern of Introversion", *Spring 1973,* New York and Zürich (Spring Publications), 1973.

W. Stekel, *Auto-erotism: A Psychiatric Study of Masturbation and Neurosis,* London (Nevill), 1951.

W. S. Taylor, "A Critique of Sublimation in Males: A Study of Forty Superior Single Men", *General Psychological Monograph,* Worcester, Mass., 1933.

S. A. A. D. Tissot, *An Essay on Onanism,* Dublin (James Williams), 1772.

R. H. van Gulik, *Sexual Life in Ancient China,* Leiden (Brill), 1961.

(Various Authors), *Die Onanie: Vierzehn Beiträge zu einer Diskussion der "Wiener Psychoanalytischen Vereinigung"*, 1912.

(Various Authors), *Mystique et continence,* Les Etudes Carmélitaines, Bruges (Desclée de Brouwer), 1952.

J. H. Weakland, "Orality in Chinese Conceptions of Male Genital Sexuality", *Psychiatry* 19, 1956, pp. 237-47.

H. Wendt, *The Sex Life of Animals,* New York (Simon & Schuster), 1965.

"Regulations governing the admission of candidates into the United States Naval Academy as Midshipmen", Washington, D. C., U.S. Government Printing Office, 1940, p. 15.

Delivered in Montreux as a Paper at Third International Congress for Analytical Psychology, September 1965, and printed in the Proceedings of that Congress, *The Reality of the Psyche,* J. Wheelwright ed., New York (Putnam's), 1968, and in *The Journal of Analytical Psychology* 11/1, 1966, pp. 49-62.

VIII

ON THE PSYCHOLOGY OF
PARAPSYCHOLOGY

Psychological Reflection

As you know I come from psychology. Psychologists have long been interested in their "para" cousin; the early modern naming of the field brought *psyche*
into it from the beginning, e.g., "psychical research". William James, William Mc-
Dougall, C. A. Mace, Cyril Burt, Gardner Murphy, as well as Freud and Jung are
representatives of psychology whose work in the parapsychological field is well
known. To extend the list would make only more evident the omissions.

Despite this long-standing interest of psychology in psychic research and the
eminence of its bearers, psychology has mainly made contributions of only two
sorts: operational and critical. It has suggested methods and provided accounts
for operations of different kinds, and it has thought critically about many areas
of parapsychology in relation with the psyche as studied by psychology. There

126

is an approach, however, which psychology has not to my knowledge yet made, and it is in this direction I would like to venture this morning.

It has seemed to me that psychology could make a deeper contribution were it to approach the field from the perspective of *depth* psychology. Let me at once hasten to add that I do *not* mean another theory based on a "subliminal self", an unconscious mind, an autonomous complex, an oversoul, or psychic energy, etc. I do not mean to provide another account for ESP events by means of the conceptual apparatus of depth psychology. Nor shall I begin an analysis of a psi-factor, or personality correlates with psi-behaviour, or any of the psychological or psychologistic approaches to our problems. There is no reason to insist that the conceptual apparatus of depth psychology can be applied to events other than the ones of psychotherapy, nor even that our apparatus is so valid and so valuable that it should be applied in other areas.

Rather, there is reason to believe, as Ian Stevenson has suggested, that parapsychology may be useful for "accounting for" phenomena of therapy. Here I refer to transference and also to the possibility that complexes may account for psi events, but perhaps psi events may help account for an "ancestral" factor in complexes. Perhaps the things so hard to shed are residues of other lives?

So I would prefer to begin a process of reflection upon parapsychology itself, rather than upon its disparate phenomena. Could we examine the psychology of the *field* and not only the psychology of the mediums, the gifted, the experimenters, and so on.

Depth psychology has applied its method to the study of alchemy, myth, religious dogma and ritual, scientific theory, primitive behaviour, cosmologies, psychiatric ideas — all in terms of the archetypal fantasy therein contained and expressed. All fields work with certain models of thought or root metaphors; so too parapsychology must have root metaphors. If this conference has been called in order to review the continuing doubts and affirmations about psychical research, then it might be useful to reflect upon the psychic impetus of the field — not what are its problems, but what are its fantasies, what is its dream?

Problems and Fantasies

I have made a distinction between not being interested in the problems of psychical research and being interested in its fantasies. Let me make this clearer.

127

Psychic life is a complexity. We can imagine this complexity as a group of complexes. Following Jung we can take these complexes to be the root of all psychic life, the nuclear fundamentals. We are each a multiplicity of voices speaking from a multiplicity of souls, and Jung refers to these complexes as "the little people". They populate our dreams, create the dissociation and internal conflicts, and give us our problems.

A complex can be taken from two sides: one is the realm of problems and the other that of fantasies. When a complex is experienced from its problematic side, it becomes a knot, a worry, a discord of complexities demanding resolution. It pushes itself into life, infects and dominates the psyche, accumulates associations, demands to be fed by attention, perseveres against our will. All these factors are familiar from the descriptions of psychology and the evidence gained through the association experiments. On the other hand, the complex is also a fantasy; it figures in our dreams as themes and personages, building hopes, illusions, depressions, projects. It fabulates tales and makes myths, playing us into all sorts of roles, making life quite exciting, and "unreal". These fantasies are like a procession of images and leitmotifs governed ultimately by basic archetypal patterns.

Usually we speak of the two sides of the complex as the "real" and "unreal" sides; problems being "real", "hard", "tough", "difficult", while fantasies are only fantasies, mere, wispy, insubstantial nonsenses.

Problems call for strong men to attack them, for hard-thinking, and tough-mindedness. Parapsychology, like all respectable, serious fields, is full of "thorny" and "knotty" problems. The word *problem* is rooted etymologically in the idea of a hindrance, barrier, blockage, connected with armor and shield. It is something that juts out, getting in the way. So, problems are to be overcome, penetrated, knocked down and solved, got rid of. Problems appear in the realm of math and logic, of chess, physics, and also war and logistics. Problems belong to the fantasies of will and thinking and our usual notion of the ego as coper, problem-solver.

Quite possibly those fantasies which we take most concretely and unpsychologically, which we endow with the most "reality" become problems. The obdurate fantasies that jut forth and annoy us — as complexes tend to do — become problems to solve. In this sense, we might say that every problem is just one more fantasy that has become hardened into an object or objection for the ego to deal with. A problem would be that fantasy to which the complex has diverted the most energy, paid the most attention, given the most credit, love and will. The complex believes in its problem and takes it seriously. In general we believe more in problems than fantasies. If the psychological therapy I am suggesting for our field of parapsychology is to have effect, a first step would be in regarding our problems as stages of fantasy, in recognizing the fantasy aspect of the problems, and remembering that we tend to perceive fantasy first in the hard-shell of problems, where it juts forward into our attention.

Fantasies are no less valid, real or serious than problems; by resolving problems into fantasies, searching for their archetypal sense so as to dissolve them rather than solve them, we do not mean that the continuing problems of parapsychology are not real. Nevertheless, I do suggest that they could be approached more psychologically, not only as persistently continuing problems, but also as *recurrent fantasies inherent to the field and part of the complexes which make up the field* — and therefore necessary to the existence of the field. In other words, the problems of parapsychology refer to fantasies, which in turn reflect the basic archetypal dominant which drives and governs our subject.

The Fantasies of Parapsychology

By turning now to these problems, and regarding them as fantasies, we may discover certain archetypal motives operating in parapsychology, which, until they become recognized as such, may be responsible for the continuing dissatisfaction with the results in the realm of problem-solving. Since problem-solving itself is a favorite fantasy of the operating, striving ego, sometimes its *raison d'être,* there is a great investment in defending these problems as legitimate, real and tough, and calling for heroic work.

So, the first of the fantasies I wish to single out is that of *work.* Often and again papers in psychic research end with an exhortation for more work. We need larger samples, more laboratory experiments, more trained workers, more pedestrian day-to-day collections, more follow-up studies over a longer period of time, more down-to-earth work. ESP workers in the field, grubbers; a kind of peasant fantasy. There is a lurking hope that spontaneous and playful events, ephemeral, odd and fantastic, reported as anecdotes and cases could be caught by more "work", thereby disciplined into an order, made to obey law, become habitual and regular, able to be displayed in public demonstration, and thus become respectable within a certain ethical universe called rational or scientific. The playful to be caged by the serious, the spontaneous by the systematic.

Correlate with the fantasy of work is that of *will.* ESP events are generally not only extrasensory, but extra-voluntary. We generally seem unable to make them happen. Could we, then we would have them under control and predictable. The fantasy of will is quite a strong one; it enters into the core of the idea of personality. When Lodge leaves a packet behind, the contents of which he alone knows, it is with the post-mortal will that he will try to communicate to the living; T. E. Wood intends the same, by communicating after death the code to a cipher he has printed. To what extent the identification of personality with conative-cognitive aspects of what we call the ego affects parapsychology's fantasies in most of its problems, I leave in order to pass on to other fantasies. Yet, it is hard to align the fantasy of willing psi events with the heaps of events that are so apparently unwilled, i.e., repetitive, automatic, undirected.

A fantasy of will appears in the experiments of mind over nature. PK presents this fantasy most acutely, but so does the healing of wounds or the growth of seedlings. Not only can willing and thinking make something occur, but the concentration of mental stuff through the focus of the operator can perform work and move matter. In psychoanalytic language this might be called an omnipotence fantasy; in psychiatry, de-reistic or delusional; in anthropology, magical or prelogical thinking. But let us not insist on those terms for putting down this fantasy. These negative descriptions, like omnipotence fantasy and magical thinking, are taken from the rational viewpoint of the last century when psychoanalysis, psychiatry and anthropology invented their terms, so loaded with nineteenth-century bias. We need not go on describing this fantasy in that language. However we account for it, the idea of *mind over nature* remains a basic idea which parapsychology seems to have an interest in confirming. Unfortunately this belief is expressed in causal, concrete experiments, the fantasy in the hard shell of psychokinesis problems. Yet, a very old and widespread fantasy and one important to the psyche is being expressed by PK. It occurs in us at one time or another quite spontaneously, as for instance when I see someone in a boat stand up, and I think he is going to fall in the water, and just then he does — and then I have the feeling-fantasy that my thought caused his falling. Psychiatry might call this a delusional idea, yet there is evidently some need for the psyche to conceive things in this way, to put *a direct relation between thought processes and external events.* The mode of this relation has been con-

ceived in many ways: causality, correspondence, coincidence, magic, occasional-
ism, synchronicity. The theory of this relation is here less the issue than is the
dominant fantasy of a direct relation between two events, thereby overcoming the
limits of the sensible, material world. Parapsychology maintains this fantasy and
provides a place for it, and by this recognition, serves psychic reality.

The next set of ideas might be called expressions of an *intimacy* fantasy.
Cases so often seem to arise from the intimate sphere, touching emotional depths:
a dead or endangered beloved, a lost child, out-of-body visions at death's door,
crisis apparitions. The clairvoyant is called upon to help with an intimate problem
of despair and bereavement. So often the events have to do with death and love —
events which touch the soul most deeply. The intimate sphere of personal values —
what one calls soul, anima, psyche — is occasion for most powerful fantasies. Here
we find ideas of the independence of the soul from all circumstances, and the belief in its indestructibility and its substantial reality. This fantasy is concretized
into visual representations of the soul's substance, its undefeatedness by death, its
freedom from the circumstances of time and space and all contingencies whatsoever. Parapsychology confirms this fundamental sense of soul, whether sentimental
or scientific, and admits fully the sacredness of intimate reality.

Gabriel Marcel has raised the fantasy of intimacy to supreme importance,
considering love to be the fundamental principle in his ideas of parapsychology.
He has said that no theory in this field can begin to be adequate unless it be based
upon a theory of love. William James said that those who have had religious experiences show afterwards "a temper of peace, and in relation with others, a pre-
ponderance of loving affection". Frederic Myers quotes the speech of Diotima
from Plato's *Symposium* on Eros, and defines love as a kind of generalized telepathy, or fellow-feeling, not bounded by divisions and separatedness. Separatedness is caused by the organization of consciousness through space, time and causality, which divides things up into discrete particles. We find here a fantasy that
parapsychology is a way of partaking in love, the cosmogonic Eros, and the end
of separated and limited human existence. In as much as the devil is traditionally
that which brings about all divisions, this fantasy also touches upon a strong Christian theme of overcoming evil through love.

Our colleagues show another dominant pattern in their writings. We may
call this the "upward drive". The men from outer space are *above* us; with their
superior intelligences they descend to earthlings. In out-of-body experiences, we

learn of people disembodied upwards. They look down as they float up. Why do they not go to the underworld, also a traditional place of ghosts and spirits? They are not shades as much as lights. In apparitions are not the appearances often white, light and usually a bit off the ground? Do they have shoes and feet? Do the observers ever look for their shoes and feet? Some souls in some traditions are called chthonic; they sink down at death, joining the ancestral demons below the earth. Yet our fantasy tends to present an upward drive towards a locus reminiscent of Heaven.

This upwardness is sometimes inseparable from an onwardness in the literature. Burt refers to the doctrine of "posthumous spiritual evolution". The activity of the human spirit continues to evolve after death through successive stages. The disembodied spirit catches glimpses of his post-mortem existence by occasional admission into the spirit world while still in this life. Swedenborg or the Iranian mystics reported upon by Corbin communicate with higher powers, are given detailed instruction about the successive and improving stages upward and onward. This fantasy of *évolution* we find in many places, and it is quite fetching, witness the degree of enthusiasm surrounding the ideas of Teilhard de Chardin. Knowledge of the other world is a knowledge of both a higher world and a better world. Evidence to the contrary, such as the trivia reported by mediums in their communication with the spirits of the departed, or the memories of minor incidents as reported in Stevenson's cases of evidence for reincarnation does not affect the force of this fantasy. Instead, the idea of a better world, beyond and above, is buttressed by death-bed visions of crossing over, fearless, to a better condition.

Depth psychology once spoke of an "immortality drive". Not all parapsychology directly shows this sort of fantasy, yet a good deal of it does. The communication with the dead has been a major part of psychic research from its inception, and attempts to establish survival in one form or another continue to occupy our energies in parapsychology. Here, the "immortality drive" is not sublimated, as the psychoanalysts say, into a cultural objective (writing a book, making a statue), nor is it transferred into the family (having descendents), but is taken at face value as a problem. One searches for direct evidence for the survival of human personality, its immortal aspect.

We come now to what seems to me to be the major fantasy, and the one which perhaps lies within the others. Let me read you two passages from the Tenth Frederic W. H. Myers Lecture, one from J. B. Rhine, the other from S. G. Soal.

. . . the devastating influence of a physicalistic view of man has affected more of our social institutions than religion. . . I will call attention to the fact that materialism seems to be the most fundamental principle of the philosophy of Russian Communism today. The Soviet system is attempting to build a society on a theory of man as matter. It is especially significant, I think, that Western society, with all its various attacks upon the communist system, has not seriously assailed this basic premise. Is it not a fact that until it utilizes the findings of parapsychology it has little with which to attack the materialistic state philosophy of the U.S.S.R.?

If we have — and of course we concluded long ago that we do have — scientific refutation of materialism that stands the severest critical analysis, on what justification should we hold aloof from the needs of our times with these vital and relevant findings? . . . The world is today facing what may be its greatest crisis, largely because we have not socially and civically faced up to the menace to our value system growing out of the overtowering domination of modern life by the philosophy of matter.

. . . If this is too large a claim [for the importance of psi research] . . . then I have grossly misunderstood the nature of our field and its significance.[1]

In the Introduction to this paper of Rhine's Soal writes:

Today a devastating materialism is creeping like a blight over large portions of the globe. Concentrating as it does on only the *sensory* [italics mine] aspects of human existence with a complete negation of all spiritual values, this system of though will, if not counteracted, end by destroying what is best in human life. . . Never at any time in history have we had more urgent need of an answer to the question, "What is man's place in the cosmos? " . . . is he an immaterial being who, when he puts off "this muddy vesture of decay" continues to live and feel and share in a freer and finer consciousness? . . . Of all studies pursued by man I believe that parapsychology is the most likely to provide an answer to the questions . . . the pursuit of happiness and the immortality of the soul.[2]

It is questionable to me whether the refutation of materialism as a hypothesis for *interpreting* data can be accomplished by the *data* of parapsychology, or by any data whatsoever, since materialism as a theoretical model — and it is not a mono-lithic idea, but a complex and subtle expression of an archetypal fantasy concerning the primacy of the symbol of "matter" — shows itself highly viable, resilient and resistant. Yet, this *anti-matter fantasy* is perhaps the most persistent and deep-going in our field. I see it in the upward movement, the transcendence of the categories of matter (time, space and causality), in the immortality drive, in the light, white ghosts without feet, in the redemption through love.

In a short and essential paper given at Harvard in 1936, Jung spoke of three basic psychic modalities that determine human behaviour in any field whatsoever. One of these primary modalities is the functioning of the psyche consciously and unconsciously; a second modality is the directions of the psyche's energy, introverted or extraverted.

> The third modality points, to use a metaphor, upward and downward, because it has to do with spirit and matter. It is true that matter is in general the subject of physics, but it is also a psychic category, as the history of religion and philosophy clearly shows. And just as matter is ultimately to be conceived of merely as a working hypothesis of physics, so also spirit . . . is in constant need of reinterpretation. The so-called reality of matter is attested primarily by our *sense*-perceptions, while belief in the existence of spirit is supported by *psychic* experience [italics mine]. Psychologically, we cannot establish anything more final with respect to either . . . than the presence of certain conscious contents, some of which are labelled as having a material, and others a spiritual, origin. . . From the existence of these two categories ethical, aesthetic, intellectual, social, and religious systems of value arise which in the end determine how the dynamic factors in the psyche are to be used. Perhaps it would not be too much to say that the most crucial problems of the individual and of society turn upon the way the psyche functions in regard to spirit and matter. [3]

Conclusions

The upward-downward polarity as conceptualized in the matter-spirit opposition seems to be an archetypal orientation schema basic to the psyche. Attempts at a unified field theory are attempts to join these polarities. Even if matter is re-defined so as to be more spiritual, or spirit redefined so as to be a property of mat-ter, the psychic tension of the upward and downward pulls remains as background factors to our formulations.

It seems to me that the anti-matter, pro-spirit fantasy of parapsychology oc-curs in many of its problems. The field itself, characterized as *extra*sensory, *para*-psychological, *super*natural, emphasizes that it is neither mainly interested in the sense experiences on which a materialistic universe depends, nor even mainly inter-ested in psychological events where the psyche is the middle region between spirit and matter. Both words, "extrasensory" and "parapsychological", imply a spiritual position outside of regions considered material and psychological.

Furthermore, the struggles over method and demonstration — whether to use the material methods of sense and measurement for psi events, and then how to jump from the methods of matter to theories of spirit — these and other strug-gles contain the tensions of the upward-downward pulls. The upward proclivity may also account for the sundry topics accumulated in the parapsychological bag: dowsing and trance, mystic and religious experience, PK with dice, haunting, rein-carnation, hypnosis, glossolalia, etc. All in one way or another reflect or derive their energy from a fantasy of the spirit.

I therefore think that parapsychology is engaged in an activity of the spirit. Further, I think that the spirit is irreducible to any other component, and is a basic modality of human nature, and perhaps of all nature. What "spirit" is, and how to define it, is far beyond the range of this paper, or any paper. In fact part of its es-sence is that it is "beyond". Classical descriptions of spirit claim that it shows it-self in emotion and that its nature is spontaneous, free and upward-seeking. It announces itself in transcendent categories. It has also been maintained that its effects call the individual out, beyond, above entropy, inertia and gravity — the downward pull. If so, I doubt whether any method will ever altogether capture it, organize it or lay it flat in explanation. Perhaps as someone here remarked, quot-ing William James, the Creator does not want us to understand. Perhaps parapsy-chology refers not to what we do not yet know, but what we may never know, be-cause it is unknowable. Spiritual events traditionally bear witness to spontaneous and individual cases or certain mass phenomena. (I think "spontaneous" belongs to the qualities of spirit and "random" is its correlate adjective in the realm of matter.) As Sir Alister Hardy would like to show through his new research project, this spontaneous factor may re-orient and revitalize a life that has lost its spirit; it may intrude and throw into question the one-sidedness of only material methods and hypotheses; it may even open the doors of belief in those symbols associated with spirit.

Because of this spirit fantasy, parapsychology is inevitably tied with matters of faith and skepticism, which appear for instance in the "sheep" and "goat" imagery of believers and skeptics. The archetype of spirit evokes questions of faith. Therefore, even this peroration of mine has overtones of a statement of faith — which it is not. It is an attempt to reflect the constellation that I think grips parapsychology.

It is questionable whether our field can ever "solve its problems" until it has fully taken into account the potency of this archetypal fantasy of the spirit. One aspect of the spirit has been called "creativity"; the spirit creates problems. Perhaps one of the tasks of parapsychological research might be the investigation of the nature of this fantasy which creates these particular conundrums and dilemmas of parapsychological research. *Perhaps our problems are different from those of science because they are driven by another sort of fantasy.*

A main difficulty we shall encounter in any examination of the spirit idea as background to our field is that the notion of spirit is always influenced by the culture in which it appears. Parapsychology suffers not only from formulations of matter in terms of nineteenth-century materialism and science, it suffers even more from the replies to this materialism in the spirit's cultural carrier: nineteenth-century Christianity. We have noted this in our fantasies of will and work and love and immortality and resurrection upwards. St. Paul might well have been a founding member of the Society for Psychical Research! The inspirational mission of parapsychology also belongs here since mission and spreading the word also belong to the classical activities of the spirit, even if not necessarily in the mode of Protestantism's fantasy.

When addressing ourselves to the problems of ESP, such questions as "How is it possible"? and "What is its cause"? tend to keep us in the realm of problems. The questions: "Do you believe it"? and "Would you swear to it"? already show the effects of the spirit fantasy. Perhaps, we could ask other questions, such as "Why did it happen, and why to me"? and "What does it mean"? "What is its 'informational content' "? We might shift our focus from the technical and practical "How" to the philosophical "Why".

Philosophical wonder asks about the necessity of events; sometimes philosophers have said that things do not occur unless there is sufficient and necessary ground for their occurrence. Even the Greek Gods obeyed a law, not of space, time and causality, but of necessity. In this pre-Christian fantasy, the dominants of the spirit (the Gods) are presented as conforming to necessity. On the level of human events, then, no matter how unwilled, irrational, incredulous and intensely personal parapsychological happenings may be, they yet follow a law: necessity. They are necessary. And our task then might be to ask questions in terms of the spirit: if necessary, then what do they mean? And our other task would be to discover less "how" they happen than to envision them as messages telling us something necessary in a form that is also necessary, and could not occur in any other form. I believe it was to the wider realm of necessity that Jung was pointing with his concept of synchronicity.

———

NOTES

1   J. B. Rhine, *Telepathy and Human Personality;* introduction by S. G. Soal. Tenth Frederic W. H. Myers Memorial Lecture (London: Society for Psychical Research, 1950), pp. 36-37.

2   *Ibid.,* pp. 7-8.

3   C. G. Jung, *The Structure and Dynamics of the Psyche.* Collected Works, VIII, §251.

From *A Century of Psychical Research: The Continuing Doubts and Affirmations* (edited by Allan Angoff and Betty Shapin), Proceedings of an International Conference, Le Piol, St. Paul de Vence, France, September 2-4, 1970, New York (Parapsychology Foundation), 1971, pp. 176-187.

I X

WHY "ARCHETYPAL" PSYCHOLOGY?

An Editorial Postscript to Spring 1970

Jungian, analytical, and complex are the three generally used terms for the psychology represented in this publication during the past thirty years. The subtitle of *Spring 1970* introduces a fourth, *archetypal.* Quite likely there are contrasts in these terms that are more than accents, and it seems worthwhile to characterize some of these differences.

The eponym Jungian is more than a common adjective; it evokes the emotional attachment to a man, to a history, to a body of thought and, especially, experience. Some who speak of themselves as "Jungians" had personal experience with Jung; nearly all have had experience of Jungian analysis. Because "Jung" continues to play a numinous role in the ideas, dreams, and fantasies of Jungians, the term musters psychic energy as an intimate symbol, stirring vital beliefs and feelings of loyalty. The name touches upon what Grinnell elsewhere in this volume *(Spring 1970)* discusses as "psychological faith" and "personality".

Since the appearance of "Jung" is unique to each person, so is this designation intensely subjective. What makes a Jungian? Is "being a Jungian" truly a kind of being, that is, a way of existing in accordance with certain beliefs (even if unformulated) and practices (even if uncodified)? Or, have we become Jungians through association in a community of interests, through professional qualifications, or through tracing psychological lineage back to Jung by means of an analytical family tree? This last question raises further ones, since many feel themselves sympathetic to "the Jungian thing" and take part in it, and yet they have never been analyzed. Moreover, strictly speaking, "Jungian" derives from a family name and belongs to an actual family rather than to a following.

By meaning many things to many people, Jungian, like any symbol, provides an emotional atmosphere. But just because of the emotions which the word conjures, Jungian also constellates *kinship libido* with attendant passions of family feeling, sometimes called transference, sometimes called sibling rivalry, trailing eros and eris along. This shows in the exogamous hostility between the Jungian community and its ideas and "non-Jungians", and it shows within the Jungian community itself. Whitmont and Guggenbühl above *(Spring 1970)* have each reflected upon aggression and destruction in relatively closed situations. The aggression and destruction released by Jungians against Jungians in the name of Jungian psychology may not be resolved merely through shifting terms, but it might be ameliorated by reflecting upon this familic designation and what it can imply. These thorny issues have led us to use *Jungiana* to refer to the actual person of C. G. Jung, and *Jungian Thought* in tribute to a tradition that is difficult to describe otherwise.

═══

The difference between complex and analytical was made clear in 1935 by T. Wolff:[1]

> Recently Jung uses the term "complex psychology" mostly when he speaks of the whole area of his psychology particularly from the *theoretical* point of view. On the other hand, the description "analytical psychology" is appropriate when one is talking about the practice of psychological analysis.

As the name indicates, complex psychology builds upon the complex for its theory.

This basis is empirical because it takes up the complex mainly through the association experiment, where measurements play the major role. Perhaps, because of this empirical origin, complex psychology inclines towards models from the natural sciences and their fantasies of objectivity. The association experiment is that part of Jung's work which can best be measured and demonstrated publicly. It is independent of therapy, an objective method that can be used with anybody. Upon it a theory of the psyche can be presented that attempts general validity and does not need the witnessing material of analytical cases. Individuals and their psychic material provide data for collections with which to advance psychology in general, rather than the psyche of a specific analytical case. However, when theory follows scientific models, there are corresponding methods: statistics, questionnaires, measurements, and machines for the study of dreams, types, psycho-somatics and -pharmaceutics, and synchronicity. The patient now may become an empirical subject and the clinic a laboratory-setting in the interests of objective research into the general laws of complex behaviour. A hope of complex psychology is to establish Jung's hypotheses, objectively and among a wider audience of the scientific and academic world beyond the one limited to Jungians or by analysis.

One could still use the description "complex" psychology, conceiving theory, not on the models of science, but in regard to the archetypal core of the complexes. Then we would be engaged more with symbolic thinking, and then psychological theory might better reflect both Jung's concerns with the metaphysical and imaginal, and the soul. Nevertheless, the designation has one great disadvantage: it evokes Jung's first idea of the complex as a *disturbance* of consciousness. Despite all that he wrote afterwards concerning its value in all psychic life, the word retains pathological connotations — power-complex, Oedipus-complex, mother-complex.

In 1896, Freud[2] first joined the word analysis to psyche in his new term "psychoanalytic" for describing a new method of therapy. Jung commented upon the naming of the new psychology in 1912:

> One could describe the psychology invented by him [Freud]
> as "analytical psychology". Bleuler suggested the name
> "depth psychology", in order to indicate that Freudian

psychology was concerned with the deeper regions or hinterland of the psyche, also called the unconscious. Freud himself was content just to name his method of investigation: he called it psychoanalysis.[3]

In 1929 Jung wrote:

> ... I prefer to call my own approach "analytical psychology" by which I mean something like a general concept embracing both psychoanalysis and individual psychology [Alfred Adler] as well as other endeavours in the field of "complex psychology".[4]

In the following paragraphs Jung says that "analytical" is the word he uses for all the different psychological attempts "to solve the problem of the psyche". Clearly, analytical refers to the practice of therapy as problem-solving, to analysis as the work of making-conscious. When "analytical" defines our field, we are mainly occupied with what used to be called "the practical intellect". Several consequences flow from this.

With the practical in the foreground, analytical psychology is naturally interested in therapy and in the many questions of profession. It will also be searching for improved methods for problem-solving. New directions are mainly practical: therapeutic techniques, groups, clinics, provide fantasies for new ways "to solve the problem of the psyche". There is also an obsessive focus upon analysis itself, especially the transference. Then, too, analytical psychology has interests naturally aligned with pastoral psychology and the "cure of souls", another path of problem-solving.

Unlike Freud's earliest use of the term, analysis today is more than a method. We are as well a profession, a mentality which analyzes (people, their "material", their "relationships"), and we have a big stake in a system: analysts, analysands, and an unconscious to be made conscious. Indeed, we can hardly get along without the unconscious. What is by definition a hypothesis has reified into a hypostasis filled with "real", "hard" and "tough" problems to be analyzed. If the unconscious calls for analysis, analytical psychology necessitates an unconscious.

In analytical psychology, the analyst is the psychologist and our psychology consists mainly in insights gained through analysis. This tends to limit our horizon. The idea of amplification may show what I mean. Even when analytical psychology extends into wide areas, such study is for the context of therapy. We feel that amplification must be brought down to actual cases, else it becomes speculative fantasy. For analysts, the problem of the psyche is "located" in the soul of the individual and his situation as a case.

———

Jungian, analytical, and complex were never happy choices nor were they adequate to the psychology they tried to designate. It seems right to turn to a word that does reflect the characteristic approach of Jung, both to theory and to what actually goes on in practice, and to life in general. To call this psychology today *archetypal* follows from its historical development. The earlier terms have, in a sense, been superseded by the concept of the archetype, which Jung had not yet worked out when he named his psychology. The archetype is the most onto-logically fundamental of all Jung's psychological concepts, with the advantage of precision and yet by definition partly indefinable and open. Psychic life rests upon these organs; even the self is conceptually subsumed among the archetypes; and they are the operative agents in Jung's idea of therapy. This designation reflects the deepened theory of Jung's later work which attempts to solve psychological problems at a step beyond scientific models and therapy in the usual sense, because the soul's problems are no longer problems in the usual sense. Instead, one looks for the archetypal fantasies within the "models", the "objectivity" and the "prob-lems". Already in 1912 Jung placed analysis within an archetypal frame, thereby freeing the archetypal from confinement to the analytical. Analysis may be an in-strument for realizing the archetypes but it cannot embrace them. Placing arche-typal prior to analytical gives the psyche a chance to move out of the consulting room. It gives an archetypal perspective to the consulting room itself. After all, analysis too is an enactment of an archetypal fantasy.

According to Jung[5] myth best represents the archetypes. But myth proceeds from a realm which cannot legitimately be considered altogether human. Like the mythical, the archetypal too transcends the human psyche, which implies the psyche's organs do not altogether belong to it. A true depth psychology is obliged by the nature of the psyche to go below or beyond the psyche. This fortunately offers a way out of the impasse of psychologism, which has hindered the collabora-tion of some who too take their perspective from the archetypes but do not allow their location *in* the psyche. But we do not have to take the archetypes as only or altogether *psychic* structures; the psyche is only one place where they manifest. By psychologizing I also mean the tendency to attribute too much to the human and the psychic, burdening our lives with an overweening sense of responsibility for matters that are not ours, but are archetypal, i.e., historical, mythical, psychoid – or instinctual in the sense of Robert Stein above (*Spring 1970*).

Insights for this approach call for an archetypal eye that is difficult to acquire through focus upon persons and cases. This eye needs training through profound appreciation of history and biography, of the arts, of ideas and culture. Here, amplification becomes a valid way of doing psychology, necessary and sufficient in itself. Amplification can be a method of soul-making, by finding the cultural in the psyche and thereby giving culture to the soul. A great deal can be done for the psyche and its healing, indirectly, through archetypal elucidation of its problems.

The mythical perspective may get us around another kind of psychologism: the humanization of the Gods which goes hand in hand with an awesome esteem for the personal psyche in its concrete existence – confrontations, reactions, immediacy. A psychology that is designated archetypal dare not be only a secular humanism; anyway, involvement is basic for all psychology, for all human existence, and hardly needs inflating by still more emphasis. The problems of the psyche were never solved in classical times nor by archaic peoples through personal relationships and "humanizing", but through the reverse: connecting them to impersonal dominants.

The dominants in the background permit and determine our personal case histories through their archetypal case histories which are myths, the tales of the Gods, their fantasies and dreams, their sufferings and pathologies. The plurality of archetypal forms reflects the pagan level of things and what might be called a polytheistic psychology. It provides for many varieties of consciousness, styles of existence, and ways of soul-making, thereby freeing individuation from stereotypes of an ego on the road to a Self. By reflecting this plurality and freedom of styles within the structures of myth, the archetypal perspective to experience may be furthered. In this spirit *Spring* hopes to proceed.

Post-Postscript:

Gerhard Adler (London) and Wolfgang Giegerich (Stuttgart) in written communications have each pointed out that my use of "complex psychology" is not the way that Jung or Toni Wolff originally meant. As the quote from Wolff shows, Jung used the term to refer to the whole area of depth psychology as a theoretical field of complex problems requiring complex methods. He called this field complex because it was complicated; his intention was the study of phenomena of complexity in distinction to simple, partial, elementary phenomena. Moreover, as Giegerich reminds me, referring to the same Toni Wolff article from which I quote above, the complexity of the psyche has to be met with a "complex method".[6]

Unfortunately, as so often happens in the history of thought, movements, and words, this original intention has turned into its direct opposite, and my sense of "complex psychology" derives from the way the designation is mainly used today. And today, it is just in those who most speak of Jung's work as "complex psychology" that we find the fractioning of complexities into simple events which can be handled by quantitative and mechanical methods: association experiments, typological tests, physiological dream research. This is not *theoria* but empirics, as C. A. Meier calls his work, *Die Empirie des Unbewussten,* the first volume of his projected *Lehrbuch der Komplexen Psychologie,* thereby expressly limiting Jung's multifaceted field requiring a variety of methods to one literalization, the method of natural science.

The designation can no longer be employed in Jung's (and Toni Wolff's) original sense, owing both to the implications of the word "complex" in English (which is not the equivalent of the German *komplexe,* complicated), and to the subsequent historical events that now color "complex psychology" so that we see it in the light of the empiricism fantasy.

=====

NOTES

1   T. Wolff, "Einführung in die Grundlagen der Komplexen Psychologie", in *Die kulturelle Bedeutung der Komplexen Psychologie,* Berlin (Hrsg. Psychologischer Club Zürich), 1935, p. 7, translation mine.

2   S. Freud, "Heredity and the Aetiology of the Neurosis", *Coll. Papers I,* London, 1953, p. 148.

3   C. G. Jung, "New Paths in Psychology", CW 7, 2nd ed., §410.

4   C. G. Jung, CW 16, 2nd ed., §115.

5   C. G. Jung, CW 8, §325; 9, i, §260.

6   T. Wolff, *op. cit.,* p. 20f.

X

PLOTINO, FICINO, AND VICO
AS PRECURSORS OF ARCHETYPAL PSYCHOLOGY

ON page 158 of the American edition of *Memories, Dreams, Reflections,*[1] Jung
tells the story of the dream he had while travelling with Freud in 1909 to the
United States. This was "the dream of the two skulls", the dream which was signal in his separation from Freud. This dream presents Jung with "his house", a
house of two storeys. The upper storey where the Jung-ego first finds itself in the
dream is furnished with fine old paintings and in a rococo style. Descending to
the ground floor, he finds it a mixture of Renaissance and Medieval; below this
is a Roman cellar, and then yet below in a deeper and darker cellar lie primitive
archeological remains, and the two skulls. For Jung (p. 161) the dream

> ...obviously pointed to the foundations of cultural history —
> a history of successive layers of consciousness...a structural
> diagram of the human psyche; it postulated something of
> an altogether *impersonal* nature...and the dream became

> for me a guiding image... my first inkling of a collective
> *a priori* beneath the personal psyche... as forms of instinct,
> that is, as archetypes.

Jung (p. 162) goes on to say that the dream of the house in 1909 "revived my old interest in archeology". (In his student years his first love was archeology; psychiatry came second, *faute de mieux*.) And he turned to books on excavations and myths. Then he says:

> In the course of this reading I came across Friedrich Creuzer's
> *Symbolik und Mythologie der alten Völker* — and that fired
> me! I read like mad, and worked with feverish interest through
> a mountain of mythological material, then through the Gnostic
> writers, and ended in total confusion... It was as if I were in an
> imaginary madhouse and were beginning to treat and analyze
> all the centaurs, nymphs, gods, and goddesses in Creuzer's book
> as though they were my patients.

He then came upon Flournoy's publication of the Miller fantasies[2] and began that extraordinary work — *Wandlungen und Symbole der Libido,* the first part published in 1911, (CW 5) — which inaugurates a direction in thought and culture now called Jungian. Before this work by Jung he had made contributions bearing his original stamp, but only from this work onwards does psychology itself take a new — or as I hope to show, recapitulate — an old direction. "The Two Skulls" motif, I believe, not only signifies the immediate issue of the separation from Freud, but finds further and more fundamental reflection in "The Two Kinds of Thinking", that chapter with which the argument of *Symbole und Wandlungen* begins and on which it rests, a chapter which opens by referring to the symbolic method of interpretation.

If the psychological source of the events that led to the theory of archetypes lies partly in Jung's dream of the house, the historical source of this archetypal psychology lies partly in the work of Friedrich Creuzer.[3] This was the author who set Jung's imagination on fire and whose book Jung read "with feverish interest". What is this book? Who was Creuzer? And what is it about his work that made such superb combustible material? How did it conform on the level of written data with the vision of archetypes presented through the dream of the house?

Creuzer was born in 1771 and died in Heidelberg in 1858, an extraordinary 87 years — a birth almost contemporaneous with Beethoven's and a death two years after Freud was born. He was a pupil of Schiller, thick in the Romantic movement of Heidelberg, the awakener of one of the period's most notorious romantic and suicidal passions (in Caroline von Gunderode), the originator of Greek historiography — and for us of main importance, he edited the Neoplatonic texts of Proclus and Olympiodoros (Frankfort, 1820-22) and of Plotinus (Oxford, 1835), and, based upon this Neoplatonism, Creuzer invented the then new symbolic approach to myth and comparative religion. His work

> ...was an attempt to give a scientific basis to the Neoplatonic
> interpretation of Greek mythology. Though soon dismissed by
> responsible philologists, it was greeted with enthusiasm by
> philosophers like Schelling, lastingly influenced the erratic
> genius of Bachofen, and altogether played a very important
> part in the development of mythological studies.[4]

All images, all statues, all tales were symbols to be researched for their hidden meanings. For Creuzer research into myth and religion stops when it arrives not at a historical origin, a causal explanation, a naturalistic account, but when the symbolic meaning is reached. To discover the symbolic meaning required what he considered to be the hermeneutic gift, *the ability to imagine mythological-ly,* an art similar to that of the poet.[5] The deepest level to which symbolic perception could penetrate was the Neoplatonic implication of the image before him. Creuzer was a Neoplatonist.[6]

I do believe that Jung's response to his dream in 1909 drew support from what he found in that same year in Creuzer; for Jung's response is Neoplatonic. By this I mean that the issue which overtly separated Freud and Jung in 1911-1913 was the psychology of incest. Was it to be taken literally or symbolically? Against Freud's literal positivism, Jung took the traditional Neoplatonic position: "Usually incest has a highly religious aspect, for which reason the incest theme plays a decisive part in almost all cosmogonies and in numerous myths. But Freud clung to the literal interpretation of it and could not grasp the spiritual significance of incest as a symbol". (MDR, p. 162, British ed.) Neoplatonic writings — such as those of the authors we shall be examining — attempt to show the symbolic spirit at work in natural events. They read "incest as symbol". The most famous of these expositions is Proclus' *An Apology for the Fables of Homer* (in English translation by Thomas Taylor).

Furthermore, I believe that Jung's separation from Freud meant the liberation of his own soul from the personalistic and literalistic interpretation which

Freud had given to Jung's "cellar", a liberation equivalent to the Platonic movement out of the Cave. Essential to the psychology of Platonists is the movement
of seeing through the illusions of literal and personal reality in terms of archetypal
verities. In Neoplatonism, Plato's Cave is the realm of *physis,* the perspective of
natural reality, where incest is sexual, literal, personal, where the two skulls in the
cellar refer to actual personal contents and their emotions. By re-interpreting his
cellar dream, Jung stepped out of confinement in the Cave of physicalistic hermeneutics which, in Neoplatonism, are the enemy that blinds the psychological eye.

The greatest of the Neoplatonists was Plotinus who lived and taught in this
your city, Rome (where his Enneads were composed) from the year 244 until his
death in Puteoli in 270. Now I do not want to make a case for the historical connection between Plotinus and Jung via Creuzer.[7] I am not here attempting an historical exercise about sources and influences. An historical approach would not
be an archetypal approach, and it would insult the a-historical method and work
of our subjects, Plotinus, Creuzer, and Jung. (Nor do I want to venture into the
"Roman cellar" of Jung's dream, hoping to discover the relics of Plotinus in its
crypt — this cellar deserves caution for us who come down from above the Alps —
Jung himself, we know, never made it to Rome.) But I do want to suggest, and
strongly, that the reason Jung was so fired by Creuzer was because he and Creuzer
shared the same spirit, a profoundly similar psychological attitude, an archetypal
attitude, which tradition calls Neoplatonist.

Jung's references to Plotinus and Neoplatonism are few. Plotinus appears
not to have been one of Jung's direct or favourite sources, and at least two standard works on Plotinus in Jung's library stand there still with pages uncut.[8] Where
then is the similarity between Jung — the protestant, medical empiricist, enemy of
metaphysics and champion of the dark and the feminine — and Plotinus who has
gone down in the history of philosophy as the great detester of matter because his
concern was with the supramundane world of the transcendent spirit.

But wait: let us not be deceived by the history of philosophy in regard to
Plotinus (to leave quite to one side the possible deception of Jung about his medical empiricism to the exclusion of metaphysics). The history of philosophy after

all is not written by psychologists so we can hardly turn to it for a psychological viewpoint toward philosophers. Philosophy's view of Plotinus of course will perceive in him precisely the philosophy (spiritual, metaphysical, theological) which Jung abhorred. Moreover, the editors of Plotinus' texts have been for a very large part Christian theologians, such as Cilento in Italy, Arnou and Henry who are Jesuits, the French Abbé Trouillard, and the British Dean W. R. Inge. There is an inherent tendency to bring out, or read in, the inspiring and inflating and Christianity-conforming aspects of his work. But psychology may turn to Plotinus and see there his major concern with soul, the question that was also foremost in Jung's mind: *what is the nature of psychic reality?* Besides, Plotinus wrestles with such psychological questions as anger, fate, happiness, suicide, as well as those which his great opus, the *Enneads,* opens: "Pleasure and distress, fear and courage, desire and aversion, where have these affections and experiences their seat"? and after elaborating upon corollary questions and possible answers, he goes on to say (I, 1, 2): "This first inquiry obliges us to consider at the outset the nature of the Soul". Clearly we have a psychology book before us. But, whether we do or do not is less important than is remembering that: to learn psychology we do not have to read psychology books; we have but to read books psychologically.[9]

Let me now lay out the bare bones of half-a-dozen basic structures in Plotinus' thought that parallel the basics of archetypal psychology. In order to present these structual themes briefly I must be abstract, and I apologize in advance for the dryness of this anatomical demonstration.

1) Man can act unconsciously. There can be consciousness at one level of the soul simultaneous with unconsciousness at another level. The psyche has memories of which it is unconscious (IV, 4, 4). There are both unconscious actions, or habits, and unconscious memories.[10] As Plotinus has been called "the discoverer of the unconscious", so has his one universal psyche been compared with Jung's collective unconscious.[11]

2) Consciousness is mobile and multiple.[12] Consciousness may not be attributed to only one center or subjective activity such as a single ego. The psyche requires a description in terms of multiplicity, "for man is many" (I, 1, 9). Jung presents a similar multiplicity of consciousness in his idea of the dissociability of the psyche into many complexes each with its light of nature, its spark or scintilla (CW 8, §388ff.). For Plotinus consciousness may be associated with one or another of these parts. The "we" (or what we call the "ego") takes its identity, its being,

from the level of activity it is enacting. The "we" moves through the soul, like the dream-ego in Jung's dream house, consciousness existing now at one level, now at another.

For both Plotinus and Jung, soul is not ego; true consciousness refers to the soul's awareness of itself as a reflection of the universal collective psyche, and certainly not an awareness of itself as a separated ego subjectivity. What we today call "ego-consciousness", the daily level of habitual actions in the realm of *physis,* or natural sensible perception, taking the world literally at face value, is for Plotinus the lowest level of activity and a kind of unconsciousness. [13] He shows us that most psychology today puts the psyche upside down. The psychology of ego-development and of ego-strengthening can only defeat its own aim, leading rather to less consciousness than to more. Because, for Plotinus, there is no "fixed fulcrum of self-consciousness as the center of our world and our activities", [14] we become precisely the activity we enact, the memory we remember; man is many, Proteus,[15] flowing everywhere as the universal soul and potentially all things. To strengthen the "we" at the level of *physis,* the level of ability to cope with hard "reality" plunges consciousness into a realm where by definition it cannot be conscious. [16]

3) Consciousness depends upon imagination and imagination holds a central place in the soul. "Imagination is the *terminus ad quem* of all *properly* human conscious experience; it is that faculty of man without which there can be no conscious experience". [17] When the imagination is in the right place, when it is functioning correctly, it works like a mirror (I, 4, 10; IV, 3, 29) so that by means of it the reflection of consciousness takes place. [18] And, though it is a mirror, imagination is an active power of the soul alone, independent of organs,[19] and thus a purely psychic activity. Plotinus' simile of mirror-like imagination implies the idea, so valuable for archetypal therapy, that disorders of consciousness must be attributed to disorders in mirroring, for if consciousness is based in imagination, then too are its disorders. One of the signs of disturbance is *thought without image,* or an awareness of concepts and ideas without reflection of them in their psychic substrate, the mirror images. [20] Therapy of consciousness requires scrutiny of the imagination, of the functional relation between consciousness and imagination, and of conscious ideas and concepts so that they correspond with and may be corrected by the images of the soul.

Plotinus' psychology of consciousness is thus a true *psych*ology, and not a disguised physiology in which consciousness derives from brain processes. This approach is characteristic also of Jung. Jung never stresses the separability of psyche from physiology, but he certainly never emphasizes the connection, attempting always to keep psychology free of organological models.[21] At the base of consciousness there are psychic (archetypal or primordial) fantasy-images.[22] Plotinus and Jung agree in declaring for a wholly psychic base to consciousness, a base in the imagination, of what Ficino later was to call fantasy or *idolum.* By holding to this tenet — the independent power of the imagination — Jung separates his psychology from those of Freud and Adler.[23]

Several passages from Jung, condensed and mentioned only in passing, may bring out what I mean by the comparison with Plotinus in regard to image and imagination as the base of consciousness: "Every psychic process is an image and an 'imagining', otherwise no consciousness could exist..." (CW 11, §889). "Psychic existence is the only category of existence of which we have immediate knowledge, since nothing can be known unless it first appears as a psychic image... To the extent that the world does not assume the form of a psychic image, it is virtually non-existent" (CW 11, §769). When Jung defines "image" (CW 6, §743ff), he stresses a notion of it as independent from the perception of external objects. Instead, he speaks of the "fantasy-image" ("a concept derived from poetic usage"), arising internally, unconsciously, as the condensed expression of the psyche as a whole.[24] Like Plotinus' imagination, the image of Jung mirrors the soul's condition, reflects its state of consciousness. Unlike Plotinus' imagination, Jung's images are the precursor and matrix of the soul's higher processes (thought and ideation).[25] The fantasy-image, by shaping meaning out of merely unconscious natural processes — (in both Plotinus[26] and Jung nature is not itself conscious) — makes consciousness possible, both as structured awareness into patterns and as freely disposable energy. In short, the essential activity of the psyche, that which characterizes its very essence, is the continual creation of fantasy-images.[27] These primordial fantasy-images are the archetypes.[28]

4) Plotinus has a way of speaking in one and the same breath of the psyche of individuals and of the psyche as *anima mundi,* the collective psyche beyond its individual carrier.[29] If one is Aristotelian or Cartesian in outlook, one asks, when reading Plotinus, is he talking about processes in persons or processes in psyche in general? Is he talking psychology or metapsychology? This mode of doing psychology was also Plato's, but not Aristotle's; he always began as a biological em-

piricist with individual cases and located psyche in particular bodies. Most psychology today is Aristotelian in this approach. But Plotinus' psychology never is. Nor is Jung's. Jung attempts to support from below his vision of the impersonality and universality of basic psychic processes, by collecting in an Aristotelian fashion empirical evidence from alienated souls and exotic cultures. Plotinus does not make any attempt of this sort. (He supports nothing from below; for him, no support can come from that direction.) Thus Jung speaks as a Plotinian when he explains the view of Sendivogius (a view that I take to be also his own): "The soul functions in the body, but has a greater part of its function outside the body...(and) imagines many things of the utmost profundity outside the body, just as God does".[30]

When archetypal psychology discusses the imaginal processes in myth, it is at the same moment describing the precise operations going on in an individual psyche, albeit there, there will be shadings and accretions from personal life. Because myths display the psychology of the world soul, and consequently also the individual soul, archetypal psychology does not require a collection of case material to exhibit psychodynamics. Exemplifications of this sort would be the Aristotelian approach. The strength of the Aristotelian approach lies in observational or organizational power and not in *imaginative or interpretative power* which is Platonic and to be found in such Platonists as Creuzer, Thomas Taylor, Vico — and also Jung.

5) As one might expect there is a similarity in *style* between Plotinus and Jung. What has been said about Neoplatonism — "that strange medley of thought and mystery, piety, magic and absurdity"[31] — is echoed in much the same words in attacks on Jung. Plotinus and Jung share a root vision based on the primary metaphor of soul, so that everything said is both a statement of the soul and by the soul as well as a statement on and about the soul. Soul is both subject and object of their concern. Moreover, in Neoplatonism we find the idea that the soul is ever-writing on itself, that psychologizing is a perpetual operation. As Dodds puts it: "In each of us, he [Plotinus] believes, there is a secret 'inner man' who is timelessly engaged in *noesis* (IV, 8, 8; V, 1, 12)".[32] Ficino called this "perpe ual ratiocination" the true activity of the psyche. It is ceaselessly reflecting about its own nature, because its essential nature is reflection. Therefore, this essential psychological activity that cannot come to an end as long as the psyche is alive must be the true formal cause of endless analysis beyond whatever ideas we may have of therapy, transference, and individuation.

Psychology itself then can come to no ultimate conclusion, no system, nor can it even make any statement that is for sure. Each dream interpretation, each psychological law, each insight is both an answer and a new question. And, all subjective psychologizing reflects the archetypal processes of the *mundus imaginalis,* so that the more imaginative – in actual images – is this psychologizing, the more basic it is and the more it truly reflects the psyche. So we find Jung referring to his imaginative psychological speculations always hypothetically, "as-ifs", as fantasies, what he called "mythologizings". Plotinus too turns to myth to exhibit an insight (V, 8, 13 – Kronos; V, 8, 10 – Zeus, Apollo, Muses; III, 5, 5f – Eros, Poros, Penia; VI, 9, 9 – Aphrodite; I, 1, 12 – Hercules).

What Jung did differently from Plotinus and from all previous Neoplatonists is told in the passage of his biography with which I opened. Jung approached the storehouse of the imagination with its mythical beings as if it were an imaginary madhouse, treating the inhabitants as if they were patients. Mythology became for him psychology – more, psychopathology. In this way, Jung took Neoplatonism one fundamental step further. By connecting the images of myth and the Neoplatonic mode of symbolic perception with psychiatry, he could link Gods with diseases (CW 13, §54) and so was able to devise an archetypal basis for the therapy of our psychic suffering.

Let us move now to the second of our three Mediterraneans. Marsilio Ficino is even less considered, less taught than Plotinus. Scarcely anything of his works and little on him exists in English.[33] North of the Alps university courses on the history of Western thought generally pass directly from the philosophy of late antiquity (Stoics and Epicureans) to Descartes and Bacon, omitting both Medieval thought (because it is supposedly Catholic theology – not philosophy) and Renaissance thought (because it is supposedly diletantish rhetoric – not philosophy). Neither theology nor rhetoric found their relevant evaluation until the appearance of depth psychology which is able to turn to them for another sort of significance. So, Ficino is a psychological writer, a kind of depth psychologist. When his father, the Medici's physician, first took the boy Marsilio to court, Cosimo remarked that Ficino's destiny was to cure men's souls as his father's was to heal their bodies.[34]

And, as Panofsky said, the movement of ideas which he started had an "impact which can be compared in range and intensity only with that of psychoanalysis today".[35] But it is not just the force that can be compared with psychoanalysis. The content of Ficinian ideas also deserves this comparison.

"Ficino, who had borrowed many elements of his scheme from Neoplatonic tradition, consciously modified it in this decisive point, the central position of the human soul".[36] Ficino writes:

> This (the soul) is the greatest of all miracles in nature. All
> other things beneath God are always one single being, but
> the soul is all things together... Therefore it may be rightly
> called the center of nature, the middle term of all things,
> the series of the world, the face of all, the bond and juncture
> of the universe.[37]

By placing soul in the center, Ficino's philosophy became a psychological philosophy, and he recognized that philosophy is based upon, is modified by, and modifies psychological experience.

A true education is thus a psychological education. Traditional methods of teaching philosophy — logic, empirical methodology, theological metaphysics — require as well a counter-education of soul. This proceeds by "the introspection of interior experience which teaches the independent existence of the psychic functioning in abstraction or separation from the body".[38] By "body"[39] we must understand the Neoplatonist notion of a *mode of seeing the world* that is non-psychological, stuck in the cave of naturalistic, literalistic, and materialistic unconsciousness.

Ficino's counter-education[40] is thus a psychoanalysis, teaching one to place psychic reality first and to consider all events in terms of their meaning and their value for soul. His position, that mind has its home *in the soul,*[41] is like Jung's — an *esse in anima* (CW 6, §§66, 77). The reality of human being is the reality of psychic being, and this is the only reality which is immediately known, immediately presented. Everything known is known *via* the soul, i.e., transmitted through psychic images, which is our first reality (CW 11, §769).

The effect of *esse in anima* (being-in-soul) is the breakdown of compartmentalization, which treats the psyche as if it were only one faculty of man and psychology based on it as if it were only one faculty of the academic world. Thus, the psychological vision which moves within a true universalism such as that of

Ficino and Jung always threatens university academics, whose universe is departmentalized. Since soul is everywhere, Ficinian thought, like that of all depth psychoanalysis, seeps through all academic barriers between "departments" and "faculties". Therefore, too, anti-psychological academics attack Ficino (as they attack Jung) either from the orthodox Catholic side (Etienne Gilson) or from the orthodox scientific side (George Sarton and Lynn Thorndike) because his writing is "rhetoric", "valueless as philosophy" — mere "mystical fancies". [42]

Instead of separately considering theology on one side and natural science on the other, or Christianity on one side and Platonic paganism on the other, Ficino and Jung would read all statements whatever the compartment from which they come, for their significance for soul, the "bond and juncture of the universe". "The one fundamental science" of the Renaissance, according to one authoritative scholar, was "knowledge of the soul".[43] This was what Ficinian Neoplatonism was all about. (And if this be so, then why, O why, I ask you, my Italian colleagues who have the Renaissance on which all Europe lives to this day, in the blood of your psyche, do you turn to us up North for psychology, to Marxism and Existentialism, to Adorno and Marcuse, to Freud or even Jung — to say nothing of Mao or the Hindu Gurus — all these secondary substitutes, when an extraordinary psychology is buried in your own soil?)

But to return to Ficino. What were the "mystical fancies" of this strange man who played Orphic hymns on his lute, who studied magic and composed astrological songs, this hunchbacked, lisping, politically timid, loving and loveless, melancholic translator of Plato, Plotinus, Proclus, Hesiod, the Hermetic books, and the author himself of some of the most popularly influential ("Commentary on the *Symposium*") and scandalously dangerous (*Liber de Vita*) writing of his time? Here, we can do nothing more than touch upon one little spot of his massive work. But this point is one which perhaps makes his whole work possible and connects him again to Jung. This focal point is his idea of fantasy.

Ficino conceives the psyche to consist in three divisions. The first, mind, or rational intellect; the second, *idolum* (imagination or fantasy) through which each of us is linked with fate; third, body, through which each of us is linked with nature. Let us look at the second and third, the relation between fantasy and body. It corresponds remarkably with Jung's idea of the relation between archetypal image and instinct. [44] In both men, fantasy shows the capacity of the psyche to dominate and direct the compulsive course of nature — "body" in Ficino's language, "instinct" in Jung's. Fantasy-images are therefore the soul's means of superimpos-ing fate over nature. Without fantasy, we have no sense of fate and are only natur-al.[45] But through fantasy the soul is able to lead body, instinct, and nature into the service of an individual fate.[46] Our fate is revealed in fantasy, or, as Jung might put it: in the images of our psyche we find our myth.

From Florence we move to Naples, from the fifteenth century to the eigh-teenth, from Ficino to Vico, but the Platonic thread is unbroken. As Ficino was translator of Plato and Plotinus, so Vico was a reader of those Ficino translations — as Jung by the way was a reader of Ficino's translation of Synesius.[47] Vico looked back upon Ficino with reverence, lamenting in his autobiography that serious study in his day had so radically shifted from the manner of Marsilio Fi-cino and an interest in Plato and Plotinus to the narrowness of René Descartes.[48]

Another kind of thread continues besides the Platonic one, and one of some importance to psychology; I mean the pathologizing one. As Plotinus suffered from chronic intestinal complaints[49] and Ficino from melancholy, Vico cracked his skull in a fall in childhood which kept him out of school for years, and again, like Ficino, Vico considered himself a melancholic.[50] Furthermore, it is again most unusual to consider Vico as a psychologist.[51] Are these three thinkers truly not psychological? Or is it more likely that psychology has never been truly psychological until Jung, who provided both a bridge to these isolated un-recognized sources and a means of drawing from them. It is through Jung that we can discover them as psychologists.

Vico has been claimed as a progenitor of innumerable branches of modern thought: mathematics, linguistics, sociology. He has been compared with Hegel, Marxism, Existentialism, and with Lévi-Strauss, and been considered the inspirer of Coleridge and Joyce.[52] It is easy to see his general significance as originator of humanistic method,[53] of anti-positivism and anti-Cartesianism, and of *verstehende* psychology as later developed by Dilthey, Cassirer, and Jaspers. Here in this gen-eral sense Vico is an ancestor of the Jungian approach. It is also easy to see small particular points of contact, as for instance: Vico uses the terms anima and ani-mus;[54] Vico, like Jung, assumes the autochthonous origin of myths which arise

157

independently (without diffusion from one source) "among entire peoples unknown to each other" (SN, §144), and that such fundamentals as are expressed by common sense, common maxims, and folk-wisdom are part of a language of "mental universals",[55] "a mental language common to all nations" (SN, §161); Vico considered the development of mankind to proceed through stages of consciousness, an idea now so comfortably taken for granted that we miss its revolutionary nature unless it is placed against the static styles of thought of Medieval and Cartesian philosophy.

However, it is neither only in his general humanistic nor only in his more narrow parallels with Jung in thought and language that Vico is a precursor of archetypal psychology. He deserves the attention of those concerned with Jung mainly because of his *elaboration of metaphorical thinking.* For him such thinking was primary, just as with Jung fantasy-thinking is primary.[56] Vico elaborates Ficino's emphasis upon fantasy further and with more precision through his doctrine of poetical characters. I would try to explain this main idea of Vico's and ask you while considering it to bear in mind Jung's notion of the archetypes.

In the fashion of the Renaissance (Petrarch with his letters to dead eminences of antiquity, Machiavelli with his imaginary dinner conversations with the persons of the past), Vico too had his four "great authors" (Plato, Tacitus, Grotius, Bacon), his personal cult-fathers, and he too *personifies.* Jung's entire psychological structure overtly and deliberately rests upon personified concepts − complexes as "the little people",[57] shadow, anima, old wise man, to say nothing of the personified substances and processes of alchemy.

In his *New Science* (SN, §§205-209) Vico presents typical aspects of the human mind as *universali fantastici* (§381), or universal images such as those found in myths. These are poetic characters, not mere inventions of a creative artist such as Homer; *for the true Homer is a state of mind,* a mode of perceiving the world in the universals of God and Hero, each of whom is a type or a class concept and also a statement of metaphysical truth, a true account (*vera narratio*) (§401). "Achilles connotes the idea of valor common to all strong men, or Ulysses an idea of prudence common to all wise men" (§403).

Moreover Vico is the first in modern times and in a modern eighteenth-century mind to attempt to set out the twelve Gods of Olympus (SN, §317) as basic structures, each with historical, sociological, theological, and I would add psychological, significance.[58] This was a bold undertaking for a pious Catholic university professor in the Kingdom of Naples at a moment when his own friends had been condemned by the Papal Inquisition.[59] On the one hand his undertaking reaches back to the polytheistic imagination to be found in the Neoplatonist approach to the psyche,[60] while on the other hand it adumbrates forward to Jung's thought in which daemons and Gods are indeed fundamental real structures because they are psychically prior to the minds which believe they project them. For Jung, the Gods were *not* projections. Jung says: "... instead of deriving these figures from our psychic conditions, we must derive our psychic conditions from these figures."[61]

These mythical persons are the archetypes, the metaphysical realities, to which physical reality conforms, and must conform. When Torquato Tasso imagines the poetical character of Godfrey as a "true war chief", "all the chiefs who do not conform throughout to Godfrey are not true chiefs of war" (SN, §205).[62]

Vico's doctrine of poetical characters gives hints for an archetypal mode of therapy. The poetical character, a Hero or a God (or Goddess), becomes the psychic structure by means of which we place events and see how well they conform with their universal types, or archetypes, of the *mundus imaginalis.*[63] The poetical character would be what we call the archetypal image with which events in your or my case history can be compared, the lacunae discovered, and a rectification take place.

Archetypal therapy of this sort proceeds by means of "likeness". In Neoplatonic thought especially as worked out by Proclus,[64] events can be recognized for what they truly and essentially are, and thus "redeemed" through this recognition, by "reverting" them to their true cause in the divine ideas. These divine ideas become in Vico the *universali fantastici,* or poetical characters, and in Jung the archetypes.

The method called return or reversion (epistrophé) in Neoplatonism compares with what Vico called *"ricorsi".* *Ricorsi* is not only the idea that history recurs and recapitulates itself in cycles. Psychologically, *ricorsi* is a *method*[65] for understanding present events in terms of their poetical characters, their archetypal background. *Ricorsi* is a perspective, like Neoplatonic reversion, for seeing present historical events in terms of myths and myths in present historical events.

The rectification and reversion process of archetypal therapy means approximating one's personal behaviour and fantasy to an archetypal figure and process, to a myth in Vico's language, and to recognize all behaviour and fantasy as metaphorical expression. It is one's understanding that is thus rectified by the image against which the behaviour and fantasy is placed. The poetical characters provide the means for understanding the very widest range of human behaviour, of human fantasy and human psychopathology. In the mirror of these images we recognize ourselves. [66]

Conclusion

By drawing attention to three Italians (let us consider Plotinus such by adoption), I am following a motif in Jung's own dreams. You may recall that Jung had three most vivid and peculiar experiences in connection with Italy — the parapsychological visions at Ravenna (MDR, pp. 284ff); the dream in Arona that abruptly ended a bicycle tour near Lago Maggiore and sent him hurrying back to Zürich (MDR, p. 306); and the faint at the Zürich Bahnhof (MDR, p. 288) while buying a ticket to Rome which he never succeeded to visit, an "omission" he had long "wished to repair". Pompeii, he says, was almost too much for him, and of Rome his autobiography says:

> ...Rome, the still smoking and fiery hearth from which
> ancient cultures had spread...There classical antiquity still
> lived in all its splendour and ruthlessness. I always wonder
> about people who go to Rome as they might go, for ex-
> ample to Paris or London. Certainly Rome...can be en-
> joyed esthetically; but if you are affected to the depths of
> your being at every step by the spirit that broods there...

Jung *was* so affected, for, besides these three unusual experiences in regard to Italy, four crucial dreams recounted in his biography take place in dream-Italy or have Italian motifs. (MDR, p. 159 [Roman cellar]; pp. 164f; pp. 171ff; pp. 202ff.) Although I am sure you are familiar with them, perhaps you have not regarded them in terms of their Italian component, or what we might call Jung's "Italian complex". [67]

By this term I do not mean Italy merely as the underside, the compensatory land of "the unconscious" for transalpine, hence Protestant, peoples. I mean rather the specific geographical and historical [68] psychic complexity that is implied in the image "Italy" and which Jung sensed in the meanings and emotions released by the image "Rome". An investigation of this "Italy" by exploring its thought, its culture, and its images, would help complete that omission, that lacuna in Jung's own perspective, and thus Jungian psychology, in regard to "Italy". [69] An investigation into the "Italian" and from the Italian would therefore be one of the lines of research necessary for extending the field of Jung's psychology. [70]

━━━━

NOTES

1   C. G. Jung (with Aniela Jaffe), *Memories, Dreams, Reflections,* New York (Pantheon), 1961. (MDR)

2   Jung (MDR, p. 163) says that the Miller fantasies "operated like a catalyst upon the stored-up and still disorderly ideas within me. Gradually, there formed out of them, and out of the knowledge of myths I had acquired, my book...". Evidently *Wandlungen und Symbole der Libido* reflects the confluence of two main sources, Miss Miller's pathology and Friedrich Creuzer's mythology. Creuzer is mentioned in CW 5, §§354-55. There is a further reference to Creuzer in the first publication of *Wandlungen und Symbole (Jahrbuch f. psychoanal. u. psychopath. Forschungen* III, 1, 1911, p. 146) in regard to sexual practices in Egypt (reported by Herodotus). This paragraph with the Creuzer reference does not occur in the revised edition (CW 5), where, following the 1911 edition, it would belong immediately after §34 and before the quotation from Ferrero.

3   The edition of Creuzer in Jung's library is: *Symbolik und Mythologie der alten Völker besonders der Griechen* (called also a *"Handbuch alter Theomythen"*), 4 vols., Leipzig und Darmstadt (Karl Wilhelm Leske), 1810. Many passages are marked in the margins, including the one which Jung refers to in CW 5, §§354-55. However, we do not have conclusive evidence that the marks are Jung's, since the edition he owned had been acquired second-hand and so the pencillings could have been made by previous owners. Although this early edition of Creuzer was not as fully "Neoplatonic" as later revisions, it is from the approach there displayed that Jung seems to have found his own symbolic approach. Jung considered his readings in Creuzer and mythology to be an equivalent to psychology, for he writes (MDR, p. 288), "...I had acquired, through my studies of 1910 to 1912, some insight into the psychology of classical antiquity". In a letter to Freud (159J, November 8, 1909 in *The Freud/Jung Letters,* ed. Wm. McGuire, Princeton [Princeton Univ. Press], 1974), Jung says: "One of the reasons I didn't write for so long is that I was immersed every evening in the history of symbols, i.e., in mythology and archeology... Now I am reading the four volumes of old Creuzer, where there is a huge mass of material. All my delight in archeology (buried for years) has sprung into life again. Rich lodes open up for the phylogenetic basis of the theory of neurosis". As Jung said repeatedly in his later works, the two main ways of gaining knowledge of the collective unconscious is through individual case studies and through the study of myths, i.e., the personal psyche and the psyche as world soul whose patterns are depicted in myths. (Platonism never made a sharp separation between your or my personal soul and the soul in general, just as archetypal psychology cannot separate the personal and the collective unconscious, for within every complex, fantasy, and image

of the personal psyche is an archetypal power.) In this sense mythology is psychology, and the investigation of myths à la Creuzer is indeed an investigation of the archetypal patterns in psychological behaviour.

4   A. Momigliano, "Friedrich Creuzer and Greek Historiography", *Journal Warburg and Courtauld Institutes* 9, 1946, p. 152. Momigliano (p. 153n.) reports on the modern revival of interest in Creuzer's *Symbolik* in relation with the modern interest in symbolism and the symbolic method. Passages from Creuzer are excerpted by K. Kerényi in his *Die Eröffnung des Zugangs zum Mythos,* Darmstadt (Wissenschaftliche Buchgesellschaft), 1967; a thorough and fair review of Creuzer's system and school and a shorter account of his life and works is given by O. Gruppe, "Geschichte der klassischen Mythologie und Religionsgeschichte", supplement 4 in W. H. Roscher, *Ausführliches Lexikon der griechischen und römischen Mythologie,* vol. 7, 1921, pp. 126-37.

5   Gruppe, "Geschichte", p. 131, citing Creuzer's biography.

6   When I use the term "Neoplatonism" it is with awareness that recent scholarship has differentiated many varieties through the course of centuries and in the teachings of several significant figures. But for the purposes of this paper Neoplatonism is used in the usual traditional sense, referring to the philosophic thought and psychological attitudes in regard to the soul as developed mainly by Plotinus, Porphyry, Iamblichus, and Proclus. It is in this sense that Creuzer was a Neoplatonist for which his work was later widely detested, as for instance by Kerényi (*Die Eröffnung,* p. xiv). Creuzer's savaging by later mythographers was mainly for his symbolic etymologies and interpretative flights which found little sympathy with the literalism of rational classical scholarship. Much of the criticism against Creuzer – his use of wrong etymology, his finding universal similarities in historically different religious contexts, his searching for hidden meanings, his interest in Gnostic and Hellenistic religion, the subjectivity of his vision, his penchant for pantheism – we find repeated in some criticism against Jung.

7   The historical connection is anyway doubtful since Creuzer's edition of Plotinus came out in 1835 while his *Symbolik* was printed 25 years earlier – not that he could not have already come under Neoplatonist influences long before he himself edited the original texts.

8   The two uncut volumes are: Th. Whittaker, *The Neo-Platonists, with Supplement on the Commentaries of Proclus,* Cambridge (Univ. Press), 1918; St. MacKenna transl. of Plotinus' "On the Nature of the Soul" (Enneads IV), London and Boston (Medici Society), 1924. Of the score of scattered references to Plotinus and Neoplatonism in the indexes to Jung's *Collected Works,* three in particular strike me as highly relevant for Jung's thought as a whole: CW 5, §198 where Jung makes use of Plotinus' thought for "freeing psychic energy from the bonds of too narrow a definition" (§199); CW 12, §113 where Jung compares the autonomous psychic development in a series of dreams with the view held by Neoplatonism that such historical reminiscences and their development within the soul was indeed possible and even normal; CW 14, §761 where Jung refers to *Enneads* IV, 9, 1, saying, "I mention Plotinus because he is an earlier witness to the idea of the *unus mundus*". Jung then gives this his usual "empirical" twist, saying, "The 'unity of soul' rests empirically on the basic psychic structure common to all souls, which, though not visible and tangible like the anatomical structure, is just as evident". Cf. CW 8, §927 on Plotinus in relation to synchronicity.

9   One who has read Plotinus psychologically is E. R. Dodds (comments in *Sources de Plotin,* Entretiens V of Fondation Hardt, Geneva-Vandoeuvres, 1960, p. 384): "I have sometimes felt that the most important contribution which Plotinus has made to European thought does not lie in his grandiose construction of the Three Hypostases... but rather in these more modest contributions to psychology... I think he was an extremely acute psychological observer". Dodds gives several examples and draws parallels between Plotinus and modern depth psychology.

10   On unconscious action cf. E. W. Warren, "Consciousness in Plotinus", *Phronesis 9,* 1964, p. 95; on unconscious memory, cf. H. J. Blumenthal, *Plotinus' Psychology,* The Hague (Nijhoff), 1971, pp. 95-7 and E. W. Warren, "Memory in Plotinus", *Classical Quarterly* 15, 1965, pp. 255-56.

11   Cf. H. R. Schwyzer, " 'Bewusst' und 'Unbewusst' bei Plotin", *Sources de Plotin,* pp. 342-78. In the discussion following (pp. 379, 390) Plotinus is called "discoverer of the unconscious" and his notion compared with Jung's. P. Merlan, *Monopsychism, Mysticism, Metaconsciousness,* The Hague (Nijhoff), 1963, pp. 55f, also draws parallels between Jung and Plotinus in regard to the collective unconscious.

12   On the mobility of consciousness and the changes of "we", see Blumenthal, *Psychology,* pp. 109-12, 140; on the multiplicity of consciousness, Warren, "Consciousness" *passim.*

13   Warren, "Consciousness", pp. 86-8; also E. R. Dodds, "Tradition and Personal Achievement in the Philosophy of Plotinus", in *The Ancient Concept of Progress and Other Essays,* Oxford (Clarendon), 1973, p. 135, who writes: "He was apparently the first to make the vital distinction between the total personality *(psyche)* and the ego-consciousness *(ēmeis)...* on this distinction between Psyche and ego his whole psychology hinges". Cf. Jung, CW 5, §335, where symbolic consciousness is contrasted with empirical, literal, sense-perception. Jung's passage there is Neoplatonic in this distinction.

14   W. R. Inge, *The Philosophy of Plotinus,* vol. 1, London/New York (Longmans, Green), 1929, p. 248.

15   That man is many, and that the soul of each individual person is also the universal soul and so *"We* are potentially all things" (Inge, *Philosophy,* p. 248), is the Neoplatonic thought expressed through the figure of Proteus, the image that was most commonly employed during the Renaissance to present the nature of man. Proteus, like Mercurius, shows the psyche ever in flux, never fixed into one stance or image, and the Protean ego truly reflects all the shapes of the imagination. Thus, we should reconsider the clichés about the ego-inflation of Renaissance man. His "strong ego" was altogether different than one conceived along Northern and Protestant lines. Cf. A. B. Giamatti, "Proteus Unbound: Some Versions of the Sea God in the Renaissance", in P. Demetz, T. Greene, L. Nelson (eds.), *The Discipline of Criticism,* New Haven (Yale Univ. Press), 1968, pp. 437-75.

16   Warren, "Consciousness", p. 84; Inge, *Philosophy,* p. 247.

17   Warren, "Imagination in Plotinus", *Classical Quarterly* 16, 1966, p. 277.

18   Cf. Warren, "Imagination", p. 284; and Blumenthal, *Psychology,* pp. 88-9.

19   Warren, "Imagination", p. 280.

20   "The images of thoughts are needed for their conscious apprehension by the human being". Ibid., p. 281. "If the mirror-activity of imagination is disturbed in any way,

then there is no image, but there is thought without an image". Ibid., p. 284.

21   CW 8, §368: "It is extremely difficult, if not impossible, to think of a psychic function independent of its organ, although in actual fact we experience the psychic process apart from its relation to the organic substrate. For the psychologist, however, it is the totality of these experiences that constitutes the object of investigation, and for this reason he must abjure a terminology borrowed from the anatomist". CW 11, §789: "Some include instincts in the psychic realm, others exclude them. The vast majority consider the psyche to be a result of biochemical processes in the brain cells. A few conjecture that it is the psyche that makes the cortical cells function. Some identify 'life' with psyche. But only an insignificant minority regards the psychic phenomenon as a category of existence *per se* and draws the necessary conclusions".

22   CW 6, §§78-84, 743.

23   CW 6, §93.

24   CW 6, §745.

25   Ibid., §750. With Plotinus, thought, especially *dianoia* or discursive reason, does not depend on imagination.

26   "For Plotinus nature is unconscious-to-itself; it can never be conscious". Warren, "Consciousness", p. 94.

27   "... the primordial image expresses the unique and unconditioned creative power of the psyche" (CW 6, §748). "This autonomous activity of the psyche, which can be explained neither as reflex action to sensory stimuli nor as the executive organ of external ideas, is, like every vital process, a continually creative act. The psyche creates reality every day. The only expression I can use for this activity is fantasy" (CW 6, §78).

28   CW 6, §747.

29   F. R. Jevons, "Dequantitation in Plotinus's cosmology", *Phronesis* 9, 1964, p. 70: "Plotinus in general followed the Socratic tradition of regarding souls as the seats of human personalities. It is true of course that he thought less of individual souls pertaining to particular bodies than of a soul divided among living bodies (I, 1, 8); the two are far from sharply separated in a philosophy in which 'all things are forever linked' " (IV, 8, 6).

30   Jung refers to Sendivogius in a letter to Kerényi (12. VII. 1951) *B* ii, p. 225; in another letter to Rudin (14. V. 1950) *B* ii, p. 188, Jung states: "... der Mensch nach meiner Auffassung in *der* Psyche (night in *seiner* Psyche) eingeschlossen sei". He also says: "... it often seems advisable to speak less of *my* anima or *my* animus and more of *the* anima and *the* animus" (CW 16, §469). That the individual soul has become divided from the world soul, so that we conceive ourselves personalistically and not mythologically, Jung attributes to the development of Western (Cartesian) philosophy (CW 11, §759). But I believe this separation is an archetypal perspective exhibited long before modern Cartesian consciousness, as for instance in Aristotle. For another alchemist, like Sendivogius (to say nothing here of Paracelsus), to whom Jung refers regarding the unity of individual soul and world soul, see his discussion of Richard White, CW 14, §§91-4.

31   T. R. Glover, *Conflict of Religions in the Early Roman Empire*, Boston (Beacon), 1960, chap. 3.

32   Dodds, "Tradition...", p. 136.

33   The sole writer in English who has dedicated himself to Ficino scholarship is P. O. Kristeller: *The Philosophy of Marsilio Ficino*, New York (Columbia), 1943, (reprint Gloucester, Mass.: Peter Smith, 1964); various papers in his *Studies in Renaissance Thought and Letters*, Rome 1956/1969; *Renaissance Thought* (vol. 1, New York, 1961; vol. 2, New York, 1965). Parts of Ficino's *Theologia Platonica* have been translated by Charles Trinkaus in his *In Our Image and Likeness*, vol. 2, Chicago (Univ. Chicago Press), 1970. Also in English, S. R. Jayne, "Marsilio Ficino's Commentary on Plato's *Symposium*" (Text, Translation, and Introduction), Columbia, Mo. (Univ. Missouri Studies), 1944.

34   Jayne, "Commentary on Plato's *Symposium*", p. 16n., from Giov. Corsi, *Marsilii vita* (edit. G. Galetti), Florence, 1847.

35   E. Panofsky, "Artist, Scientist, Genius: Notes on the 'Renaissance Dämmerung' ", in *Renaissance: Six Essays*, W. K. Ferguson *et. al.*, New York (Harper Torchbook), 1962, p. 129. By 1488 Ficino wrote in a letter that all Europe was demanding his works, and in 1491 he wrote that he had correspondents in France, Germany, Spain, and Hungary. R. Marcel, *Marsile Ficin*, Paris (Belles Lettres), 1958, p. 534 and following, on the relations of Ficino with European intellectuals, and his biography in detail.

36   P. O. Kristeller, *Studies in Renaissance Thought*, p. 268.

37   Kristeller's translation (from *Theologia Platonica*) *ibidem*.

38   Trinkaus, *Image and Likeness*, p. 473.

39   Plotinus had distinguished between the soul's motion and the body's motion *(Enneads* II, 2, 2). Soul rotates circularly; "the forward path is characteristic of the body". By taking "body" to mean the natural, straight-on, face-value, directly literal approach, we see that the counter-education of the soul means another style of reflection, one in which circumambulation is primary. Thus, "body" in Ficino is not something to be separated from, in a literalistic sense. Rather, Ficino means a separation from the naturalistic and simple "forward path" bodily point of view, which is tangential to the soul's ever-recurring cyclical concerns.

40   The term is from Ficino, *Theol. Platon.* VI, 2, and reads in English (Trinkaus, *Image and Likeness*, p. 473): "We begin to recognize that the error of the uneducated life is for the most part born from the experience of the body when we conceive of a certain education contrary to it". The analogue to this counter-education in Jungian psychology is called "symbolic thinking" (Jung), "symbolic perception" (Whitmont), "psychic consciousness" (Layard). The analogue in Vico he calls "negative discourse". In all, the way of psychological education is conceived as an *opus contra naturam*.

41   Ficino, *Commentary on the Symposium* VI, 9 (Jayne): "The soul itself is the home of human thought. The spirit is the home of the soul, and the home of the spirit is the body. There are three inhabitants and three homes. Each of these is exiled when its natural home is lost".

42   R. R. Bolgar, *The Classical Heritage*, Cambridge (Univ. Press), 1954, pp. 287-88.

43   Nesca A. Robb, *Neoplatonism of the Italian Renaissance*, London (Allen and Unwin), 1935, p. 43.

44   CW 8, §§408-20. Jung there stresses that we cannot transform the compulsive aspect of instinctual nature directly (§415). But nature is amenable to transformation through

archetypal fantasy images, and through an exercise he calls "active imagination" (§414). A similar line of thought occurs in Ficino and partly accounts for his occupation with astrological songs and magic as a mode of healing his "nature" (melancholy) through active occupation with archetypal images.

45   Jung is also Neoplatonist enough to have disdain for merely "natural" man. He writes: "Natural man is not a 'self' – he is the mass and a particle in the mass, collective to such a degree that he is not even sure of his own ego" (CW 12, §104; cf. CW 5, §335). In Ficino's sense, natural man has no connection with a fate, which Jung would probably call individuation. Thus, the appeal to nature, or to the natural instinct in oneself as having the "answer" or as "guide", is to lose the perspective of soul. Soul turns not to nature but in its perplexity to images.

46   "... the nature of the body is entirely subject to the movements of the soul". (Ficino, *Theologia Platonica* XIII, 1.) Thus, intellectuals of sensitive soul are often ill (Ficino follows here the old theory of the melancholic sensitivity and illness of the philosopher), e.g. Aristotle, Carneades, Chrysippus, Plotinus, etc. Where a powerful "fate" is constellated, according to this view, nature must take a second place, not only in a life as a biographical whole, but in any intense psychic moment of any life which exhausts the natural body. His view has a psychotherapeutic consequent. One cannot treat physical symptoms without taking into account that they are "ruled" by the soul, and further, that intense work with soul – such as what goes on during a deep analysis – will have symptomatic effects upon bodily nature. The symptoms produced during an analysis are thus not only the re-activation of past events, but show the work of a specific fate being constellated by fantasy. The pathologizing process might then be considered as an inherent part of the soul's involvement with a specific fate. (Further on "Pathologizing", see Chapter Two of *Revisioning Psychology*, New York [Harper and Row], 1975.)

47   CW 6, §174n.

48   *The Autobiography of Giambattista Vico,* transl. and with notes by M. H. Fisch and T. G. Bergin, Ithaca (Cornell Univ. Press), 1963, p. 137.

49   Porphyry, "On the Life of Plotinus and the Arrangement of His Work", in MacKenna, *Enneads,* p. 1.

50   *Autobiography,* p. 111.

51   For one paper on Vico and psychology see F. Dogana, "Il Pensiero di G. B. Vico alla luce della moderna dottrina psichologiche", *Arch. di Psicol. Neurol. e Psichiat.* 31, 6, 1970, pp. 514-30; also R. Flint, *Vico,* Edinburgh (Blackwood), 1884, pp. 129-35. Although A. R. Caponigri, *Time and Idea: The Theory of History in Giambattista Vico,* (Notre Dame [Univ. Press], 1968), does not mention psychology in his index, his chapter "The Modifications of the Human Mind" is relevant. The massive proceedings of the international symposium in honour of Vico's tercentenary (G. Tagliacozzo and H. V. White, *Giambattista Vico,* Baltimore [Johns Hopkins], 1969) has no paper on psychology, and psychology is mentioned in the index in but two general contexts, and these are irrelevant.

52   For some modern praise heaped upon Vico, see: Elizabeth Sewell, *The Orphic Voice,* London (Routledge), 1961, p. 181f.; O. Barfield, *What Coleridge Thought,* Middletown (Wesleyan Univ. Press), 1971, p. 205, n. 2; E. Cassirer, *The Logic of the Humanities,* New Haven (Yale), 1961, pp. 52-55. Cassirer emphasizes the subjective, psycho-

logical value of Vico's work, which keeps him in the Neoplatonic tradition where knowledge is ultimately self-reflexive, for the sake of self-knowledge, rather than abstractly physical, mathematical, or logical.

53   I. Berlin, "Vico's Concept of Knowledge", in Tagliacozzo, p. 376, best sums up Vico's huge importance for all humanities including psychology through his elaboration, in the face of the rife Cartesian thought of his time, of a new epistemological method called now after Dilthey "verstehen": "It is a species of its own. It is knowing founded on memory or imagination. It is not analyzable except in terms of itself, nor can it be identified save by examples... This is the sort of knowing which participants in an activity claim to possess as against mere observers: the knowledge of the 'inside' story as opposed to that obtained from some 'outside' vantage point; knowledge by 'direct acquaintance' with my 'inner' states or by sympathetic insight into those of others, which may be obtained by a high degree of imaginative power; the knowledge that is involved when a work of the imagination or of social diagnosis or a work of criticism...is described not as correct or incorrect, a success or a failure, but as profound or shallow, perceptive or stupid, alive or dead". If, as Berlin says, this is Vico's great original achievement, the method of depth psychology goes back to him.

54   Flint, *Vico*, p. 129; *The New Science of Giambattista Vico* [*SN*] (1744), transl. and ed. by T. G. Bergin and M. H. Fisch, VII, 2, §§695f., Ithaca (Cornell Univ. Press), 1968, p. 263.

55   D. Bidney, "Vico's New Science of Myth", in Tagliacozzo, p. 274.

56   CW 6, §§78, 84, 174, 743.

57   CW 8, §209; cf. §§202-208.

58   We find a similar idea in Ficino ("Commentary *Symposium*" V, 13) where each of the twelve Gods of Olympus is associated with one of the twelve signs of the Zodiac, an archetypal psychology attempting to show "which Gods bestow which arts upon men". In *Theol. Platon.* XIV, 1 (Trinkaus, p. 487), Ficino further elaborates these twelve structures to show how they govern the ways in which the soul strives to become God-like. Jung indicates that these structures have now been "internalized". "Instead of the lost Olympian Gods, there was disclosed the inner wealth of the soul which lies in every man's heart". (Passage is originally in the last paragraph of section 3 of the Eranos Lecture, "Transformation Symbolism of the Mass", but does not appear in the CW 11, §375.) But the Olympian Gods do not appear only internalized in the heart: Jung also sees these structures as re-appearing in psychopathology, the Olympians having become diseases (CW 13, §54).

59   *Autobiography*, pp. 34-5.

60   "Polytheism is a most subtle mode of apprehension of 'facts of mind', incomprehensible only to those who, like Locke, regard mental processes as mere elaborations of sense impression...". This passage by Kathleen Raine is part of a longer explanation on the role of the polytheistic approach deriving from the most important English Neoplatonist (and like Creuzer and Ficino translator of Plotinus) Thomas Taylor. K. Raine and G. M. Harper, *Thomas Taylor the Platonist*, Princeton (Princeton Univ. Press, Bollingen), 1969, p. 40. Miss Raine adds in a footnote (p. 41), "C. G. Jung's archetypes may also be described as composing a 'pantheon' of the divine natures as these are manifested and diversified in the psyche". Cf. further my "Psychology: Monotheistic or Polytheistic?", *Spring 1971*, New York and Zürich (Spring Publ.), 1971, pp. 193-208 and Miss

Raine's comments, pp. 216-19.

61   CW 13, §299; cf. CW 9, ii, §41.

62   The elaboration of classical, literary, historical, and mythological figures as ideal types, even as Platonic forms or archetypes, was a convention of Renaissance rhetoric and it did not originate with Tasso. A source is Hermogenes (second century A.D.) and his Strassburg editor Johannes Sturm (1571). Cf. A. M. Patterson, *Hermogenes and the Renaissance,* Princeton (Univ. Press), 1970, p. 37. But prior to Sturm was the translation and elaboration of Hermogenes by that neglected genius, Guilio Camillo Delminio (ca. 1480-1544) whose precise examination of images into a "theater" for encompassing the entire *memoria* (or imagination) is described brilliantly by Frances Yates, *The Art of Memory,* London (Routledge), 1966, pp. 129-72. Giulio Camillo's system is a primary document for archetypal psychology inasmuch as it lays out a ground plan of what is still so limpingly called "the unconscious". A promising venture in the direction of drawing insights for archetypal psychology from this Renaissance "theater" of the psyche was begun in 1972 by Rafael Lopez in a series of seminars in Zürich.

63   Cf. H. Corbin, *"Mundus Imaginalis,* or the Imaginary and the Imaginal"*, Spring 1972,* New York and Zürich (Spring Publ.), 1972, pp. 1-19.

64   Proclus, *Elements of Theology,* ed., transl., annotated by E. R. Dodds, 2nd ed., Oxford (Clarendon Press), 1963, pp. 218-23 (Props., pp. 29-34). The process of reversion to likeness *(epistrophe)* has its parallel in the Avicennian *ta'wil* the method of interpretation which leads both text (dream, behaviour, symptom, vision) *and interpreter too* into the correct relation with soul (cf. H. Corbin, *Avicenna and the Visionary Recital,* New York [Pantheon, Bollingen], 1960, pp. 28-34).

65   Caponigri, *Time and Idea,* p. 131: " 'Ricorsi' appears in Vico, in the first instance, as a methodological notion. It designates a methodological device for making effective his discovery of the primacy of poetry and, with this, of the genuine time-structure and movement of history. It consists in the employment of the categories of poetic wisdom for the interpretation of the cultural and social structures of post-poetic times. By this employment there is determined abstract contemporaneity between time-form structures". In other words: archetypal persons transcend historical limitations even as they manifest themselves in historical time. These poetic figures are the ultimate categories for understanding human existence.

66   I use the word "recognize" on purpose for it is this word which Jung has sometimes used to describe what he means by "integration", cf. CW 13, §62; also CW 7, §337; CW 14, §616; CW 9, ii, §58.

67   Cf. Letter 206J, 11 August 1910 *(Freud/Jung Letters):* "...I have secret obligations to my unconscious ('inconscient supérieur') as regards Rome and the south, which makes a quick run through the country altogether impossible. Rome in particular is not permitted to me, but it draws nearer and I even look forward to it at odd moments". For Freud's "mysterious inhibition" in regards to Rome, see H. F. Ellenberger, *The Discovery of the Unconscious,* New York (Basic Books), 1970, p. 447.

68   I have taken the conception of a geographical and historical psyche from Rafael Lopez who has developed it in keeping with a peculiarly Spanish tradition (Ortega y Gasset, Unamuno, Santayana, Madriaga) of understanding ideas in terms of the geographical and historical temperament in which they have their home. The conception is comparable in some respects with Jung's valuable notion of a racial unconscious, or the

racial level of the collective unconscious, and which led him to speak of the German psyche, the Jewish psyche, the Mediaeval or Modern psyche, etc. By considering "Italy" and "Rome" as genuine psychic geography and history, they become areas of the cultural imagination, genuine expressions of regions of the soul and are no longer images of the south, freedom, song, catholicism, dark irresponsibility, and the like. "Italy" is not merely an area for projection of the repressed and unconscious, but itself refers to an arena of Western culture that belongs to the collective psyche of every Western person.

69 Cf. L. Zoja, "Observations in Transit between Milan and Zürich", *Spring 1973*, New York and Zürich (Spring Publ.), 1973, for some beginnings in this direction.

70 A re-appraisal of the Italian Renaissance in order to suggest its value for psychology, and thus to move psychology itself from the geographical and historical limitations of the Judeo-Protestantism of Northern and Central Europe, was one of the aims of my Terry Lectures (IV, "De-Humanizing"), *Revisioning Psychology*.

Delivered as a Lecture at the Conference "Jung and European Culture" in Rome, May 22, 1973, and published in an Italian translation by Priscilla Artom in the *Rivista di Psicologia Analitica* 4/2, October 1973, pp. 322-40.

X I

ARCHETYPAL THEORY: C. G. JUNG

> Every exposition cannot help
> but be an apology, a critique,
> and also a confession.

Prefatory Note: I shall be following Jung's own approach to theory. For him it was always related to therapy of the soul because ideas cannot be separated from life without damaging both. As we go along I shall be pointing out the therapeutic implications of the theories of archetypal psychology.

Calling Jung's psychology after its principal structural idea, the archetype, emphasizes the theoretical work of his mature and late periods (ca. 1928-1961, *aet.* 53-86). Usually his psychology is called "analytical", a term coined in the early days in relation with Freud's "psychoanalysis". But "archetypal" more adequately corresponds with his own construction as a whole and its wide range of concerns besides actual analysis. Also, "archetypal" more accurately describes Jung's approach to the fundaments of the psyche.

Throughout my account I use the word "understand". Understanding is perhaps the most operational of all Jungian concepts, implied throughout all others, and places Jung's approach within the tradition of *psychologies of understanding* (Dilthey, Nietzsche, Jaspers), rather than psychologies that are explanatory, descriptive or medical in the narrow sense. Jung set out from the beginning, not to compare or measure or explain or redeem personality, but to understand it and bring understanding to it. His was the myth of meaning (Jaffé 1971).

The Idea and Nature of Personality

Individuality. Jung writes: "My life has been permeated and held together by one idea and one goal: namely, to penetrate into the secret of personality. Everything can be explained from this central point, and all my works relate to this one theme" (MDR, p. 206). Towards the end of his late essay on the plight of contemporary man, he asks the rhetorical question of each individual threatened with doomsday extinction: "Does the individual know that *he* [and she] is the makeweight that tips the scales"? (CW 10, §586.) What happens to the individual and to the world at large depends on the individual personality. No other idea in Jung's work holds as much importance as does personality. "The sole and natural carrier of life is the individual, and this holds true throughout nature" (CW 16, §224). "All life is individual life, in which alone the ultimate meaning is to be found" (CW 10, §923).

Individuation. Jung coined the term "individuation" for the activity of personality realization, a term which "denotes the process by which a person becomes a psychological 'in-dividual', that is, a separate entity or whole" (CW 9, i, §490). More simply he calls individuation the process by which a person "becomes what he really is" (CW 16, §11). Individuation is the supporting theoretical construct, or vision, from which proceeds a rich proliferation of other ideas about personality, some of which we shall now examine.

Jungian theory does not ask the question "What *is* personality"? as an entity to be defined and explained. Rather, it is dynamic and pragmatic in its questioning, asking "In what way can a person know who he is, discover his personality, develop and refine it, and become him- or herself"? Personality itself is given with the psychic reality of the questioner, so the idea of personality is taken for granted in the common dictionary sense of a "personal being", as distinct from an abstraction or a thing, and the organization of that being into a *qualitatively differentiated unit.* (Individuation is a "process of differentiation" [CW 6, §757] which means "the development of differences, the separation of parts from the whole" [CW 6, §705].) Where philosophers and churchmen account for the essence of personal being in their metaphysical language and embryologists and geneticists account for its origin in their physical language, Jung's hypotheses attempt to describe it and further it – psychologically.

Value. Part of this description is in terms of value. One way of giving value to personality is to connect it with transcendent factors, especially God. By doing so the Jungian idea of personality is in keeping with the Greek, Roman, and Judeo-Christian tradition. Each personality is potentially a self that embodies and reflects something more than itself. It is not self-sufficient, but in relation with others, both other persons and "the other" which is not personal and not human. The very word personality from the Greek, *persona,* implies a mask through which sounds something transcendent. Without this "other" which stands behind ego-consciousness, independent of it, yet makes personal consciousness possible, there would be no individualized personality, no subjective center to which events relate and become experiences. This inner conviction in oneself as a personality Jung also calls "vocation" (CW 17, §300ff; cf. Grinnell 1970).

The condition clinically called depersonalization demonstrates what Jung here means. There can be a loss of personal reality and identity even if all ego functions remain intact; perception, orientation, memory, association, etc., are each undisturbed (Meyer [ed.] 1968). Depersonalization indicates that the sense of personality, the very belief and conviction in one's reality as an individual, depends on a factor transcendent to the ego-personality, beyond its sensorium and its powers of will. Sometimes Jung calls this factor, on which the individual depends, the "self". This term can be taken as a description of substance and as a description of value. I prefer the latter usage.

Self. The self in Jung refers to: (a) the fullest extension of the individual, and (b) experiences of the highest value and power beyond one's own extension, that is, experiences of the transcendent and other. Such experiences and images of great value and power have traditionally been given the names of Gods. By giving "self" this double meaning, both personal and transcendent, Jung suggests that each person is by definition connected to something transcendent, or even

172

has a transcendent supreme value beyond his ego-personality. This gives worth to all manifestations of human nature. Even the most debased conditions have a wider significance and are not merely human faults because they point to transcendent collective, archetypal, and non-human factors. The double meaning of self suggests also that personality cannot be understood by a personal approach alone. One eye needs always to be focussed upon the impersonal, non-human background.

Evil. This background is not only positive, not only good. Non-human means also inhuman. Personality reflects disorder, destruction, and shadow values as well. These powers are as effective in the psyche as the apparently creative, constructive ones, so they are psychologically just as real. Jung's position here in regard to the place of evil in personality is not at all moralistic, even if religious. This distinguishes his from other psychologies that are moralistic, but not religious.

Because the individual personality has such worth, because it is the locus of all values — consciousness, conscience, life, meaning, soul as well as destruction and evil — work with individuals, whether others or oneself, statistically insignificant as such work may be, remains nonetheless a most valuable kind of occupation.

Religion. These religious aspects of Jung's personality theory derive partly from his personal make-up and partly from his notion, gained through practice and research, that religion is constitutionally based on personality and no more an illusion than is sexuality. Further, the religious metaphors he uses belong to his style of giving value to psychic facts, just as other psychologists imply their value system by employing other kinds of transcendent metaphors such as "nature", "evolution", "authenticity", "maturity", etc. Jung's religious language in no way implies orthodoxy of creed, membership in church, or observance of ritual.

Psychic Reality. The world of reality that personality inhabits is *psychic reality.* In Jung "reality" finds an altogether different definition than in Freud, where the word refers mainly to what is external, social, and material and where psychic reality is decisive only in the realm of neuroses and psychoses (Casey 1972). Jung states: "Reality is simply what works in a human soul" (CW 6, §60). All sorts of things work in the soul — lies, hallucinations, political slogans, outmoded scientific ideas, superstitions — and so these events are real, whether true or not. Many other conscious events — good advice, historical facts, ethical codes, psychological interpretations — may not have any effect in the psyche's depth, and so these events may be considered as not real, whether true or not.

Fantasy Images. At the most basic level of psychic reality are fantasy images. These images are the primary activity of consciousness. This ongoing fantasy activity, a vital process that Jung states cannot be explained as mere "reflex action to sensory stimuli", is a continuously creative act — through fantasy "the psyche creates reality every day" (CW 6, §78).

Jung reverses the familiar theory that holds reality to be external, images to be the imprint of externals, and fantasies to be decayed or distorted impressions. He also departs from psychoanalytic colleagues who hold fantasy to be a substitute reality. Fantasy *is* reality, even creates it by giving instinctual conviction (Santayana's "animal faith") to whatever area of experience we believe is real. By creating reality into the shapes and notions that we actually perceive and by which we apprehend the world, formulate it and deal with it, fantasy is evidence of the negentropic activity of consciousness. *Images are the only reality we apprehend directly;* they are the primary expression of mind and of its energy which we cannot know except through the images it presents. When we perceive a fantasy image we are looking into the mind of instinct, seeing the libido itself ("Fantasy as imaginative activity is identical with the flow of psychic energy" — CW 6, §722, cf. §§711, 723ff; CW 11, §§769, 889; CW 8, §389).

Instinct and Archetype. The primacy of images means that they are in the realm of cognition what instinctual activity is on the conative-affective level. In the realm of mind, instinct is perceived in images. In the realm of behaviour, images are enacted in instinct. Behaviour is always the enactment of a fantasy, and fantasy is not merely something going on privately in the head but presents itself in our behavioural stances. Psychic and behavioural events are distinct, but indivisible. One is not the sublimation of the other since they are coexistent. To conceive instinct independent of image-patterns is to make it blind, and to conceive images independent of instinct is to deprive them of vitality and necessity. Imagination then would become a sublimated luxury rather than the instrument of survival.

The principle which organizes imagery, the principle which gives psychic reality its specific patterns and habitual forms — universal, typical, regular, conservatively repetitive through centuries — Jung calls the "archetype". These same qualifiers apply to instinct, too. The energy of the archetype is instinctual because the archetype is instinct itself; the archetype is instinct's "pattern of behaviour", its "meaning" or, as Jung says too, its "psychic equivalent" (CW 8, §§397ff).

Jung's analogy here is taken from animal behaviour. He hypothesizes that every inborn release mechanism (or instinct) is both organized in a pattern and implicates a fantasy image that either releases it or represents its goal. Instinct misfires when there are disorders of imagery. Jung (CW 6, §765) defines instinct as "an impulsion towards certain activities" which is compellingly necessary, inherited, reflex in character, uniform, regular, and unconscious (CW 8, §§267, 233ff, 378f). That instincts are so specific and typical points to a principle within them of order, meaning, and purposefulness. These are the archetypes. The psychic life of personality is governed by them.

The idea of the archetype is fruitful for therapy. Because fantasy is never merely a wisp of unreality, because it expresses personality's archaic, emotional and creative aspect and is a person's primary reality, by focus on fantasy we touch what really is at work in the soul. The qualitative transformations in fantasy such as go on in a long dream series or meditative discipline represent transformations of the archetypes that rule personality and are its basic nature.

Schizophrenia. We also see such transformations in fantasy in the course of schizophrenic degeneration which point to changes in the basic nature of personality. Jung's theory of schizophrenia is based upon the same psycho-physical interaction. Even if we posit that psyche and body are one, our direct knowledge is only of psyche. Our knowledge of body always comes through psychic images. Although these images from all evidence depend on neuro-chemical systems, whatever we say about or do with these systems again depends on psychic images. We cannot reduce either one to the other. They are interdependent and interacting.

Jung was the first in modern psychiatry to suggest a psychological origin for schizophrenia. As early as 1907 (and as late as 1958) (CW 3) he considered schizophrenia to be an autointoxication, a metabolic disturbance owing to a pathogenic complex whose intense affects involve somatic processes. The archetype at the core of the complex would be that psychosomatic factor which induces both the psychological disorders and the somatic "toxin". Therapy of schizophrenia, also pioneered by Jung, focusses mainly upon these archetypal factors.

Personality in its Context

Individuality presupposes something beside itself and within itself from which it differs. Individuality does not mean solidarity and so it cannot be considered alone, without its contexts.

Amplification. Jung calls his method for gathering the context *amplification.* The aim is not to reduce psychic data to its simplest element or single meaning, but to approach it from many sides until its meaning becomes stronger and fuller. *Nothing psychic means only one thing.* Ambivalence of value and ambiguity of content is basic to every piece of psychic data, and amplification is designed to show this. Personality is set within cultural, symbolic, and historical processes. These impinge upon the psyche's images. Personal associations to dream images are never enough because they are limited by the ego's bias and they return every image to the ego through the links of association. The ego personality can never by itself give full due to the dark tunnel, or the lion, or the image of a lake that appears in a dream. These images have an inexhaustible echo and yet have a highly specific significance.

Moreover, each dream belongs to a series of dreams which in turn is set within personality and its context. Extended, the idea of amplification means that no single consultation can diagnose in depth, nor even provide a competent opinion. It cannot do justice to the complexity of personality. At best one has gained information from only one contender (ego) and drawn conclusions in terms of its partiality.

Anamnesis. The context is gained just as in medical practice through a case history, an *anamnesis.* But an anamnesis does not equal the context, and this for several reasons. The anamnesis is mainly *conscious,* a record of what a person remembers in his ego personality. Depth psychology in general assumes that there is more to the context of a case than the string of chronologically presented memories. The anamnesis is mainly *external,* a record of what happened to one through life — family, education, work, illness. The context, however, includes internal events, as we shall soon explain. The anamnesis is *factual.* At its most simple level a case history begins with date of birth, height in inches and weight in pounds. It attempts to pare away interpretations and get to the factual core. But the context of personality includes shades of feeling, half-remembered and distorted events. These are aspects of one's personal complexity that are far from facts and hard to put into words. Finally, an anamnesis is *historical.* It refers to the past. But the context of personality is conditioned also by what lies ahead in the form of ambitions and anxieties, as well as avoidances in regard to the present.

Jungians also take the following factors into account in amplifying the basic case history.

    1. *Ancestral.* "Family" in Jung's psychology includes more than the actual members one now lives with or the family one lived with as a child or as a parent (CW 17, §93). "Family" does indeed include these actual persons, but it extends as well to the circumstances of the parents' parents, for one is searching not only for the family history, but also the *family fantasy.* In my analyses I ask about grandparents and even their parents, what they did, what was odd about them, what they hoped for and died of. I ask about their interrelations with one another, the racial stock, religious belief, physical constitution, and economic position. I may ask an analysand to work out a family tree to uncover similarities in repetitive patterns or striking differences between the patient's life and that of the family, to see where he or she fits in with the family fantasy. By means of this investigation we are not looking for inherited psychic factors. Rather we are recreating a genealogy or a mythology of "my own" family. This helps create in an individual a sense of roots, a context within which his personality belongs and to which it has emotional affinities. This investigation of family, the respectful care one gives to every detail of fantasy and scrap of evidence (old photos, souvenirs) revivifies in a modern clinical setting a worldwide practice lost in our culture called ancestor worship.

    Psychological Level. This amplification exposes as potential areas of stress any extreme disparities between personality parts. To the psychological level of a person belong: psychological age; quality of self-awareness, humor and insight; capacity for emotion, especially depression; intelligence quotient; quality and quantity of imagination; the lacunae or holes (where we draw a blank); nature of sensuousness; gifts and accomplishments; areas of fear; general culture in the use of language and relationship with symbolic modes, ranging from dreams to art, travel, music, crafts and skills, food and drink; tragic experiences undergone (war, death, disease, betrayal, failure, etc.).

    The question here that comes to mind is: is a person living in general above or below his economic class, innate gifts, social milieu, cultural background, psychological age. The answer helps indicate where the shadow problems can be expected. Too far above one's level can point to strongly regressive counter-pulls and manic defenses to maintain the pitch. Too far below can mean that the presenting complaint may be a strong developmental urge in disguise.

    Wholeness. Investigation of the person's psychological level makes operational in therapy the richness of personality posited in theory. By calling attention to hu-

man complexity through the theory of amplification, Jungian therapy is obliged
to amplify its attention to the whole warehouse of inventory that constitutes personality and to coax the whole crowd into the encounter, otherwise Jung's idea of
wholeness remains an abstraction, a circle, an empty egg, the number four. Personality is revealed not merely by two persons in chairs talking problems. This
shrinks personality, and psychology too, into the narrow boredom recorded by
countless taped therapy sessions and textbooks. Jung's theory implies that therapy
engages as many as possible of the partial personalities. This brings the confusion
of life itself into the psychological container of therapy. "Individuation does not
shut one out from the world, but gathers the world to oneself" (CW 8, §433). The
alchemical description for this process was putting a *massa confusa* of active substances into a closed transparent vessel for the sake of soul-making.

Soul. Jungian theory presupposes an independent factor which once was
called depth of soul. A personality may have attained a high educational or economic level and yet be a psychological dunce, below himself in culture, insight,
sensuousness, emotional capacity, and so on. Depth analysis goes about soul-making through *deepening* psychic events, whether they be feelings, insights, pathological peculiarities, or fantasies. It fills up the holes and deepens the superficiali-
ties in a person's psychological level. Depth takes slowness and holding on, living
things in as images more than acting them out onto others. It is in terms of dis-
parities and shallownesses in psychological levels that Jung speaks when he fears
for "modern man in search of a soul" as one of his books was called.

2. *The Actual.* One way Jung's psychology differed from Freud's was in
terms of past and present, Freud asking about early memories, Jung turning to the
"here and now". Whether Jung was right or wrong in his characterization of Freud
is less my point here than is his insistence upon the actual situation. Here Jung's
thought precedes later schools — Existentialist, Rogerian, Gestalt, Encounter.

Compensation. First, actual means current. The present problem is explored
in terms of its present significance: What is the problem interrupting? What does
it (not you) want? What and how is it a *compensation?* Here we operate with the
principle of *self-regulation:* Personality naturally attempts to balance itself between
various opposing complexes. Every presenting complaint belongs to the present situation, fits into its archetypal meaning, and expresses an aspect of it in metaphorical
language. All dreams, symptoms, emotional tangles, and failures are also asked the
question of *finality* — what is their purpose and intention, what are they pointing

towards — in preference to questions about causation.

The current situation has an archetypal significance. So the investigation of context must expand and deepen to the eternal actualities of human life. Amplification brings in the deeper context by turning to myth and religion, philosophy and fiction, art and folklore in order to give full value and psychological understanding to the archetypal significance.

3. *The Collective.* Personality is of course situated in a living concrete person, who gets up each morning in a specific room, leads a specific pattern of life among certain other persons, is surrounded by definite objects, and receives the input of subliminal information from social, political, and economic "forces", and so to sleep, and dream, where again personality is subject to immersion in a second collective with its specific scenes, friends and enemies, input and information. In both realms a personality acts and is acted upon. This interaction between the individual and the collective is a theme running through Jung's entire description.

On the plain naive level of experience, there is an opposition between individual and collective: I can't be myself when doing crowd things, and the crowd can't function with a unified purpose if it must take into account each individual's style and needs. The philosophical antinomy between individual and universal (CW 16, §§1-5) is itself an archetypal situation that enacts in each person's life.

When Jung's idea is examined more carefully we find:

(a) Not all that is collective is actual. The psyche is highly selective as to what moves it. Only a small area of "the collective" impinges actually and is therefore psychically real. We shall return to this shortly.

(b) The collective is also the common, what we all hold in common and what holds us universally together as human beings. The hypothesis of the *collective unconscious* means for therapy that *all people can communicate on this commonly human level,* both today, and with the peoples of the past, in the language of emotion, fantasy, dream, and archetypal imagery and situation, despite individual differences of age, sex, sanity, culture. Similarly, the hypothesis of *collective consciousness* establishes community through roles (persona). We can understand our fellow citizen also in terms of his and her collective activity (postman, salesgirl, patient, nurse, etc.). These are also contexts in which personality is situated and by which it is made more understandable.

(c) The collective is neither only inside or outside, nor only subjective or objective. It is both. I am collectivized as much by the role of my outer job as by the mood of my anima complex. The moods and opinions of the lover, the salesman, the messianic hero or the therapeutic guru show little individual differences. All trippers, whether on a public bus tour or private drug session, bring back similar collective reports. Inwardness and outwardness can both be collective, and Jung shows in several papers (on flying saucers, on the Germany of Hitler — CW 10) that the two collectives reflect each other. The *Zeitgeist* (spirit of the times) affects both inner and outer through archetypal images and emotions.

Therefore, to know individual personality means to know where it varies from its collective context. *Deviations thus become cues to essence of individuality.* This is also what it means in Jung's view *to be* an individualized personality: to be called into differentness. But this personality, ideally, will not have to deny collectivity, for it will have found a differentiated style of performing the roles. Adaptation in the Jungian view means not effacing individuality, but rather an innovative collectivity. Living a collective vocation in an individual manner is precisely the way in which the patterns of one's myth can be fulfilled.

Mythology. To complete the collective context, personality is amplified by mythological parallels. Myths give another dimension to the present plight. For Jung, myths describe the behaviour of the archetypes; they are dramatic descriptions in personified language of psychic processes. As universal presentations of psychological dilemmas, *myths are the basics of archetypal psychology.* Besides their drama, myths are dynamic, effectively moving personality out of its fixation on itself, its problems in isolation, and the desperate "hows" of immediate solutions. Besides giving a generally human background to one's particular mess, we discover that the archetypes in a myth are the selective factors which arrange the particular pattern in which one finds oneself. So to understand one's mess, one seeks the mythical pattern, for its mythical personalities (the archetypal figures) and their behaviour give the clues to what is happening in our behaviour. The ultimate context of personality are the myths which the personality is enacting.

Structure of Personality

Descriptive Method. Jung's presentation of the structure of personality is radically original in one respect. His model is in terms of personality itself, that is, he describes the structure of the individual person as a composite of partial

180

personalities. He thereby avoids the difficulties of transposing to human experiences biological, metaphysical, or mechanical models.

For Jung there is nothing more "basic" than the psyche itself. It is the only thing we experience directly and know immediately. All other fields are derived from psychic experiences. The concepts from other fields which some psychologies use to account for the structure of personality and its processes are secondary inventions. They are abstractions from primal images in the psyche at its pre-conceptual level.

Besides, models that rely upon analogies from other fields also tend to insinuate, for instance, a biological, or physical, or moral point of view towards psychological processes. If I conceive the parts of my personality as so many mathematical forces or instinctual drives or independent factors, I will understand myself accordingly, devising means of treatment for personality disturbances that will rely on the same sort of thinking. I will be abstract and mathematical, or like an animal trainer, or a preacher, or a census-taker of personality inventory.

By grasping the processes of any personality as the interaction and relation between different partial personalities, there is at once set up *through theory itself* a wholly psychological field, an interior community. There are relationships. There are contrasts and conflicts — not between traits or drives or forces or brain regions, but between individual persons, each as worthy of respect, each as complex and difficult to understand, each as influential in the body politic of the whole psyche as I (the ego personality). Jung's theories definitely do not present an ego-psychology, since the ego, too, is, and must always remain, but a partial personality by definition.

Opposites. These interior relationships call for psychological understanding within the community of each of our personalities: between masculine and feminine members, between superior developed parts and those that have been neglected and repressed, between healthy and sick, moralists and criminals, young new enthusiasms and old fears, high spiritual aims and savage physical impulses. These problems between all these parts Jung conceives as the struggle of opposites. But "the opposites" is merely a way of putting the tumultuous contention of persons that compose each individual human being.

Dream and Drama. Jung puts the same interior contention also in terms of drama. His theory of the dream states that it has a dramatic structure from opening scene, characters, plot, crisis, to resolution. Since he regards the dream as psychic reality laid bare, or the self-portrayal of the complexes, the psyche's structure is therefore a dramatic one. If psychic structure is fundamentally a dramatic process, then a person's whole life history is a story and personality cannot be grasped in any more accurate way than in narrational form. From this perspective, personality is a theater of archetypal figures, some downfront and center, others waiting in the wings, and the contests show heroic, commercial, comic, tragic, and farcical themes.

How the ego personality relates *internally* with the others, whose side it takes and whom it opposes, will also show in one's relations with the social environment. If I am repressively domineering toward my interior weaknesses, I will tend to be the same way to others, not listening to the needs of my associates and patients any more than my egoism is able to listen to my internal needs. If I play favourites, preferring inner companions that seduce and charm and flatter the ego, then chances are that I will drift into that same sort of milieu in the world at large, avoiding criticism and confrontation. In Jung's theory, the roles we play with each other are given by the partial personalities. *Interpersonal relations are based on intrapersonal relations.*

Personified Multiple Personalities. The *personified* (Hillman 1975) way of regarding personality structure is valuable for therapy, or, better said, it is already therapeutic in its effect. "Drives", "processes", and "factors" remain abstract. They lend themselves to intellectual rationalizations and to defenses against direct experience. But with personifications I can communicate directly. In Jungian therapy the technique, "active imagination", does precisely that. It is an encounter between parts of the personality; it is a battle, a dialogue, a symposium, a drama, among the complexes.

However, before we move into the detailed account of personality structure, there are several theoretical consequences of a general nature to be considered. Of these, most important is Jung's idea that every *personality is essentially multiple* (CW 8, §§365f., 388f.). Multiple personality is human nature. Therefore, every personality is potentially dissociable into the partial personalities which compose it. This is both a regressive threat and progressive differentiation. Individuality (which in Jung's mind means undivided) is the counterpole of natural dissociability. Individual personality means a contained diversity, a differentiated unity that is neither single nor simple. Wholeness of personality means a highly complex tension of parts. Multiple, dissociable personality remains a lifelong tenet of Jung's theory. We see it in his early work on schizophrenia, his interest in parapsychology, in hallucinatory visions, and dissociation, as well as in his autobiographical account of himself in terms of personality number one and personality number two (MDR, pp. 45, 68).

Although the idea of partial personalities is a hypothetical construct and no less a metaphor than other such explanatory constructs as drive, factor, need, etc., the actual partial personalities are given directly to consciousness and are not only inferred. We meet these persons in our dreams and hear them as inner voices. We experience them in our peculiar reactions to which friends say "that isn't like you at all", in moments when we see ourselves looking exactly like mother or father, when we are out of ourselves or beside ourselves with rage, when we say what we do not intend to say, or cross ourselves up in any of a hundred ways. For Jung these partial personalities are also the foundation for the worldwide belief in spirits and demons (CW 8, §§570ff.).

Archetypal Figures. Jung insists that his constructs be formulated in experiential terms and so he names the partial personalities in accordance with their imagery. His method is both that of phenomenology, sticking close to things as they present themselves, and that of naive realism, taking psychic events at face value as fully real. He holds that primitive descriptions (personifying and demonizing) are the most empirically accurate way of talking about psychic facts. It is in the personifications of sweetly seductive nymphs that we experience what we learn to call "sexual desire" and in the shape of shaggy night demons that we meet what the textbook labels "anxiety".

The partial personalities are collected under the names shadow, persona, ego (hero), anima, animus, puer (eternal youth), senex (old wise man), trickster, great mother, significant animal, healer, divine child, self. On the one hand, these are the names of archetypes, that is, typical figures in myth, art, literature, and religion the world over. On the other hand, they are the typical figures in dreams, family roles, personal emotions, and pathologies patterning our behaviour. They can be found wherever the human imagination elaborates its products, from religious dogma to delusional beliefs, from the sublimest art to a hallucinatory psychosis. These figures are the stances which each personality can assume when one or another of them dominates, and these are the viewpoints that rule our ideas and feelings about the world and ourselves. Of course all of them and their variations do not appear at once, so it is not a matter of memorizing the cast of a variety show in order to know the psychology of personality. But in Jung's view it is a matter of recognizing that personality is archetypally conditioned, or that personality is a dialectical scene where during a lifetime many imaginal characters play their part, have intercourse, and argue it out. (It is beyond our scope here to do anything more than sketch how the partial personalities generally work.) More detailed studies examine most of these figures, their phenomenology and pathology. Some of these recent studies, besides Jung's own, are Neumann 1955, *great mother;* Guggenbühl 1971, *shadow;* E. Jung 1957, Adler 1961, de Castillejo 1973, *animus;* E. Jung 1957, Hillman 1973/74, *anima;* v. Franz 1970, *puer;* Hillman 1970, Vitale 1973, *senex.* This by no means complete list offers a serviceable introduction to the archetypal figures and their effects on behaviour.

Let us take the shadow as an example. It is the image of all sides of personality that I could become. In my dreams he may be a brother, a schoolfriend I feared or envied, an outcast or a success, or a professional colleague whose traits are those I most dislike — but which are closest to mine. Because of my identification with a personality I call "my ego", the shadow usually appears as inferior and as rejected by society. The development of one partial personality, the ego, builds a shadow at the same time. Ego development in our culture proceeds through choices between good and bad, right and wrong, like and dislike. The bad, the wrong, and the disliked then fall into the shadow, becoming fearful. Soon the suppressed side becomes the repressed side; the shadow archetype which is a potential of destructive values, an "instinct to evil" or "destrudo", is activated by the cast-off impulses of daily life. The more right I become, the more the shadow is fed with contrary motives until the extremes of a Dr. Jekyll and Mr. Hyde can result. Because the shadow is an archetypal figure, and not merely a cover-name for the repressed, it is a living personality with intentions, feelings, and ideas.

By keeping innocent and self-righteous in ego-consciousness, I force the shadow into the dark where he archetypally belongs anyway as the devil is depicted in hell and the criminal fantasied in the night. So, in dreams, he will show in ghettos, as a welfare case, an invalid, crippled or diseased. He appears also in the images of power politician, fake guru, street gang, or person of darker skin. It is easy to see how problems of society can be referred straight back to individual partial personalities.

The shadow also determines the ulterior motives in plans, the schemes for professional advancement, the nasty gossip, the sellouts, all beyond and in spite of our honest intentions. Although I have described him mainly in terms of ethics, the shadow can as well carry any incompatible aspect — one's unlived sexuality or primitivity and one's unlived potential achievements and cultural sensitivity. Especially, the shadow presents images of one's pathology: sadism, hypochondriacal complaining, or any of the various psychotic syndromes that reflect in caricature one's overall personality structure.

Therapeutic work cannot avoid meeting the shadow. An aim of Jungian therapy is a mutual accommodation of the two brothers, ego and shadow, and a relativization of their previous antagonistic attitudes, lightening the dark and darkening the light. However, the shadow is never wholly overcome any more than we ever achieve all that is potential in us or ever have done with the destructive and malevolent aspects of human nature. The shadow is particularly relevant for understanding the difficulties that can occur between doctor and patient. They can mutually project shadow on each other, so that one remains perpetually strong, healthy, and knowing, the other weak, self-destructive, and inferior (Guggenbühl 1971).

Archetypal Situations. Just as significant as archetypal figures are archetypal situations. Although not strictly a part of personality structure, they are basic for understanding behaviour. By recognizing which archetypal situations a person is actually living, we are better able to understand what he or she is undergoing. As an example we might consider *initiation*. Many cultures have initiation rituals to help the individual pass from one stage of life to another. According to Jungian theory (Henderson 1967), a person without the psychological equivalent of initiation may well be at a loss when confronted with a transition for which he is not psychologically prepared. At such moments a massive regression can take place in which the entire personality seems to recoil from a critical task (examination, military service, marriage, parturition, menopause and mid-life, death of a beloved, one's own death). There can be an acute psychotic episode. When we look at the fantasies, fears, behaviour, and dreams during this crisis they may show the person to be going through a psychological initiation, giving to the peculiar behaviour a ritual import — the magnified fears of the physician, the fantasies of torture, the sense of isolation, the images of birth or transformation to a new condition, and the hallucinatory voices giving instruction, all may be appropriate to the archetypal situation of initiation. By confirming the events as archetypally significant, the person in close touch with the case may aid, not only in deterring

185

senseless disintegration or suicide, but also in making the episode psychologically significant.

Another archetypal situation is the *temenos* (Greek for sacred precinct) or enclosed area in which overwhelming problems can be placed, a center of order can be experienced, or the personality itself be protected while vital changes are going on. Jung has illustrated the temenos with geometrical illustrations, mainly from Oriental *mandalas.* Their spontaneous appearance in extreme disintegrative stress and their relevance for understanding counterphobic rituals are only two aspects of their importance.

In the *descent,* another archetypal situation, there is often a depressive darkening or a confused clouding of consciousness, even a loss of orientation, for the sake of experiencing hitherto unknown aspects of personality. *Sacrifice* often helps clarify bizarre mutilations or feelings of radical deprivation. *Abandonment* is familiar clinically in emotions of separation, loneliness, and helplessness, which, as shown by the myths of Hercules, Moses, Jesus, etc., refer to a necessary pre-condition for the emergence of a new kind of strength which belongs archetypally to the same pattern.

Archetypal Substances and Processes. Alchemy. Many discussions of Jung find his alchemical writings an embarrassment. But to present him without this part of his theory would be a gross distortion. Jung devoted the last thirty years of his research to this subject, published perhaps a quarter of his printed pages on alchemical texts and themes, and said in his autobiography that it was alchemy which provided the true background to his psychology (MDR, pp. 205, 212, 221). Alchemy is thus not merely of scholarly interest and a separate field of research, nor is it Jung's quirk or private passion. It is in fact fundamental to his conception of personality structure. Jung saw alchemy as a prescientific psychology of personality disguised in metaphors. He understood four basic substances of alchemy (lead, salt, sulphur, mercury) to be archetypal components of the psyche. Individuation, or the full realization of personality, requires a long series of operations upon its basic stuff, expressed metaphorically by these substances. Personality is a specific combination of dense depressive lead with inflammable aggressive sulphur with bitterly wise salt with volatile evasive mercury. The alteration and integration of these experiences form phases in the combination of the two principal oppositions: gold and silver, sun and moon, king and queen, active consciousness and reflective unconsciousness. The alchemical formulations correspond with

186

the archetypal figures mentioned above (anima, animus, senex, etc.), filling out with pathological detail and subtle psychological understanding those more general personifications.

The processes that go on in personality are also archetypally depicted in alchemy as a series of operations. The names of many of these have found their way into clinical psychology. Projection, dissolution, sublimation, fixation, and condensation were all alchemical terms. The two main processes — solution and coagulation — are another way of putting the main work of psychotherapy: taking apart and putting together, analyzing and synthesizing. Thus methods which modern analysis believes it has invented for furthering personality development were already known to alchemy as descriptions of the autonomous movements of psychic processes. The goal of the alchemical work — and in Jung's mind goals are but signposts, to be valued for their impetus as ideals not meant to be attained literally (CW 17, §291) — is a series of unions of the various contending psychic substances. These unions he calls the "integration of personality" and the work, "individuation of the personality".

Types (A) – Introversion and Extraversion. Beyond the structures of personality is the overall characteristic tendency of its energy. Is its basic dynamic orientation outward, flowing toward its world and the things, people, and values in its surroundings? Or is its primary movement inward towards its subjectivity, the claims of its internal nature, images, and values? This distinction between the objective and subjective orientation of personality, between introversion and extraversion, is one of Jung's major contributions to psychological theory. It was soon employed by Hermann Rorschach, whose widely influential work began primarily as a further investigation through projective methods of the introvert-extravert polarity (Klopfer 1972), and it was developed in many publications by H. J. Eysenck, both theoretically and experimentally.

As so often happens with successful ideas (evolution, entropy, relativity), they become popularized. Thereby they lose much of their original precision and subtlety. It is now all too easy to characterize introverts as withdrawn and schizoid, extraverts as manic and superficial. We facilely believe introverts are maladapted and extraverts overadapted. This opinionated way of regarding the attitudes of personality itself derives from the prejudices of the observer and one's own typical attitude. Therefore, activity or object-dependency as keys to extraversion, or antisocial hostility and desire for power as keys to introversion may be quite deceptive. The introverted attitude requires a good deal of involvement with the world in order to draw stimulation for its subjectivity. And the extraverted personality may strongly turn against its environment, be shy at large social events, or be innovative in regard to ideas and systems. This behaviour, though seemingly introverted, actually reflects an orientation toward the object and accurate appreciation of it. ("Toward" the world or "against" the world are movements in the same dimension; they are still in terms of the world, and therefore both reflect the predominance of extraversion.)

Because introversion and extraversion are energetic phenomena, it is best to think of them as "facts of nature", given with existence like right and left, expansion and contraction, morning and evening, each having its necessity.

Introversion and extraversion are concepts of practical value for diagnosis, treatment, and clinical prediction. Therapeutic measures always need to be relativized according to the attitude type of the patient — one man's meat is another man's poison. Sometimes Jung prescribes compensation through the opposite attitude, while at other times Jung hints that the treatment of choice is "more of the same". The preferred therapy of extreme introverted conditions, for instance, is less a forced extraversion to compensate than it is a thoroughgoing investigation of and empathy with the subjectivity of the patient through understanding the fantasies. The attitude types are also valuable conceptual tools for understanding people in all sorts of situations: work with colleagues, life with family, choice of scientific method and projects, leisure-time preferences. Even politics and religion come under the influence of the introverted-extraverted bias.

Types (B) – Functions. Besides these two fundamental attitudes in "energetic" language, there are four functions: *thinking, feeling, sensation,* and *intuition.* These functions are theoretical constructs derived from the terminology of traditional psychology. Ever since Kant (1724-1804) and the modern psychology of the Enlightenment, functions (usually called faculties) of the human mind have been described by academic psychologists. Jung's work on types (1921; CW 6) offers the hypothesis that each personality functions preferentially, structurally and typically by means of one or another of these faculties. We are not merely typically extraverts or introverts; we are also typically introverted thinkers or feelers, say, or extraverted intuitive types. The four functions are *modes of consciousness,* whereas the attitudes of introversion and extraversion refer to the basic *energies of the person.* The four functions describe the way in which consciousness shapes experience. The function of sensation, for instance, is assumed to work mainly through perception, either inwardly of images and proprioceptions of the body, or extravertedly in accurate observation and esthetic sense. So, with thinking, feeling and intuition – each presents a typical modality, and a typical pathology, of consciousness.

In recent years a spate of publications (Marshall 1968; Shapiro 1972; von Franz and Hillman 1971; Mann *et al.* 1972; Plaut 1972) express the recurrent interest, both clinical and experimental, in this aspect of Jungian personality theory. However, within Jung's work as a whole, the typology is only one of the twenty large books constituting his collected works and *typology remains but an introductory approach* to the complexities of personality. Typology is elementary, both in the sense of fundament and also in the sense of preliminary, merely a primary step into the nature of individual differences and into the theories of Jung.

Complexes. Jung's most important theoretical construct is that of the complex. The term is his, and was first used by him and his co-workers at Burghölzli, the psychiatric clinic of Zürich University, to account for interferences in verbal associations in an experimental situation – the Association Experiment. A list of a hundred words – verbs, nouns, adjectives – is read, one by one, to a subject (S) who is asked to reply as quickly as possible with the first word (and only one word) which comes to mind. After recording the one hundred associations to test-words and the reaction time (in fifths of seconds) to each, the experimenter again goes down the list of the stimulus words, asking S to repeat what was said the first time. Deviations between the first association and recall are also recorded. Patterns of disturbance are then examined in the protocols, as, for example, prolonged reaction times, perseveration of the same verbal reaction, forgetting of the original reaction the second-time through, peculiar or bizarre associations, rhyming, or affective reactions, etc. (cf. CW 2; Hull and Lugoff 1921; Rapaport *et al.* 1946; Cramer 1968).

Jung hypothesized that disturbances in association reflect an unconscious group of ideas, images, and memories, intertwined in an individual way, permeated by a single feeling tone (longing, anxiety, anger, painfulness, etc.), and charged with strong emotion. This he called the complex. Despite the best intentions of the ego personality to pay attention and follow instructions, there were interferences. This experimental work that went on during the first decade of the present century brought him into contact with Freud. At that time experimental and clinical psychology and psychiatry all worked closely together in fraternal felicity.

Jung's work gave Freud's theory of repression a second leg to stand on. The first leg is anecdotally empirical, a collection of psychopathologies from everyday life — slips of the tongue, parapraxes, forgetting, absent-mindedness. But the second leg, disturbances of attention, can be shown experimentally. The theory of repression was now on an empirical footing, and as well, the wider conclusions drawn from it — a second system of mental functioning, or the unconscious psyche. In this way Freud and Jung support each other. Freud's idea of the unconscious used Jung's complex for its empirical grounding. Jung's idea of the complex used Freud's theory of repression and of the unconscious for its theoretical account.

In all of the work of that period, especially in regard to psychopathology (theory of schizophrenia), criminology (lie-detector test), and psychosomatics (psychogalvanic phenomena, or changes in the resistance of skin-conductivity when complexes are struck), there is one paper particularly relevant for personality theory (CW 2, §§793ff). There Jung shows the connection between the content of the disturbance that appears in the association experiment, the hysterical symptom, and the dream. All three can be accounted for through the hypothesis of the complex. One and the same complex disturbs the association, is the underlying meaning of the symptom (as a bodily conversion of an emotionally charged bundle of ideas and images), and appears as a personified figure in dreams. Jung's vision of personality as a multiplicity of interacting partial personalities, "splinter psyches" (CW 8, §203) or "little people" (*ibid.*, §209), can of course be traced to his association experiments and the hypotheses of complexes, which for him are the basic realities, elements, nuclei of psychic life.

Experienced *figuratively,* the complex is a personality with feelings, motivations, and memories. Experienced *somatically,* the complex is a change in heart-rate, skin-color, sphincter control, genital tumescence, breathing, sweating, etc. Experienced *energetically,* the complex is a dynamic core, accumulating ever new particles to it, like a magnet, or coalescing with other atomic units, like a molecule. It produces tension, compulsions, charged situations, transformations, attractions, repulsions. Experienced *pathologically,* the complex is an open sore that picks up every bug in the neighborhood (suggestibility), a psychic cancer growing autonomously, or a panic button, or an over-valued idea that first becomes delusional and then a paranoid delusional system, integrating to its core all dissuasive arguments.

Complex and Archetype. Analysis of any complex shows it composed of personal associations from personal experiences. But Jung recognized that the energy it could mobilize, the autonomy of its behaviour, and the archaic, universal character of its imagery, could not be accounted for altogether through personal experiences. He thus hypothesized that the core of the complex is archetypal and that the personal material is clustered around and organized by an archetypal image and charged with instinctual energy at the somatic level. For example, my mother complex is built on my experiences with my mother and my associations to her world. But the patterning of those experiences and the immense emotional charge this pattern contains, refers to the archetypal great mother imago and to the instinctual desires, taboos, and magic involved in the mother-son relationship, together with the rich collective fantasies and roles to do with nature, nurturing, growth, protection, preventing, encompassing, smothering, etc. Therapy can disentangle much of the mother complex at the personal level, freeing the personality from projections of archetypal significance upon the ordinary citizen who is our actual mother. But the archetypal foundation of the mother complex and all its faces remains as long as life, belonging to all humankind.

Personality in Therapy

All along I have been pointing out the operational meanings of Jung's concepts. To draw these meanings together into short statements will be the focus of this conclusion.

1. Since fantasy-images are the fundament of consciousness, we seek for them in therapy. Fantasies may not appear as such. Patients often "have no fantasies". The fantasy is then disguised in plans, in reports about themselves, in snatches of popular culture that especially fascinate them, in personal hatreds and desires, in relationships. The therapist listens to this material metaphorically, imaginatively, trying to "hear through" to the fantasy, rather than to the literal content. This can be called *deliteralizing*.

2. Since individuation is defined as "a process of differentiation" (CW 6, §757), analysis attempts to separate and to distinguish between the parts of personality. We ask the parts to identify themselves. This both relieves identifications

with complexes and aids in establishing intrapersonal connectedness, thus consolidating one's personal identity. We distinguish the parts of personality by asking each feeling, opinion, reaction to which complex it belongs. "Who is speaking now? Mother, Hero, Old Senex"? We attempt to develop individual self-knowledge through knowledge of the different collectivities that speak through the ego. Only as these are made distinct and identified is one able to discover who one is. This is *differentiating*.

3. Differentiating means also being different, just as individuality means being unique, and thus peculiar. So, we focus on the odd. The eccentric, that which does not fit in, occurs most evidently in psychopathological abnormalities. We see these rather as seeds of individuality than as faults to be rid of. We keep in relation with symptoms but do not focus upon them. We attempt to reconnect the various supposedly balanced or cured parts of personality with their odd aspects so as not to lose touch with (suppress) them. By keeping aware of psychopathology, which means the abnormal aspect of all so-called normalities, we hope to avoid pseudo-cures based on "therapeutic repressions". This is *pathologizing* (Hillman 1975).

4. Because the highest value in personality is expressed in Jung by the term *self* which is defined as partly transcendental and impersonal, we aim to move personality away from too personal relatedness, whether in transference or in relationships in general. Therapy works at developing relationship to impersonal affairs and at experiencing the *impersonal* aspect of relationships. We assume that the relationships in our contemporary humanistic culture are not humanly underdeveloped as much as overloaded with archetypal demands. What people expect of mothers and fathers, teachers and friends and lovers is far beyond the ability of personal human beings; people ask that archetypal qualities be present in each other which in other cultures are present only in Gods and Goddesses.

The movement towards impersonalizing relationships and relating to the impersonal is aided by the therapist in various ways: through selective attention, through interpretations, through the style of the therapeutic relationship which attempts to be both personal and impersonal, and through interest in dreams. We prefer not to translate the dream into psychodynamic explanations or concepts (even Jung's own terms — "anima", "shadow" — become misused as concepts). Instead, we reply to the dream in a similar metaphorical language, even by telling a dream in return. We move away from the personal by moving towards the story-telling and the mythological, through talking imaginative, personified speech, through allusions to fictions of all sorts (films, fairytales, theater). By concentrating upon the images of the dream (Berry, 1974) rather than their translation we hope to revitalize the imagination of the patient. This is *remythologizing*.

5. Since images and instinct are conceived as two aspects of one and the same archetypal structure (and not as a sublimation of the "lower" by the "higher"), emphasis in therapy upon fantasy images is also an emphasis upon instinct. Through active imagination instinctual disturbances are amenable to change: only symbols are as potent as symptoms. A direct approach through behavioural and body therapies is eschewed in favor of the psychological engagement with images, so that instinctual vitality and sophisticated psychic differentiation proceed hand in hand. This leads to a more immediate and passionate adaptation which is at the same time more culturally imaginative, whether achieved by means of music, painting or writing, or work on dreams, or opening the imaginative eye in daily life. This can be called *vitalizing*.

6. Jung's general theory of neurosis is simply "onesidedness". (He refused a specific theory of the neuroses other than occasional insights drawn from typology, complexes, and archetypal patterns.) Therapy of all neuroses of whatever sort aims at extending consciousness beyond the dominant onesidedness — usually of the ego — to the other partial personalities. The patient learns methods for carrying on the psychologizing process after therapy has ended. The patient does this either through intrapersonal dialogues between the parts of himself, or in his personal psychological relationships, or by reflection on dream images, carrying them around in the day, keeping them alive. Especially the changeless parts and unwelcome images that one is likely to repress are kept near. This continual work upon one's psychic ground, this familiarity with one's multiple personalities, gives increasing containment, inner space and depth to personality. It gives a sharper definition, unifying the looseness and loosening the onesided unity. This can be called *consolidating*.

REFERENCES

C. G. Jung, *The Collected Works,* Vols. 1-17, Princeton (Princeton University Press), 1954-. Abbreviated as CW with paragraph numbers, unless otherwise indicated.

C. G. Jung & A. Jaffe, *Memories, Dreams, Reflections,* New York (Pantheon), 1961. Abbreviated as MDR.

*

G. Adler, *The Living Symbol,* New York (Pantheon), 1961.

P. Berry, "An Approach to the Dream", *Spring 1974,* pp. 58-79.

E. S. Casey, "Freud's Theory of Reality: A Critical Account", *Rev. Metaphysics* XXV, 4, 1972, pp. 659-690.

P. Cramer, *Word Association,* New York (Academic Press), 1968.

I. C. de Castillejo, *Knowing Woman,* New York (Putnam's), 1973.

R. Grinnell, "Reflections on the Archetype of Consciousness: Personality and Psychological Faith", *Spring 1970,* pp. 14-39.

A. Guggenbühl, *Power in the Helping Professions,* New York and Zürich (Spring Publications), 1971.

J. Henderson, *Thresholds of Initiation,* Middletown (Wesleyan University Press), 1967.

J. Hillman, "On Senex Consciousness", *Spring 1970,* pp. 146-165.

J. Hillman, *The Myth of Analysis,* Evanston (Northwestern University Press), 1972.

J. Hillman, "Anima", *Spring 1973,* pp. 97-132; *1974,* pp. 113-46.

J. Hillman, *Re-visioning Psychology,* New York (Harper & Row), 1975.

C. L. Hull & L. S. Lugoff, "Complex Signs of Diagnostic Free Association", *J. Exper. Psychol.,* 4.

A. Jaffe, *The Myth of Meaning in the Work of C. G. Jung,* transl. R. F. C. Hull, London (Hodder), 1970.

Emma Jung, *Animus and Anima,* New York and Zürich (Spring Publications), 1957.

W. G. Klopfer, "The Short History of Projective Techniques", *J. Hist. Behav. Sci.,* 9, 1, 1973, pp. 60-64.

H. Mann, M. Siegler, & H. Osmund, "Four Types of Personalities and Four Ways of Perceiving Time", *Psychology Today,* 6, 7, 1972, pp. 76-84.

I. N. Marshall, "The Four Functions: A Conceptual Analysis", *J. Analyt. Psychol.,* 13, 1, 1968, pp. 1-32.

J.-E. Meyer (Ed.), *Depersonalisation* (fifteen papers by various hands), Darmstadt (Wiss. Buchgesellschaft), 1968.

E. Neumann, *The Great Mother, An Analysis of the Archetype,* New York (Pantheon), 1954.

J. Perry, "The Messianic Hero", *J. Analyt. Psychol.,* 17, 1, 1972, pp. 111-151.

D. Rapaport, M. Gill, & R. Schafer, *Diagnostic Psychological Testing,* Vol. 2, Chicago (Yearbook Publ.), 1946.

K. J. Shapiro, "A Critique of Introversion", *Spring 1972,* pp. 60-73.

M.-L. von Franz, *The Problem of the Puer Aeternus,* New York and Zürich (Spring Publications), 1970.

M.-L. von Franz & J. Hillman, *Lectures on Jung's Typology,* New York and Zürich (Spring Publications), 1971.

A. Vitale, "Saturn: The Transformation of the Father", in *Fathers and Mothers,* New York and Zürich (Spring Publications), 1973.

Published originally as Chapter Three of *Operational Theories of Personality,* edited by Arthur Burton, New York: Brunner/ Mazel 1974, pp. 65-98. The last part of that chapter – a case report – has not been included here.

XII

METHODOLOGICAL PROBLEMS
IN DREAM RESEARCH

When one considers the startling advances made since 1900 in the sciences, it is all the more striking how little has been achieved in dream research.[1,2] One then wonders what the grounds of this stagnation might be.

Among the many general requirements for scientific advance, three in particular might be examined for their relevance to the stagnation in dream research. The first is the need to clear away a no-longer-fruitful theory or exhausted model of thought that hinders investigation. Example here might be Ptolemaic geography and cosmology. Second, the need for more refined instruments for the gathering of new data, as for instance the telescope or microscope.

These two requirements can only lead to more fruitful prospects when, third, new methods can order the data into more meaningful coherence than heretofore.

I

In regard to the first requirement — clearing away a worn-out model of thought — we find that the model which has dominated the field of dream investigation for the past half-century is the one introduced by Freud. Meier[3] has pointed out that "...in the fifty years since the formulation of this theory of dreams, the literature, with few exceptions, has brought no new viewpoints, but has limited itself essentially to confirming Freud's theory — or simply to repeating it".

In reviewing the recent literature in dream research we find all too often that noble efforts of able men bear little fruit. As examples here: the writings on dreams and parapsychology by Servadio, Eisenbud, and others; the work of Fisher [4] (and others) on the recall in dreams of subliminally stimulated images (Poetzl phenomenon); the hypotheses of dream function and content analysis of dreams collected in the experimental situation of the Chicago school; anthropological collections of dreams. Generally, all use a Freudian framework for conceptualizing their findings. Generally, all are constricted by the same model, so that their findings only reinforce the Freudian theory in the minds of the investigators. Yet, is it not also a purpose of independent and objective research to bring into question the very model with which one is operating? For the science of dream research to advance, it would seem the time has come to examine again the Freudian theory of dreams.

The success of Freud's theory of dreams is not a mere accident in the history of psychology. His *Traumdeutung,* appearing at the end of the last century, brilliantly solved the problem of the dream as it was then formulated. During the nineteenth century, there were three dominating hypotheses concerning dreams. These conflicted with one another. The *Romantic* view held the dream to be a message from the beyond with personal significance. The *Rationalists* denied sense to dream contents altogether. But Romantics and Rationalists were agreed that the dream, because it was either poetic inspiration or nonsense, could have no place in science. The *Materialist* view favoured scientific research, but only to prove the organic origin of the dream. This research had for its aim the reduction of dream events to body activities and sense-stimuli.

Freud, by reasserting the ancient tradition that the dream has an immediate personal meaning for the dreamer, gave credit to the Romantic position. (He even compared the dream to a letter, a message.) He recognized as well the nonsense and irrationality of dream language and gave a rational account of the causality of this nonsense. Finally, through the sexual theory of the libido he agreed with the materialist position that there was an organic basis for the dream. He thus brought together the contrasting strands of the nineteenth century and wove them into a coherent system.

Within the compass of this short paper we cannot take up in detail the negative consequences of Freud's achievement and give thorough ground to Meier's assertion. It should be enough to note that the opening up of the continent of the unconscious did not lead to a corresponding gold-rush of explorative research. The new land had been mapped too rigidly and named too odiously, so that the few who dared venture only restated what had already been found by Freud. Research has tended to shy away from the night side of the mind, so that even the subject of sleep, as Webb [5] reports, has suffered neglect to this day. "The average percentage of the psychological abstracts on the topic of sleep (exclusive of dreams) between 1940 and 1959 was 0.267, or slightly over 2-1/2 articles per 1000". The *Index Medicus* shows in a recent two-year period (1958-59) approximately only one article per 1000 concerned with sleep. May we not correlate the paucity of research in sleep and dream to the growing scientific sterility of psychoanalytic theory?

Briefly, let us say that the Freudian conceptual model has hindered the further movement of dream research for the following reasons:

First, because it is elegant. The *Interpretation of Dreams,* especially Chapter 7, is an exemplar of a closed and harmonious theoretical system.

Second, because it conforms with a scientistic and materialistic *Weltbild* which today is no longer operational as it was then.

Third, because it is rooted in the positivist and associationist theory of mind.

Fourth, because it devalues the manifest contents of dreams, consideration of which is the starting point of any research on empirical lines.

Fifth, because it lays main weight on the wishes and memories of the personal unconscious, requiring the specialist in dream interpretation in order to raise them to consciousness, thereby encouraging interest in dream meaning and dream interpretation rather than in dream research as such.

Sixth, and last, because it has become – if I may say so – a cliché having a paralyzing effect on philosophical inquiry and the spirit of research.

II

Turning to the second requirement — technological advance — we find that the major contributions in this field were made *previous* to Freud's *Traumdeutung,* by Maury (1878),[6] Vold (1896, 1897),[7] Ladd (1892),[8] Calkins (1893),[9] Vaschide (1899, 1902, 1903),[10] Clavière (1897),[11] Pilcz (1898),[12] De Sanctis (1902),[13] as well as works on dreams of blind by Jarisch (1870),[14] Jastrow (1888),[15] and Hitschmann (1894),[16] to mention only some of those who investigated sleeping and dreaming with experimental and statistical methods.

The decline during the current century of significant empirical research corresponds with the ascendency during the same period of psychoanalytic hermeneutics. Although Hall[17] presents conclusions from the contents of 10,000 dreams and Junger[18] reports on 100,000 details from a ten-year dream series (his own), and though Siebenthal *(op. cit.)*, Ramsay *(op. cit.)*, and de Martino[19] report on several hundred studies in this field, none were considered of significance until the first *technological* breakthrough occurred at the Chicago Institute for Dreaming and Sleeping in 1955. (I have already reported on that work and raised questions about it at the C. G. Jung Institute two years ago, and I expect others will discuss it at this Conference.)

That research came to the result that subjective reports on "having-dreamt" correspond to a large extent with rapid eye movements during sleep, especially during what is called a period of light sleep as recorded on the electro-encephalograph. Kleitman[20] reviews the work of Aserinsky, Dement, Wolpert, Kamiya, Trosman, Rechschaffen, and himself. The literature gives the picture of a quickly growing area of research in which a great deal of experimentation is going on, and that is already subject to controversies in regard to hypotheses and counter-hypotheses (Dement 1960;[21] Barber, Ullman, and Dement 1960;[22] Malcolm 1959;[23] Hawkins *et al.* 1962;[24] Kubie 1962[25]).

The primary psychological interest in their work is that for the first time dreams can be collected immediately after dreaming. Not only is a vast amount more non-psychoanalytic material available, but also the material reported is less liable to alterations by waking consciousness. This was confirmed to me, for example, by John Watson, who compared the dream reports recorded in the laboratory during the night with those recorded of the same dream the next morning. As with the microscope and telescope, we are in a better position to perceive the data. Our technique of observation has been refined, bringing the perceiver "closer" to the object of study.

We now may ask new psychological questions, such as: why is the dream transformed from the raw report of the night into an ordered narrative in the morning (secondary dream elaboration)? In those cases when no dream is remembered in the morning, although physiological evidence of dreaming is present, can we conclude that repression is taking place? Or, as Dement and Wolpert[26] ask, is there a relation, and if so what kind, between the manifest contents of dreams during the same night?

III

We come now to the third and most significant requirement, methodology, that is, the ways we approach our findings and models we use to organize and understand them. In other words: we must be clear from the outset which questions we are asking of dream material since *prudens quaestio dimidium scientia* or the appropriate question is half of science. We examine dream material in altogether different ways when we ask, "how and what caused the dream, what are its manifest contents"?, than when we ask, "what does the dream mean, what problems and processes are being reflected in the dream"?

A main method of scientific research is to break down an object into component elements. Applied to our field this approach would allow us to compare dream elements, and then dreams themselves could be classified on the basis of a dominant element or group. Thus, dreams with the word *river* or *mother* or *gun* could be compared, and the elements themselves extracted for statistical investigation. Further, these elements of dreams could be charted according to frequencies. This sort of analysis into elements has been the major method in dream content research. For example, the investigations of dreams among school children by Blanchard[27], by de Martino[28], and by Schnell[29]. The question is asked: What do children dream about? Or: What is the main dream content of school children? Then one discovers that one group of school children dream frequently of ghosts and robbers, or that one group of male college undergraduates dream more of one kind of animal than of another kind.

Although studies of this sort may yield statistical averages of dream elements, and even provide a statistical norm for these elements, these studies do not lead us further into understanding the dream and its dynamics. They can say little about what we want to know most: what the dream means in an interpretative sense. For example: it may be far rarer to find an ostrich than a horse in a dream. The ostrich has higher statistical significance, in the sense of rarity and abnormality. But the significance of the horse is in no way lessened because it is more usual and regular. Besides, frequency tells us nothing about what ostrich and horse *mean* in the dream and to the dreamer.

The method of analysis into elements can be sophisticated by placing them in wider categories. Rather than *river* we might use Water, Older Woman rather than *mother,* or Weapon rather than *gun.* In this way we might eventually arrive at fundamental classes of dreams, as for instance, "parental dreams", "aggression dreams", "anxiety dreams", etc. The research of C. S. Hall and his pupils [30] is based largely on this method. Hall and his students have put together Technical Manuals [31] for the classification of dreams according to elements. Aggression in dreams [32] is analyzed into many types and subgroups — physical, verbal, dreamer-involved, dreamer-witnessed, etc. — and, in accordance with the usual headings of sociological statistics, aggression is further classified by age, sex, etc., of dreamer.

Let us note carefully, however, two principal difficulties with this approach. First, the move from *gun* to Weapon to "aggression" is actually a move away from the specifics of the dream, its actual imagery, into concepts and categories. This is a necessary move in the method of natural science from particular phenomena to larger groupings so as to make order. But in regard to dream images, this ordering may distort the fundamental reality of the dream: each one is a unique presentation. It could even be held that the dream is so idiosyncratic that no nomothetic system of comparative research is possible, even though analysts themselves continually do refer to similar images and situations in similar dreams, and draw heuristic conclusions from their unscientific comparisons.

Second, we should not lose sight of the fact that what determines the location of a dream in the aggressive category is the presence or absence of a particular element. Whether or not this step from element to class is justified, and what effect this step has on determining the value of the dream, limiting the many possibilities in its total gestalt, is open to discussion. Even when using larger headings and rubrics — sex dreams, animal dreams, water dreams — the method is still based upon elements.

An outstanding virtue of classification based upon elements is that these categories provide a framework within which to chart *transformations*. For example, within the class of Weapon, there might be — as therapeutic work proceeds - quantitative as well as qualitative changes. There might be an increase or decrease in the frequency of Weapon dreams in proportion to other dreams, or there might be changes within the sort of weapons: bare fists, medieval lances, H-Bombs.

This confronts us with another question. What is the methodological basis for determining *qualitative change* in dream content? Models for valuing qualitative change are given by Jung[33] in his alchemy studies where, for instance, specific colors can be read as indicators of stages in psychological development. There are many such rules of thumb which analysts use for evaluating progress, and these might be reformulated as hypotheses and tested in dream research. Besides the parallels to the individuation process given by Jung and his collaborators, Jungian literature suggests other analogs or models for judging improvement via dream content such as: (mathematical) indefinite multiplicity to primary number; (biological) primitive animal to human; (social) collective to individual; (metaphysical) disorder to order, simple to complex to simple. These are but a few of the assumptions analysts use for evaluating change in dream content. Comparative research might expose which of these assumptions are prejudices and which are confirmed by data. For instance: does the increased production in dreams of orderly mandalas conform with outer criteria of progress? Analysts, obliged to make qualitative judgments concerning regression-progression, are aided by their own and the dreamer's feelings, as well as such other factors as the dreamer's relation to the dream, etc. But the analyst might be grateful if dream research could provide some substantiation for his value scales.

This is of course a difficult area for research, not only because improvement is subjective and hard to measure, but also because a "lower" level image in low frequencies (cave-man or bee-swarm or kindergarten-child) may coincide with improvement over conditions showing high frequencies of "upper" level images such as academic or Church dignitaries. An element, no matter what it is, high or low, infrequent or normal, receives its fundamental value from its symbolic impact. Since *any element may take on symbolic significance,* it would be difficult, if not impossible, to draw objective scales for content values from dream research.

For all its seeming worth in noting frequencies and providing categories, the method based on elements is neither the only or the best. This has been borne in on me as a result of working with two small research groups. There, the lack of deeper understanding based on accurate knowledge (and the absence of a leading hypothesis) is even more apparent than in practical work where therapeutic art can substitute for scientific inadequacy.

Research based on the division of a dream into elements is severely limited. It implies a model fundamentally inappropriate to the dream. Like other mental processes, dreams are not mere associations of components. They are Gestalten, intentional meaningful wholes. Above all, they are *patterned sequences.*

The sterility of dream research — as has been stated by those who know the field best (*v.* Siebenthal) — is due largely to its split from dream interpretation. This has some of its origins in the consequences of Freud's work, as discussed above. But any research method that would produce fruit cannot ignore Freud and the role of meaning in dreams. We may not neglect dream meaning *(Traumdeutung)* in the name of dream research *(Traumforschung)* or attempt to explain without at the same time aiming to understand. Even scientific research has as its fundamental aim the search for meaning.

As another starting point for a more comprehensive method of dream research, let me refer to a passage from Jung (CW 8, §474):

> I would now like to treat briefly of some further problems of
> dream psychology which are contingent to a general discussion
> of dreams. First, as to the *classification of dreams,* I would
> not put too high a value either on the practical or on the theo-
> retical importance of this question... It seems to me that the
> *typical motifs* in dreams are of much greater importance since
> they permit a comparison with the motifs of mythology. Many
> of these mythological motifs — in collecting which Frobenius in
> particular has rendered such signal service — are also found in
> dreams, often with precisely the same significance... I would
> like to emphasize that the comparison of typical dream-motifs
> with those of mythology suggests the idea — already put for-
> ward by Nietzsche — that dream thinking should be regarded as
> a phylogenetically older form of thought.

Although the dream can be regarded at least in some aspects as a product of nature, a method suitable for investigating it must differ from one suitable for other products of nature that do not depend on the human psyche in the same way. The dream is halfway between the poem and the paramecium. Like the paramecium it is a product of nature, not created by man's will. But like the poem, it is a product of art, dependent upon man's imagination.

We have found at the Jung Institute in our research group, studying dreams with animal images in them, that ordering these dreams only according to the animal images does not ask the right question. The method must suit the object and where the object is a process, then the method must be able to delineate sequences and encompass processes. Jung's emphasis upon the dramatic structure of the dream points out that the dream, like a drama, is always an action, a dramatic performance. The dream acts (*handelt, agiert*). These action sequences are not reducible to simple actions like *running, fighting, eating* which some studies use as their categories for content analysis. Again, this is but an analysis based upon elements, but now using verb forms instead of nouns.

A classification of dreams according to animal images — dog dreams, tiger dreams, etc. — does not lead to understanding the actual processes taking place. The action sequences are best grasped as *mythologems.* These are fragmental or segmental patterns of action, analogous to the episodes that appear in other products of the human imagination. They are specifically human categories and therefore closer to the realm of *Geisteswissenschaft* (humanities), the history of art, thought, and culture, than to the realm of the natural sciences.

In dreams one finds, for example, complicated action sequences of the following kinds: reconciliation with the animal after the dreamer lowers himself (or herself) to the animal's level; taming of a wild animal by an unknown woman; an animal proves indestructible in spite of repeated attempts at killing it; an animal proves harmless contrary to the dreamer's expectations. These are but a few of many we have tried to describe. There are as well the better known motifs such as the talking animal, or the animal that transforms into a person, or the animal with unusual colors or marks — but these motifs familiar in fairy-tale and folk-lore research we need not take up here.

It is obvious that analysis of animal dreams into elements — animal images only — would not grasp the processes going on in the dreams. The elaboration of conceptual descriptions for these processes has been our main task. Conceptual language, as Bergson argued, tends to distort activities or processes into the static models of the intellect. This is especially true for the important but delicate feeling expressions and modes between man and animal in dreams. Fortunately we can follow the indications given by Jung, Frazer, Kerényi, Neumann, Campbell,

Eliade, and all those who have tried to formulate comparable dramatic episodes as mythologems, whether in dream, art, ritual, religion, fantasy — or psychopathology.

The work of von Franz and von Beit [34] in fairy-tales and that of Propp[35] in folk-tales uses the same method. Somewhat similar is the structural anthropology of Levi-Strauss and the comparative religion of Eliade and his school. In these different fields, the method seeks to grasp action-sequences. One attempts to get at the meaning of the material by laying bare the functional or structural patterns, the typical motifs. These motifs can be said to be the primary language of the unconscious mind, determining not only dreams but the patterns of behaviour of the conscious will. Mark Blum has noted this, and he suggests the same method is applicable to the study of history, in that mythologems are operative in the biographies of historical personalities. This implies that historical crises must be viewed also from the psychology of the unconscious. An understanding of the mythologem presented in a dream offers the opportunity for understanding not only the therapeutic process. The mythologem tells something also about the cultural and historical level of the dreamer. It is a method with implications for sociology and suggests a bridge between the two disciplines. (Compare Jung's psychological studies on Wotan and flying saucers [CW 10] for mythologems underlying socio-historical events.)

Dream research that bases its comparison upon mythologems — rather than frequencies of elements — has an immediate practical usefulness. Sufficient knowledge of myth, of which mythologems are the dynamic threads, will give the analyst prognostic clues. It can help the analyst follow the action-patterns taking place in the unconscious mind of the analysand. This can better guide the dreamer's attitude toward playing his role in keeping with the fundamental pattern expected of him by his "inner" drama. For example, the element "bull" and statistical norms about the "bull element" in dreams tell the analyst little. However, different conscious attitudes and behaviour are required of a person whose mythologem may call for slaying the bull in combat, eating the bull, sacrificing the bull in ritual, running from it, riding upon its back, or learning its language.

The task of dream research becomes one of extracting these motifs, comparing them among different dreamers in different analyses, or the same dreamer across a span of time, investigating the motifs to find if there is a sequential order or perhaps a developmental process (according to standards of qualitative change), relating them to age, sex, level of psychological culture, symptomatology, and the like, of the dreamer.

Our method then is to grasp phenomenologically the action sequence and to conceptualize it as a mythologem. I refrain from using the term archetypal pattern until the themes can be amplified beyond the dream context where they have been uncovered. Of course the very recognition of these sequences as mythologems implies that we are looking for them in the dream and therefore at the dream in terms of archetypal patterns.

This approach might also be useful in attempting to describe the energetics of dreams. This question has been occupying a few of us in parapsychological research. Here the question has been: how do we judge from the manifest dream content, the direction of energy and changes in potential from conscious to unconscious, and vice-versa.

If we take the dream as a drama, it is then a field of action, or as the gestalt psychologists would say, a field of forces. In order to describe the tension in this field and the direction of the energetic flow, we must examine the nodal points where the energy is tied up (peripety), intersects (crisis) and is released (lysis). Again, this cannot be adequately charted with simple dream elements like *fire* or *explosion* or *sudden movement,* but more likely by uncovering the mythologems in the dream. These might provide an understanding for the actual happening and thus for the direction and intensity of the energy involved.

The investigation of dream tension might be aided by the Rapid Eye Movement studies following Dement. Assuming that tention has to do with repression, then through the examination of repression by testing dream recall, we might arrive at more accurate knowledge of repression in relation to dream tensions.

Further, the investigation of dream tension might also lead to useful correlations with psychosomatic symptom formation. By asking the question whether extreme psychological tensions reflected in dream mythologems manifest at some point in functional physiological disorders we would be gaining evidence for psycho-physical parallelism. If we find the contrary — that the more dream tension, the less body symptoms — then we would be gaining evidence for psycho-physical inversion or conversion.

IV

Summing up we find that the abandonment of the Freudian model of thought coupled with the introduction of new techniques for "catching" dreams, leads to the need for new methods in ordering dream phenomena. A method based on dream elements, even dream images, is limited. An understanding method for encompassing dream processes is also needed. This method requires new formulations which cannot be easily conceptualized because they represent action sequences. The preferred method for describing what takes place in the dream is the mythologem, or archetypal episode. These action sequences might also be used for studying dream energetics.

Finally, the classical problem in dream research presented clearly by Siebenthal *(op. cit.)*, i.e., the opposition between *Traumdeutung* and *Traumforschung,* between *Geisteswissenschaft* and *Naturwissenschaft,* between *verstehen* and *erklären,* can be bridged through this method. Primary units can be abstracted from dreams and these can be classified and compared. But the primary unit is not a static element. It is rather a mythological action sequence which is always *meaningful.* The method for comparing these primary dynamic patterns, and their translation into our psychological lives is a task for further study.

=====

NOTES

1   G. V. Ramsey, *Studies of Dreaming,* Psychol. Bull., 50:432-455, 1953.

2   W. v. Siebenthal, *Die Wissenschaft vom Traum,* Berlin (Springer), 1953.

3   C. A. Meier, *Zeitgemäße Probleme der Traumforschung, Kultur- und Staatswissenschaftliche Schriften, E. T. H.,* Zürich, 75, 1950.

4   C. Fisher, *Introduction to "Preconscious stimulation in dreams, associations, and images"* (Classical studies by O. Pötzl, R. Allers, and J. Teler), Psychol. Issues Monograph No. 7, New York (I. U. P.), 1960.

5   W. B. Webb, *An overview of sleep as an experimental variable* (1940-1959), Science, 134:1421-1423, 1961.

6   L.-F.-A. Maury, *Le Sommeil et les Rêves*, Paris, 1878.

7   M. Vold, *Expériences sur les reves et en particulier sur ceux d'origine musculaire et optique*, Rev. de l'hypnotisme et de la psychol., Jan., 1896; *Einige Experimente über Gesichtsbilder im Traum*, 3te internat. Kongr. f. Psychol., München, 1897.

8   G. T. Ladd, *Contribution to the psychology of visual dreams*, Mind, 2:299-304, 1892.

9   M. W. Calkins, *Statistics of dreams*, Am. J. Psychol., 5:311-343, 1893.

10   N. Vaschide, *Les recherches expérimentales sur les rêves: De la continuité des reves pendant le sommeil*, C. R. Acad. d. Sci., CXXIX:183-186, 1899; *Les recherches expérimentales sur les rêves: Les méthodes*, Rev. psychiat. et psychol. expér., 1902; *Recherches expérimentales sur les rêves: Du rapport de la profondeur du sommeil avec la nature des rêves*, C. R. Acad. d. Sci., CXXXVII.

11   J. Claviére, *La rapidité de la pensée dans le rêve*, Rev. Phil., 43:507-509, 1897.

12   A. Pilcz, *Über eine gewisse Gesetzmaßigkeit in den Träumen*, Wien. klin. Rundsch., 12:505-507, 1898.

13   S. De Sanctis, *An experimental investigation of dreaming*, Psychol. Rev., 9:254-282, 1902.

14   A. Jarisch, *Die Traüme der Blinden*, Organ der Taubstummen- und Blindenanstalten in Deutschland, Dez., 1870.

15   J. Jastrow, *Dreams of the blind*, New Princeton Rev., 5:18-34, 1888.

16   F. Hitschmann, *Über das Traumleben der Blinden*, Z. Psychol. Physiol. Sinnesorgane, 7:388-393, 1894.

17   C. S. Hall, *What people dream about*, Am. Sci., May, 1951; *The Meaning of Dreams*, New York (Harper), 1953.

18   G. Junger, *Der Traumrhythmus; Ergebnisse einer statistischen Untersuchung*, Schw. Z. f. Psychol. u. ihre Anwend., 14:297-308, 1955.

19   M. F. de Martino, *Dreams and Personality Dynamics*, Springfield, Illinois (Thomas), 1959.

20   N. Kleitman, *Patterns of dreaming*, Sci. Am., Nov., 1960.

21   W. Dement, *The effect of dream deprivation*, Science, 131:1705-1707, 1960.

22   T. X. Barber, M. Ullman, and W. Dement, *Correspondence on dream deprivation*, Science, 132:1416-1422, 1960.

23   N. Malcolm, *Dreaming*, London (Kegan Paul), 1959.

24   D. R. Hawkins, *et al.*, *Basal skin resistance during sleep and "dreaming"*, Science, 136:321-322, 1962.

25   L. S. Kubie, *The concept of dream deprivation: A critical analysis*, Psychosom. Med., 24:62-65, 1962.

26   W. Dement and E. Wolpert, *Relationships in the manifest content of dreams occurring on the same night*, J. Nerv. Mental Dis., 126:568-578, 1958.

27   P. Blanchard, *A study of subject matter and motivation of children's dreams*, J. Abn. Soc. Psychol., 21:24-37, 1926.

28   M. F. de Martino, *A review of the literature on children's dreams*, Psychiat. Quar. Supp., 29:90-101, 1955.

29   M. Schnell, *Gespensterträume bei Schulkindern,* Psychiat. Neurol. med. Psychol., 7, Leipzig, 1955.

30   C. S. Hall, *Current trends in research on dreams,* In Progress in Clinical Psychology, II, D. Brower and L. Abt, eds., New York (Grune & Stratton), 1956.

31   C. S. Hall, a) *A manual for classifying characters in dreams,* TM 1; b) *A manual for classifying aggressions, misfortunes, friendly acts, and good fortune in dreams,* TM 2; c) *A manual for classifying settings and objects in dreams,* TM 3; d) *A manual for classifying activities in dreams,* TM 4; e) *A manual for classifying emotions in dreams,* TM 5; f) *A manual for classifying fears and anxieties in dreams,* TM 6, 1962.

32   C. S. Hall and B. Domhoff, *Aggression in dreams,* Preprint for Int. J. Soc. Psychiat.

33   C. G. Jung, *Psychology and Alchemy,* CW 12.

34   H. v. Beit, *Symbolik des Märchens* (3 Bde.), Bern (Francke), 1952-1957.

35   V. Propp, "Morphology of the Folktale", *American Folklore Society Special Series,* Philadelphia, 9, 1958.

Delivered as a paper in the German translation of Hilde Binswanger
to the Swiss Society for Analytical Psychology, Bern, Summer 1961,
and published in *Traum und Symbol* (ed. C. A. Meier), Zürich: Rascher,
1963. A bibliography of 195 entries listing work in dream research during the years 1956-63 has not been included here. I wish to thank Hilde
Binswanger, Eleanor Mattern, and collaborators in research on animal
images in dreams, for their contributions to this paper.

209

Also by James Hillman

Anima: An Anatomy of a Personified Notion

Anima and Eros, Anima and Feeling, Anima and the Feminine, Anima and Psyche, Mediatrix of the Unknown, Integration of the Anima, etc. — ten succinct chapters, accompanied by relevant quotations from Jung (on left-hand pages facing Hillman's essay), which clarify the moods, persons, and definitions of the most subtle and elusive aspect of psychology and of life. Illustrated. (188 pp.)

Suicide and the Soul

A classic introduction to the *experience* of depth psychology—for analyst, patient, and anyone having to meet questions of suicide. Although ostensibly a practical treatise on suicide, it opens into the profound differences between the medical model of therapy and one that engages soul. Since the book's first publication in 1964, it has enjoyed wide recognition in many languages as a teaching text. (191 pp.)

Insearch: Psychology and Religion

Widely used in pastoral counseling and psychotherapeutic training, this book sets out the fundamental attitudes of Jungian psychology in a simple, yet deeply experiential style. Sensitively addresses such topics as listening, curiosity, confession, secrecy, befriending the dream, morality of analysis, conscience, emotions and moods, problems of sexual love, and psychosomatics. (126 pp.)

Inter Views

A vivid, free, exploratory dialogue between the founder of archetypal psychology and an Italian feminist-psychologist writer, recorded and revised by the two authors. Here we follow the imagination ruthlessly and lovingly pursued down the alleys of the modern city, the soul's twisted pathologies, and the mazes of love. Extraordinary, yet practical accounts of active imagination, of writing, of daily work, and of symptoms and sufferings in their relation with loving. Index. (198 pp.)

The Thought of the Heart

This is an essay on Beauty and the relation between the heart and the world. Part One clears away imprisoning notions of the heart: as muscle and pump, as symbol of royal pride and solar will, as seat of personal sentiments. Part Two relates the heart with the aesthetic response and reactions of outrage at ugliness and injustice. Hillman traces the movements of the heart's failures and its duplicity and then presents a psychology of 'heart operations' that release it from subjectivism and sulphuric illusions so that it can respond like an animal to the ensouled beauty of the sensuous world. (50 pp.)

Spring Publications, Inc. • *P.O. Box 222069* • *Dallas, Texas 75222*